Jennie Anderson Froiseth

The Women of Mormonism

Or, the story of polygamy as told by the victims themselves

Jennie Anderson Froiseth

The Women of Mormonism
Or, the story of polygamy as told by the victims themselves

ISBN/EAN: 9783337297848

Printed in Europe, USA, Canada, Australia, Japan

Cover: Foto ©Lupo / pixelio.de

More available books at **www.hansebooks.com**

THE WOMEN OF MORMONISM;

—OR—

THE STORY OF POLYGAMY

As Told by the Victims Themselves.

EDITED BY

JENNIE ANDERSON FROISETH,

Editor of the Anti-Polygamy Standard, Salt Lake City, Utah,

WITH AN

INTRODUCTION BY MISS FRANCES E. WILLARD.

AND SUPPLEMENTARY PAPERS BY

Rev. LEONARD BACON, D. D., LL. D., Hon. P. T. VAN ZILE,

AND OTHERS.

ILLUSTRATED.

PUBLISHED BY
C. G. G. PAINE, DETROIT, MICH.
1882.

DEDICATION.

TO THE
HAPPY WIVES AND MOTHERS OF AMERICA,
WHOSE HOMES ARE PROTECTED FROM INVASION BY THE
MAJESTIC ARM OF THE LAW;
TO THOSE TO WHOM THE WAIL OF THEIR FIRST-BORN
IS SWEETER THAN THE MUSIC OF THE SPHERES,
BECAUSE THAT BABE IS THE PLEDGE OF
THE UNITED AFFECTION OF
ONE MAN AND ONE WOMAN;
TO THOSE WHOSE CHILDREN DO NOT BRING WITH THEM A
BIRTHRIGHT OF SORROW, AND WHOSE MOTHER-
HOOD IS NOT A BADGE OF SHAME,
THIS BOOK IS APPEALINGLY DEDICATED BY SOME OF THE
WOMEN OF MORMONISM.

PUBLISHER'S NOTE.

WITH an earnest desire to have some part in the great work of redeeming the large, beautiful, and populous Territory of Utah from the tyrannical and degrading evil which holds it in its mighty grasp, and which is ruining the souls and bodies of thousands of men and women, the publisher sends forth this work. He is confident that it will impart information which will astonish its readers, and hopes it will exert no small influence in molding public opinion, and thus lead to an energetic demand upon Congress for right and efficient legislation, and direct the sympathies of the people to some practical end, in increasing the means of the various "redeeming agencies" that are operating in Utah and the adjacent territories.

In order to give the work the greatest possible circulation, it will be sold only by subscription. Every effort has been made to have it thoroughly accurate and reliable, and to issue it in an attractive style. The illustrations are chiefly portraits of some of the most prominent persons who are working in various ways for the redemption of the inhabitants of Utah from the terrible bondage in which they are held, and have been engraved expressly for this work, at great expense.

EDITOR'S PREFACE.

SOME one has said that an Author's Preface is as unnecessary as absurd, because in ninety-nine cases out of one hundred it is simply an apology for having written the book. The Editor of these pages certainly does not offer any apology for this book. She only gives a few words of explanation as to how it came to be presented to the public.

A few years ago, a little band of brave and devoted women in Salt Lake City, associated themselves together for the purpose of fighting an iniquitous monster which had brought thousands of their sex to untimely and unwept graves. Some of these women had experienced personally all the horrors of the Mormon system, and when an organ for the "Anti-Polygamy Society" was established, they were willing to give their experience to the world, only stipulating that, for family and personal reasons, their names should not be made public. They were willing to make private affidavits to all the facts, (these affidavits to be held in reserve), should their veracity be questioned.

These recitals, told in the powerful language of the heart, were deemed worthy of a much larger circle of readers than the columns of a new journal afforded. Ardent friends of the cause were anxious that the narratives should be published in book form, in connection with other papers bearing upon the subject of polygamic Mormonism. Said these friends, "If the wives and mothers of America could only be made aware of the extent and character of this degradation of their sex, and informed of the need of their sympathy and support, the on-rushing tide of public sentiment, once set in motion, would sweep away the curse of polygamy in a single year."

Consequently, the Editor of the *Anti-Polygamy Standard* was empowered by the writers of the different sketches to revise, re-arrange, and prepare the matter in its present form, and send it to the WOMEN OF AMERICA, hoping that thus might be set in motion a tide which would purge our nation of this evil without such a convulsion as imperiled the national life in extirpating the other "relic of barbarism."

It will be unnecessary to add one word to the pathetic appeals contained in these pages, and, I trust, just as unnecessary to ask my countrywomen that not in vain shall sweep over the broad prairies, the cries of the "WOMEN OF MORMONISM."

JENNIE ANDERSON FROISETH.

SALT LAKE CITY, UTAH,
 January, 1882.

CONTENTS.

DEDICATION, ...	page 3
PUBLISHER'S NOTE, . . .	4.
EDITOR'S PREFACE, . . .	5.
CONTENTS, ...	7.
INTRODUCTION BY MISS WILLARD,	15.

CHAPTER I.
THE CASE STATED.

Polygamy as a Religion.—As a Social System. Address of the Gentile Women of Utah.—Appeal of Mrs. Ann Eliza Young.—Design of this Work.—Degrading Influence of Polygamy.
p. 19.

CHAPTER II.
THE ORIGIN OF POLYGAMY.

Mormon Policy.—Joseph Smith.—Crusade Against Woman.—Special Revelation.—Treatment of Those Who Rebelled against the Doctrine.—Polygamy a Curse. . p. 29.

CHAPTER III.
POLYGAMY PROPAGATED.

Polygamy Denied Abroad While Practiced at Home.—Ingenious Liars.—Danger of Admitting Utah as a State.—Relief Societies.
p. 42.

CHAPTER IV.
CLASSES OF MORMON WOMEN.

Apostates.—Anti-Polygamous Mormons.—Full Believers.—Courage of the Apostates. . . . . . p. 48.

(vii)

CHAPTER V.

WOMAN'S CONSENT.

A First Wife's Story.—Counseled to Humble His Wife.—"Wives Have no Rights in this Territory."—A Mother's Reason for Going to Utah.—The New House.—The Baby.—Persecutions.—Husband Persuaded.—Death of the Baby.—Wife Reluctantly Consents.—Consequences.—A Death-Bed Scene.—Escape.

p. 50.

CHAPTER VI.

A FIRST WIFE'S REVENGE.

Both Fanatic and Fool.—A Husband's Promise.—The Husband Ensnared.—Happiness of Polygamous Families.—Sickness.—The Vow.—English Mollie.—The Third Wife.—A Religious Enthusiast. . . . . p. 74.

CHAPTER VII.

A VICTIM OF PIOUS WORDS.

Married to a Missionary.—The Awakening.—Tempted to Murder Her Own Children.—Apostasy.—More Demon than Woman.

p. 90.

CHAPTER VIII.

A SLAVE TO THE FIRST WIFE.

Sorrows of Plural Wives.—An Elder's Importunities.—An Unwilling Consent.—Slavery.—A Disappointed Lover.—Escape from Home.—Tracked.—Driven Back.—Shameful Neglect.—Leaving Home a Second Time.—Lying Justified.—A Husband's Treachery.—Doubts and Apostasy. . . . . p. 96.

CHAPTER IX.

EVIDENCE VS. STATEMENTS.

Incident of the Endowment House.—Statement of a Mormon Bishop.—Testimony of a Victim.—Result of a Second Marriage.—Testimony of the United States District Attorney for Utah. . . . . p. 111.

CHAPTER X.

STILL IN THE TOILS.

Help of the Nation Needed.—Timidity of the Women Still in the Church.—Their Despair.—An Infatuated Wife.—A Sad Story.—Wives without Legal Rights.—The Third Wife.
p. 116.

CHAPTER XI.

FANATICISM.

Degradation of the Fanatics.—Joseph Smith's Holiness.—Brigham Young's Opinion of Joseph.—Mormonism Justifies Lying for the Truth.—No Cross, no Crown.—One Man the Husband of Three Generations.—The Mormon Elder and His Wives.—Advice of a Mormon Woman. . . . . p. 131.

CHAPTER XII.

TOOLS OF THE PRIESTHOOD.

Remarkable Statement.—Polygamy Instilled into the Young.—Apostates Become Infidels or Spiritualists.—No Sympathy for the Tools.—A Young Girl's Statement.—Attempts to Keep a Young Lady from Apostatizing.—Corruption Fund.—Woman to the Rescue. . . . . . . p. 144.

CHAPTER XIII.

AN EARNEST APPEAL.

Quotation from the *Deseret News*.—Joseph Smith's Widows.—Changed Views.—Smith's Denunciation of Polygamy.—Married or Single.—Controversy with God.—Polygamy Binding upon All, or None.—No Plural Marriage. . . . p. 155.

CHAPTER XIV.

OPEN LETTERS TO THE MORMON WOMEN.

Anti-Polygamists Animated Only by Love of Humanity.—A Revelation Cannot Release from Allegiance to Law.—Fruits of Polygamy.—Geo. Q. Cannon's Four Wives.—Ann Eliza Young's Suit.—Letter from Ann Eliza Young.—Woman in Utah and Other Sections. . . . . p. 164.

CHAPTER XV.

BEAUTIES OF POLYGAMY.

A Saintly Husband.—A Wedding and a Funeral.—The Trio Victorious.—"It Rejoices Mother Beyond Measure."—"I Prefer to Scratch for Myself *Now*."—"I am Heart-Broken."—The Black Eye.—An Eastern Lady.—Four Wives and Three Beds.—Sixteen Children Left.—Peculiar Consolation.—Would Visit His Sick Wife Next Sunday.—Would not Harmonize.—Arraignment of Polygamy by a Victim. . . . p. 174.

CHAPTER XVI.

EFFECTS OF POLYGAMY.

Affects Unborn Generations.—Young Girls.—Remarkable Statement.—Testimony of Stenhouse.—House of Correction.—An Apostle's Son.—A Bishop's Hopeful Heir.—Taylor's Refusal.—"Poor Boy."—Unfortunate Girl.—"Surprised that They Lived together so Long."—Fifty Children in the Cemetery.—Joseph Smith's Son.—"Queen of the Harem." p. 195.

CHAPTER XVII.

A HEART HISTORY.

Wedding Anniversary.—Mormon Missionary.—His Visit.—The Shock.—The Old Home.—Invalid Sister.—The Mother's Ad-

vice.—The Journey to Zion.—Bishop Parker's Wives.—A Solemn Promise.—The New Home.—Obscene Sermons.—Mrs. Parker's Friendship.—Unwelcome Visitor—"Murdered."
p. 213.

CHAPTER XVIII.

A HEART HISTORY CONTINUED.

A Happy Home Picture.—"Brother Ellis."—The Message.—A Stormy Scene.—Attempt at Reconciliation.—Mrs. Parker's Visit.—Her Advice.—Christmas.—Sealed to Jesus Christ.—Joining the Church.—"Brother Ellis" Again.—Interview with the President.—The Terrible News.—"One of Papa's Women."—Attempt to Escape.—Death.   .   .   .   247.

CHAPTER XIX.

SPREAD OF MORMONISM IN THE UNITED STATES.

The People of the Nation Have the Power.—The Let-Alone Policy not Sufficient.—Steady Influx of Foreigners.—Concealment of Second Marriages.—Mothers Will not Make Known the Fathers of Their Children.—Mrs. Young's Letter.—Danger to the Nation.—"Danger to Every Household in America."—Mormon Church at Covington, Ind.—Mormonism in Michigan.—Canton, Ill.—Young Girl in Colorado.—An Appeal.—Young Lady in Indiana.—An Infatuated Daughter in Massachusetts.—Will Another War be Needed?   .   .   p. 284.

CHAPTER XX.

WHAT ARE YOU GOING TO DO ABOUT IT?

BY THE LATE REV. LEONARD BACON, D. D., LL. D.

Something Now.—Thirty Years' Compromise.—National Sovereignty.—People Unfit for Self-Government.—No State Rights.—The First of Human Rights.—Jim Fisk.   .   .   p. 303.

CHAPTER XXI.

THE TWIN RELIC.

BY HON. P. T. VAN ZILE, U. S. DISTRICT ATTORNEY FOR UTAH.

Philadelphia Convention, 1857.—No Easy Question.—Mormons Completely Organized.—Tithes.—Polygamy not Publicly Announced at First.—Wonderful Power of Forgetting.—You Cannot Protect Me.—Proportion of Polygamists.—"Brooming a Bishop."—Polygamists Holding the Offices.—Spiritual Exaltation.—Mormon Jurors.—Congress Guilty.—Evil Results of Polygamy.—Laws Suggested. . . . . p. 312.

CHAPTER XXII.

SOME SUGGESTIVE LETTERS.

BY HON. P. T. VAN ZILE, U. S. DISTRICT ATTORNEY FOR UTAH.

Difficulties in the Way of Convicting Mormons.—How to Crush It.—Law of Limitation.—Disfranchise the Polygamists.—Punish Adultery.—"Don't Persecute Us."—Mormon Buncombe.—Treason.—No Kid-Glove Proceedings.—The Young Men.
p. 337.

CHAPTER XXIII.

VIEWS OF A STATESMAN.

BY HON. SCHUYLER COLFAX.

Mormon Defiance.—Juries.—Female Suffrage.—Right of Dower.—Abolish the Legislature.—Heed the Gentiles.—The Golden Time. . . . . p. 357.

CHAPTER XXIV.

THE REDEEMING AGENCIES.

BY C. G. G. PAINE, A. M.

Threatening Aspect.—Past Political History.—Legislation Powerless to Reform.—Congregational Churches.—Salt Lake Academy.—New West Education Commission.—Roman Catholics.—Episcopal Church.—The Hebrews.—The Presbyterians.—Salt Lake Collegiate Institute.—The Methodists.—The Baptists. The Press. . . . . 365.

APPENDIX.

Independence Hall. (By Hon. O. J. Hollister, Salt Lake City, Utah.)—The Pioneers in Providing for Social, Educational, and Religious Necessities of the Non-Mormons of Utah Territory. —Decision of the Supreme Court.—Polygamy not Religion.—The Illustrations of this Work.—Judge McKean.—Perils of a Missionary. . . . . . . 387.

LIST OF ILLUSTRATIONS.

Mrs. Jennie Anderson Froiseth	FRONTISPIECE.
Rev. Walter M. Barrows	page 24
Mrs. Sarah A. Cooke	48
Gov. E. H. Murray	80
A Happy Home Picture	95
Mrs. A. G. Paddock	112
Hon. James B. McKean	144
A Turkish Scene	163
Miss Lydia M. Tichenor	176
A Polygamous Family	184
Rt. Rev. Daniel S. Tuttle	208
Prof. J. M. Coyner	240
Innocence	246
Rev. D. J. McMillan	272
Mrs. Ann Eliza Young	288
Hon. P. T. Van Zile	312
"Brooming the Bishop"	324
Pres. John Taylor	344
A Warning of Danger	364
M. E. Church, Salt Lake City	380
Independence Hall	387

INTRODUCTION.

There are many theories about the "Origin of Evil." The women who will write theological treatises in the twentieth century, will probably explain its horrid advent into this world as being consequent upon the first assumption by man of authority over the mate or comrade who, though weaker than himself in body, was stronger in soul.

However that may be, the degradation of man has always been the inseparable result of the subjection of woman; for the stream cannot rise higher than its fountain, and it is written in God's Book of Fate, which man calls "Natural Law," that the mother's relation to the Home, Society, and the State, shall determine their degree of elevation or ignominy.

Turkey is doubtless the most debased country on earth, and there, as I was told in Constantinople by an American of twenty years' residence in that capital, a Turkish gentleman (?) who so far forgets himself as to mention his *wife* in the hearing of ears polite, always adds, "I beg your pardon for the allusion." In Syria, I learned from the missionaries that a man never calls himself a father unless he has a son, his *daughters* being altogether counted out as ciphers until a brother's birth places a significant figure before them, after which they are mentioned as "That boy's sisters."

But America need not go so far for illustrations. Turkey is in our midst. Modern Mohammedanism has its Mecca at Salt Lake, where Prophet Heber C. Kimball speaks of his wives as "cows." Clearly the Koran was Joseph Smith's model, so closely followed as to exclude even the poor pretension of originality in his foul "revelations." Man was to take his position in the future world according to the zeal with which he had "built up the kingdom," while woman's *immortality* depended on her conjugal relations here.

When we consider that the country which permits this abomination of desolation to continue, is the "bright consummate flower" of Christian civilization; when we remember what o'clock it is in the Nineteenth Century, and that the formula of Utah's monstrous lust is, "*Live your Religion*,"—we are tempted to change Sojourner Truth's famous words, "Is God dead?" from a question into a heart-sick affirmation.

If ever the incalculable mischief of excluding women from direct participation in Government had an illustration so conspicuous as to silence the blindest conservative, it is afforded by the dalliance of Congress with polygamous Delegate Cannon and his unclean constituency. Were women in the House of Representatives, the disgraceful record that must go down in history would not be even thinkable.

The same *esprit de corps* in women which led a Mormon wife to say as she touched the chilly hand of a dying man, "*Thank God, this can never again strike a woman!*" has inspired the brave woman who writes this book.

INTRODUCTION. xvii

I have read its pages with thoughts too deep for tears. Some sulphur-shrouded planet may have a vocabulary fiendish enough to fitly characterize what they reveal, but mere English is only the vocabulary of a prating parrot in presence of such pathos and such woe.

There is something chivalric as the knights of old in the Author's defense of Mormon women from the harsh criticisms made by the uninformed upon their course in submitting to this most awful form of tyranny. But with the physical strength and the money-power in the one scale, and the mother-heart in the other, there is no more mystery about the passive attitude of Mormon women than about that of unhappy wives in more favored localities, or in the mute endurance of slaves or squaws.

When Brigham Young declared that "if women would not submit to polygamy they should be eternally damned," and when history shows that women who have resisted have often been murdered, the mystery of the non-resistance policy which they commonly pursue, is certainly cleared up. "Starve them, and beat them if necessary, to bring them to submission," said the Mormon apostles; "better crucify the body than let the soul go to perdition." Well was the method of these hypocrites characterized by a Mormon woman who said of one of them, "He is a man who steps on hearts as though he stepped on stones."

The fact that Emma Smith, the first wife of Joseph, so trained her sons that they reorganized the church, and their branch prohibited polygamy, shows that the one woman who had power in this subtle hierarchy was swift to use it for a righteous end.

Surely it is time that the Christian women of this nation arouse themselves to *organized action* against this sum of all curses which can curse the sex not physically strong. To say we have been hitherto indifferent would be a libel on our womanhood no less than our religion; to say we have been idle would be unjust, when we remember the books of Mrs. Stenhouse, the *Anti-Polygamy Journal* of Mrs. Froiseth, the lectures of Mrs. Ann Eliza Young, and the great petitions which have registered where they were little heeded, the votes of the great army of women whose actual ballot would soon deliver our captive sisters on the blighted frontier.

But the hour demands a deeper, more combined, and far-reaching movement; and the instinct of self-protection no less than of philanthropy should warn the wives and mothers of this land that each woman degraded means the potential degradation of all women.

Who will lead us along the path of high endeavor which this thoughtful volume indicates, until the Book of Mormon is burned in the fierce blaze of Christian manhood's indignation and woman's righteous wrath, and the Gospel of Him who came not only to redeem the world but to restore to woman her lost inheritance, "the equality of equals," is the beloved Home Religion in every Home?

FRANCES E. WILLARD.

CHICAGO, 1882.

THE WOMEN OF MORMONISM.

CHAPTER I.

The Case Stated.

Polygamy as a Religion.—As a Social System.—Address of the Gentile Women of Utah.—Appeal of Mrs. Ann Eliza Young.—Design of this Work.—Degrading Influence of Polygamy.

"WHAT is your opinion of Mormon polygamy as a religious tenet?" was asked of an eminent divine, upon his return from a visit to Utah, where he had spent several weeks in investigating the system, with eyes, ears, and heart wide open.

"It may be good enough for a certain class of men," was the reply, "but for the women, it is a damnable doctrine. Religion was designed by the Creator to satisfy that longing for infinite good and purity, which exists, in some degree, in every human soul; its mission is to elevate and purify mankind, and a system which tends to degrade any portion of humanity is but a libel upon the sacred name of religion. The best resources of our language cannot supply me with strong enough terms in which to denounce this infamous doctrine of the Mormon creed!"

"And how do you consider Mormon polygamy as a social system?" was inquired of a philosopher, who ignored all creeds and dogmas, and expressed belief in only what he termed "natural religion."

"As a social system, it is a miserable failure," was the answer, "because it is founded on the law of retrogression, which cannot be tolerated in this advancing age. The corner-stone of polygamy is the degradation of woman, and it can flourish only where she is regarded and treated as a slave. The question suggests itself, Does this country intend going back to the conditions of semi-barbaric civilization? For, whatever degrades woman, degrades man also. The future of our race depends entirely upon the character and position of the women. If we make them slaves, how can we expect that our children will be anything else than children of bondwomen, and slaves, like their mothers?"

In the address issued by the Gentile women of Utah, to the women of the United States, asking co-operation in measures for the suppression of this great crime against nature and the law, there appeared the following statements: "Considering all our surroundings, polygamy has never taken such a degrading and debasing form in any nation, or among any people above the condition of savages, as in Utah; and there are facts which cannot be repeated, that reduce the system to the lowest form of indecency. It is degrading to man and woman, a curse to children, and destructive to the sacred relations of family. That it should be practiced in the name and under the cloak of religion, only adds to the enormity of the crime, and makes it more revolting to our common Christian principles."

Mrs. Ann Eliza Young, in dedicating her book, "My Life in Bondage," to the Mormon wives of Utah, says, "So long as God shall spare my life, I shall pray and plead for your deliverance from the worse than Egyptian bondage in which you are held. Despised, maligned, and wronged; kept in gross ignorance of the great world outside,—its pure creeds, its high aims, its generous motives,—you have been led to believe that the noblest nation on earth is but a horde of miscreants, and that every one outside of your own church is your enemy, and plotting your destruction."

In the closing chapter of the same work, Mrs. Young makes this eloquent appeal for assistance to the women of America: "And you, happier women, you to whom life has given of its best, and crowned right royally,—can you not help me? The cry of my suffering and sorrowing sisters sweeps over the broad prairies, and asks you, as I ask you now, Can you do nothing for us? Women's pens and women's voices pleaded earnestly and pathetically for the abolition of slavery. Thousands of women, some of them your country-women and your equals in moral and intellectual worth, are held in a more revolting slavery to-day. The system that blights every woman's life who enters it, ought not to remain a curse and a stain upon this nation any longer. It should be blotted out so completely that even its foul memory should die!"

It is for the purpose of making another appeal to those happier women of the United States, that the present work has been undertaken. We make another effort to enlist the sympathy and co-operation of good women everywhere in the labors of that little band of noble workers who have devoted their lives to the task of freeing our common country from a most loathsome ulcer, of liberating their sex from the most degrading bondage possible, and of inducing Congress to do something for the redemption of thousands of women who are slaves in the heart of the Republic!

And theirs is as noble a work as was ever undertaken. For if to break the fetters from the wrists of slaves was a worthy deed, how much more worthy is a struggle to emancipate enslaved souls. If the women of the United States could only realize that it is the sacred duty of every *individual woman* throughout the length and breadth of the land to aid in this work of enfranchisement, the evil would be of short duration. An active public sentiment would soon be awakened against it, as irresistible as that which made the people furious against slavery when their first dead were sent home from the war.

If the present volume is productive of no other result, it will at least make the women of America better acquainted with the degraded position of the deluded and down-trodden women of Mormonism, and this in itself is one step in the way of ameliorating their condition. It has often been asserted by those who were interested in defeating legislation against the peculiar institution, that polygamy could not be perpetuated except by the consent of the women, and if they are contented, who has any right to interfere, especially when it is practiced as a religious belief? It has always been a favorite argument with Mormon enthusiasts in defense of this doctrine, that their women are so much happier and more contented than women anywhere else in the world, and for that reason they claim to have discovered the true sphere of woman. The true nature of this "consent," how "contented" and how "much happier" (?) they are, will be learned from these pages. We shall also show that these enthusiastic defenders of woman's "true sphere" are those who in reality hold their wives in about the same estimation that they do their cattle, and who show the most indignation when outsiders call the poor slaves the deluded and down-trodden women of Mormonism.

We reiterate the words deluded and down-trodden both indignantly and sorrowfully, and we know they cannot be gainsayed,—indignantly, that such an expression should be applicable to any inhabitant of this, our boasted land of light and liberty,—sorrowfully when we think of the many broken-hearted women now lying in the dreary Mormon cemeteries, victims of this monstrous system of iniquity; and we know that those words cannot be gainsayed, because they are truths which are self-evident to the casual observer, as well as to the calm, dispassionate philosopher who has studied all phases of the question, disregarding all prejudice,—truths which can be verified by all those who have been identified with the delusion, but who have outlived it,—women whose finer feelings and womanly instincts could not longer submit to the degradation into which their superstition had led them.

The lives of some of these women have been more pathetic and full of tragedy than any of which the tragic muse has ever sung. The sacrifice of Jephthah's daughter, the immolation of the Hindoo widow, or the desolation of the lonely nun, who, through a mistaken faith gives up her hopes of maternity, and surrenders the dream which is innate in every woman's breast to sometime be the central figure in a happy home, is not a feather in the balance when compared with the sacrifices made by some of these women, and the sorrows endured by them in silence and alone. Is there not a whole volume of tragedy expressed in these simple words of a wife who had been supplanted in her husband's affections by another woman, "They say I am dying of consumption, but it is only my heart that is wasting away?"

Travelers and strangers in Utah have often asked the questions: "What is the cause of the Mormon women being in such a degraded position? Is polygamy the entire cause of it?" It may be here remarked that there is something peculiar and almost indescribable about the majority of Mormon women.

Rev. WALTER M. BARROWS.

Even in Salt Lake City, where they adopt more of worldly fashions than they do in the remoter settlements, there is little possibility of mistaking them. Especially do the first wives seem to carry the signs of care and sorrow,—a mark of Cain, as it were, which separates them from the rest of their kind. It is perceptible to even the most transient visitors, and those who tarry for any length of time can readily distinguish a Mormon woman from an outsider, though they have no personal acquaintance with either.

We have studied the subject closely for years, and believe that we understand it thoroughly. We have heard the stories of hundreds of the women themselves, both good Mormons and apostates, which is perhaps the truest criterion by which to judge. It is only a woman of marked courage and strength of character, that will acknowledge the real extent of a delusion under which she has been laboring, especially when that delusion has been accompanied by shame, and a despotism strong enough to intimidate and crush the bravest spirit. That despotism has, no doubt, deterred a great many from giving full expression to their feelings, but the testimony that has been given is strong, abundant, and conclusive. And by this testimony we purpose to prove that what the divine said was true, that polygamy is a damnable doctrine for women; that the philosopher understood the system well, when he declared it a miserable failure socially; that its corner-stone is degradation to women and infamy to children; that its annals are unequaled in shameless crimes, and that the non-Mormon women fully appreciated the evil influences that have made the Mormon women what they are when they wrote, "Polygamy has never taken such a debasing form in any nation or among any people above the condition of savages, as in Utah."

We also purpose to prove that it is a curse to children, and destructive to the sacred relations of the family, and that those who practice it in the name and under the cloak of religion are in reality those who have outlived every vestige of pure religious feeling with which their natures might once have been endowed. By this testimony of the women themselves, we also purpose to expose the arts by which women are coerced into permitting their husbands to take other wives, to show the evil results of the system so far as decency will permit, to exemplify how it destroys all that is manly, honest, and chivalrous in man, degrading him to the level of a brute; how it completely ruins all that is lovable and lovely in woman, and renders her either a dull, senseless, sorrowful, heart-broken creature, who has no interest in life, and no hope beyond the grave, or else makes of her a common virago; how it fosters all the worst passions of both sexes, and makes them but a libel on God's image; how it corrupts childhood and youth; how there is no respect nor honor shown to woman living or dead, but that she is simply regarded as the slave of a lustful and tyrannical master. We shall show how polygamy, by its lack of family unity, is a foe to every household in Christendom, and subversive of all those principles of truth and honor which promote the good of a people and which are the crowning glory as well as the safeguard of the State. We shall show the deceit and treachery, the brutality, the complete demoralization, which everywhere characterize the infamous institution which renders motherhood a disgrace, and brands with shame the innocent foreheads of little children. We shall sketch the past as well as delineate the present of the women of Mormonism, and show how they have been reduced to the position they now occupy.

Non-Mormon women are very apt to say to those who have come out of polygamy, and especially to those who had been Mormons at the time of its adoption as a tenet of the church, " Why did you ever submit to the infamous doctrine; why did you not leave the church, leave your husbands, bring them to law, kill them, do anything rather than submit?"

It is easy to ask these questions, if one is entirely unacquainted with the complete and intricate machinery of the Mormon church, but it is more difficult to explain why the women did not take any or all of these steps. But any one who understands the system, would never make these inquiries.

The longer a person lives in Utah, the more convinced he will be that these women, whom outsiders often regard with scorn and contempt, are deserving of their deepest sympathy and commiseration. Their scorn and indignation should be directed against the wicked and fanatical men, who have been instrumental in ruining the lives of these women. And perhaps a little of their indignation would not be misplaced, were it directed against our national lawmakers, who have suffered this plague-spot to grow unchecked in the very heart of the most enlightened and Christian country on the face of the globe. It will be well, too, for people to understand that polygamy is not a local evil in the sense of being confined to Utah. Polygamy is aggressive. Year by year it conquers new territory, and claims fresh victims. There are Mormon colonies in Wyoming, Colorado, Idaho, Washington, Arizona, and New Mexico, and to all these colonies polygamy is carried by emigrants from Utah. If people would only compare the area of country over which it is spreading with the area of New England or the Middle States, they would perceive that Deseret, the kingdom that can never be moved, a kingdom reared upon a foundation of lust and blood, is likely to become a formidable power in future years, if its people are not soon taught the supremacy of the national law.

CHAPTER II.

The Origin of Polygamy.

Mormon Policy.—Joseph Smith.—Crusade against Woman.—Special Revelation.—Treatment of Those Who Rebelled against the Doctrine.—Polygamy a Curse.

THE true secret of the anomalous condition of woman among the Mormons, is, that it has been Mormon policy to degrade her to the position she occupied among barbaric nations in the dark ages, before the light of civilization raised her to be what God intended at the creation,—man's equal, companion, and helpmate. If this doctrine of woman's inferiority had not been rigidly enforced, polygamy would never have gained its present strength, nor even have been established as an essential doctrine of the church. But in order to give the innovation a permanent place among the dogmas of the new religion, it was necessary to make woman believe that she was an inferior being, a lower creation than man, that her only chance of salvation, her only opportunity of entering the gates of Heaven, was as a satellite, to add glory to some male Saint. It was also taught, and is still, that a woman cannot be raised from the dead except through some man, and

in fact, the entire spirit of Mormon teachings so far as the relations of the sexes are concerned, is man's superiority to woman, mentally and morally, as well as physically.

We do not know how we can better describe the estimation in which woman is held among the Mormons, than by quoting from one of their prophets, the late Heber C. Kimball. His common expression for them was his *cows;* and when exhorting the brethren "to live their religion," as they sacrilegiously term going into polygamy, he would say, "I think no more of taking another wife than I do of buying a cow, and if you want to build up the kingdom you must take more wives." The expression "build up the kingdom" has a dual meaning, one referring to the temporal welfare of the church, the other to personal celestial glory. The more wives and children a man has, the greater will be his glory in the celestial kingdom; and the larger his family, the greater power and strength he adds to the organization here. Hence, men are constantly being urged by the leaders "to build up the kingdom."

But to return to the early history of polygamy. Any unfortunate or rebellious star, who declined the honor of being one of these satellites, and attached to the illustrious train of one of Israel's chosen kings, —all good Mormons are going to be kings in the next world, and the Gentiles their subjects,—was destined to roam forever through realms of darkness, or as the prophet tersely and less poetically expressed it, "If the women would not submit to polygamy, they should be eternally damned." These are Brigham Young's own words, often repeated in council and sometimes in the public Tabernacle. Old Mormons do not hesitate to say that the word "damned" may be interpreted as a synonym for *murdered*, and that the threat has frequently been carried into execution. There are also many instances on record where the destined victim has anticipated her doom, and precipitated it by her own hand, preferring death to shame and dishonor. Verily it is not exaggeration to declare that the annals of this horrible system can never be truly transcribed until they are written in letters of blood.

During the first few years after the religion of Joseph Smith had begun to spread and gain disciples, theocracy was not so firmly established, neither was there any difference manifest between men and women. Both were earnest, sincere seekers for truth; determined, if possible, to find in the new religion what they fancied was denied them in the old. The principles taught, appeared to be pure and good,—belief in the divinity of the Saviour, equality, brotherly love, and other tenets of revealed religion. One old Mormon said to the writer: "The Saints were all they professed to be in early days. They fed the hungry, clothed the poor, feared God, and loved their neighbors as themselves. Of course, they had the utmost confidence in and reverence for their prophet, and like all innovators and impostors, he labored to exert the greatest possible influence over his dupes. And never did impostor succeed better. Men who were intelligent and otherwise strong-minded became as submissive as children under his powerful hand.

People often say that they now look back with the utmost amazement to those days, and marvel at the strange magnetic influence which this illiterate, wicked man possessed over men and women of intelligence and education. That he was of loose and immoral character is conceded by his warmest friends, as well as his bitterest enemies. Even his successor, Brigham Young, said that Joseph was of mean birth, wild, intemperate, dishonest, and tricky; but for all that he was a prophet of the Lord. These inconsistencies may seem strange to outsiders, but they are understood by those who are acquainted with the inner workings of Mormonism. Brigham further said that these "trifling faults" were nothing against the religion which he had founded. The following are Brigham's exact words in this reference: "I care not if he (Joseph) gamble, lie, swear, run horses, and marry women every day; for I embrace no man in my faith."

But the followers of Joseph were not all so blinded by his influence, neither had they become so corrupt, nor so lost to all principles of truth and honor as to sanction his unblushing wickedness; so, in order to screen himself from the consequences of his iniquity, and at the same time retain his influence over his followers, he conceived the idea of obtaining the revelation on polygamy.

MORMON ASSEMBLY HALL, SALT LAKE CITY.

CHURCH OFFICES.   BEE HIVE HOUSE.   EAGLE GATE

RESIDENCE OF THE LATE PRESIDENT BRIGHAM YOUNG

Those who have studied closely the early history of Mormonism declare that polygamy was latent in it from its very conception, and that the practice and the revelation were no mere accidents or afterthoughts on the part of the natural-born libertine who propagated them. Stenhouse, in the "Rocky Mountain Saints," speaking of the early days of Mormonism, says, that "all through the history of the Church, during the lifetime of Joseph, may be noticed a disposition to free-loveism;" and Brigham Young is on record as having said that "the principle of celestial marriage was one of the first things the angel showed to Joseph,"—and this before Mormonism started.

It is not our purpose at present to discuss any of these theories, nor to enter into any particulars regarding its original conception. We will simply state what is an indisputable fact, that Joseph Smith, while in Nauvoo had entered into criminal relations with a number of his female disciples, and the scandal became so notorious as to threaten his influence and compromise him as a leader and teacher of religion, when he pretended to have had a revelation from Heaven commanding the Saints to adopt what is termed, "The order of celestial or plural wives." The wife of an apostle who lived in Nauvoo at that time, and who is still living in Salt Lake City has repeatedly affirmed that she was aware that such a revelation was contemplated several weeks before the date on which Joseph avowed he had received it from Heaven. It is only simple justice to those women whom Joseph deceived so shamefully, to state that he evidently taught the doctrine to them *privately,* telling them that it was a true principle, but the time had not yet arrived for its public announcement or practice. It is also only an act of simple justice to say that Emma Smith, Joseph's wife, never believed in the revelation, and her life was a constant martyrdom on account of her husband's "celestializing" propensities. Her sons are to-day the leaders of the " Reörganized Church of Latter Day Saints," or, as they are familiarly called, the "Josephites," a party who profess adherence to the original principles of Mormonism, as first taught by Joseph Smith, without the debasing doctrine of polygamy, which they condemn as severely as do the Gentiles.

Whatever the origin of the revelation, it is certain that it did not meet with a very enthusiastic reception at first, and by very many it was viewed with abhorrence; for there were men among them who dearly loved their wives, and who were jealous of the honor of their mothers and sisters. These men, notwithstanding their devotion to their leader and their religion, could not readily believe that Heaven could either command or sanction the practice of a system so dishonoring to the sex, and so contrary to every principle of morality and the usages of civilization. Some of the stronger minded, and of purer hearts, made a brave resistance, and a large number apostatized, and left the church forever. Before long, those who remained succumbed to the authority of the church, and if they did not in reality believe in the revelation, they pretended to. And when once the downward path is entered upon, descent is easy.

Then it was that the crusade commenced against women. From the very first the majority of the women had considered the "revelation" in its true light—a cloak to cover immorality—and in many cases they were strongly supported by their husbands. But the authority of the church was so complete, and the influence of Joseph so great, that the infatuation soon became uncontrollable,—a few fanatical women assumed to believe in the divinity of the revelation, and these being in high standing in the church, the rest were not long in perceiving that the struggle would be a terrible one, and almost sure to end in their defeat.

The maidens were as adverse to becoming plural wives, as were the first wives to have their rights invaded and their homes desecrated; but where flattery failed to cajole or threats to intimidate, special revelations were obtained to suit special cases. The history of Joseph Smith's revelations would prove interesting reading, and would make a volume of no mean dimensions, as he claimed to have received thirty-seven distinct communications from Heaven in the year 1831 alone. It was a great habit with him, after he had committed some particular breach of decorum, to obtain a revelation assuring him that "the Lord forgave his servant Joseph" his special sins.

We are acquainted with the facts in one case, which was not a solitary one of its kind. A prominent apostle in Nauvoo, a bosom friend of the prophet and a strenuous supporter of the new doctrine, became infatuated with a young girl who had left her family in an Eastern State to become a Mormon. He was determined to have her for a plural wife, but she was as determined in her refusal. Wearied by his importunities, she told him one day, half in jest, that she would never marry him unless she was specially commanded to do so by Heaven. A few days afterward she was summoned to attend a private meeting of the prophet and several of the high priests, and was there informed that a special revelation had been sent from Heaven, ordering her to become the plural wife of the apostle. The poor girl was astonished enough, but still she had firm belief in the honesty of her religious teachers; and although she did it reluctantly, she married him, being afraid to disobey what she thought was a direct command from God. A friend questioned as to how the revelation came, and to whom it was given; but the girl acknowledged that she had such implicit faith in the church authorities, she would not have dared make those inquiries, even had they occurred to her mind.

This blind devotion and unquestioning faith has been the great means of giving the Mormon church its present strength and power. Years afterward, when this child—for she was but seventeen years of age when the event happened—

had outgrown her delusion, she said to her friend, "How could I have been so blind and foolish! how could I have let those wicked men dispose of me, body and soul, as if I had been a calf or a dog! Whenever I think of it, I hate and despise myself for my folly, for, in my case, folly was worse than crime." This poor girl's experience in polygamy was just what might have been expected, for she was soon discarded for another favorite, who did not need any special revelation in her case. It may be imagined what kind of a life she had, when she said these words in speaking of her husband: "The happiest day I spent for twenty years was the day I saw him laid in the grave." Truly, this doctrine of polygamy is a damnable one for women!

During this crusade against woman, referred to above, nothing was left undone to compel them to accept the revelation on polygamy. Husbands were commanded to resort to all manner of severity if their wives would not consent to their taking more women, and those who objected to being taken were subjected to every conceivable persecution. Their reputations were blasted, and their souls threatened with eternal condemnation. If a woman declined to be divorced from her husband to become the concubine of the prophet, if he happened to fancy her, she was branded as an infamous character, and the Saints were warned not to associate with her thereafter. There are women living in Salt Lake City in this year of grace, 1882, who were secret plural wives to Joseph Smith or Brigham Young, deceiving their own husbands, because they dared not brave the prophet's anger and its consequences. For then, as to-day, the Mormon weapon against its antagonists was *slander*. The man or woman who has the moral courage to apostatize, becomes a target for the vilest kind of abuse and falsehood. Of this more will be said hereafter.

And yet all this persecution was conducted in the most secret manner possible. In public, the Saints denied that they either advocated or practiced polygamy, though it was the one important and all-absorbing theme of their counsels in private. Those who would not sanction or follow the revelation were denounced as traitors to their faith, whose portion should be the lake of fire and brimstone forever. One old lady who had passed through that terrible ordeal, said: "A person can scarcely form the slightest conception of what we suffered during that dreadful time; poverty, sickness, distress, or death would have been nothing compared to what we endured. Indeed, death would have been gladly welcomed by many of us; but, alas, we cried in vain; he would not come!

"Our husbands were enjoined to treat us with the utmost severity if we objected to their 'living their religion;' not alone to withdraw all marks of esteem and affection, but also to deprive us of the necessaries as well as the comforts and luxuries of life. 'Starve them and beat them, if necessary, to bring them to submission,' was the counsel; 'better crucify the body than let the soul go to perdition.'

"If, by chance, the men were rebellious, they were dispatched on missions, and their wives commanded to receive the attentions of other men during their absence. I dare not repeat the counsel given on this point, it is so grossly indelicate and immoral. If a wife fell a victim to the snare, and her husband found more children in his home when he returned than when he left, it was all 'religion.' If she remained true and loyal, her reputation was ruined among the Saints. And when the Mormons came to Utah, and were so completely isolated from the influences of the outside world, there was no help or redress for the women. Those of us who rebelled against the doctrine were treated without tenderness, or even respect. In fact, we were regarded as simply brood animals. Brigham Young frequently told the women that they must not expect their husbands to love them, it was enough honor to be allowed to bear children to a Saint. Then when that reign of terror known as the 'Reformation' was inaugurated, thousands were compelled to enter polygamy in order to save themselves from being 'blood-atoned.' Then a single woman could scarcely be found in the length and breadth of the Territory; and when the supply of marriageable girls had given out, others were recruited from the ranks of the children. It was a very common affair for a little girl of thirteen or fourteen years to be forced into polygamy with some wretch old enough to be her grandfather! After long years of such tyranny and inhuman treatment, is it any wonder that our women became reduced to the lowest depths of degradation?"

The same lady said upon another occasion: "Polygamy is the direst curse with which a people or a nation could be afflicted. I could tell you stories enough to fill volumes, of its vile workings, its unholy influences, its horrible results. It completely demoralizes good men, and makes bad men correspondingly worse. As for the women—well, God help them! First wives it renders desperate, or else heart-broken, mean-spirited creatures; and it almost unsexes some of the other women, but not all of them, for plural wives have their sorrows too. An elder once said to me, 'Sister Sarah, you are a regular Satan.' I had been giving my views in regard to polygamy and polygamists. I answered him, 'There are only two classes of Mormon women, devils and fools.'

"Talk about the lost women of the outside world! Are any of them so lost to all sense of shame that they will parade themselves before the wife, and rob her unblushingly not only of the affections of her husband, but of every particle of his substance, even the bread out of her children's mouths? They at least have shame enough to keep themselves hidden from the women they may happen to wrong. But I have known my husband's concubines to enter my home, after I would not have them in the house with me any longer, and deliberately take away the food and clothing I had earned with my own hands, and my husband stand by without a word of expostulation or reproof. He was not in a position at that time to give them what they desired or needed, and he did not care if they robbed me of my last penny, even if my little children went hungry or naked in consequence. Yet before he became a polygamist he was as kind and tender a husband as ever lived."

But alas for the consistency of the Latter-day religion! A husband like this will often descant for hours upon the advantages of the "divine ordinance," especially for the benefit of distinguished strangers. There is one apostle in particular who is frequently chosen to fill this office, who, as the Mormons say, becomes completely lifted out of himself in expatiating upon the benefits of the divine order of marriage, and its ennobling influences upon the women. This holy apostle has never provided properly for any of his wives, two or three have left him, he has deserted as many more, one of whom died of sheer destitution under the most heart-rending circumstances; and yet he is perfectly fanatical on the subject of polygamy.

Is it any wonder that those who have suffered, or seen others suffer, from the horrors of this system, should wish it "blotted out so completely that even its foul memory should die?"

CHAPTER III.

Polygamy Propagated.

Polygamy Denied Abroad while Practiced at Home.—Ingenious Liars.—Danger of Admitting Utah as a State.—Relief Societies.

WHILE Joseph and his deluded followers were practicing polygamy in Nauvoo, the missionaries abroad were sedulously preaching against it, and in pursuance of the prophet's private orders, were positively asserting that no such tenet was recognized by the Latter-day Saints. They were afraid to advocate the principle openly, because they knew it would bring upon them the just condemnation of the entire world, and prevent converts from embracing the new religion. Consequently, they were obliged to resort to the vilest kind of deceit, in order to screen themselves and their nefarious doctrine from the abhorrence so justly merited. They were afraid to acknowledge the truth, because they knew it would be their death-blow at that time, and it is a well-known fact that even to this day the missionaries in foreign countries are very reticent upon this point.

There was considerable excitement in Europe when the rumors of the new ordinance were brought to their shore, but the American missionaries assured the European Saints that the rumor was only started by their enemies to injure their cause. The most eloquent and remarkable denial was made by Apostle John Taylor (the present head of the Mormon church), at Boulogne, in France, where he presided over a large and successful mission.

Apostle Taylor was at that time the husband of five wives, two of them sisters. A missionary who was laboring with him there had for wives a mother and daughter. The French converts were determined to know the truth in regard to polygamy, consequently Apostle Taylor preached an eloquent sermon, denying the charge emphatically, and quoting extensively from the "Book of Mormon" and "Doctrines and Covenants,"—works containing the articles of faith of the Mormon church. Being very earnest and impressive, he convinced his audience, without a doubt, that the Latter-day Saints had been vilely slandered by the accusation of polygamy. What a religion, which permits a man to lie so unblushingly, and that in the name of the God of truth, who cannot lie!

One reason why a great many honest, straightforward Mormons declare against polygamy is because it involves such a sacrifice of truth. It makes a man a deceiver in spite of himself, in defiance of his better nature. Men who would scorn a falsehood in any other relation of life, who are faithful to the end in friendship and just in business to the uttermost farthing, do not scruple to descend to the lowest grade of falsehood when polygamy is concerned. As a Mormon lady once said to a distinguished traveler, "A polygamist is the most ingenious liar imaginable, because he dare not tell the truth, that is, if he wishes to preserve a semblance of peace in the family. If the first wife remains the favorite, and he desires to please her without totally neglecting the others, he will invent the most plausible stories in regard to his absences from home, to avoid telling her that he has been visiting them. If he is an old man, and the slave of some concubine, there is no end to the falsehoods he will have to tell. But the deceit and treachery are most practiced when the men are looking for other wives." If you will talk with Mormon women you will find that the testimony on this point is overwhelming. Almost every woman, either first or plural wife could tell the same story of some kind of deception having been practiced upon her. Many of them were married to missionaries in foreign lands, thinking they were first wives, only to find upon their arrival in Zion, that two, three, or more women, as the case might be, had a previous right to call the same man husband.

It was necessary to revert to the early history of polygamy, and show, for two reasons, how the women were forced to submit to it. First, to illustrate the principle which has made the women of Mormonism what they are to-day, and which can find no parallel anywhere on the face of the civilized globe; second, to show that if Utah were admitted as a

State, unless polygamy were abolished as completely as slavery now is, the same things would be repeated. Given Statehood under the present condition of affairs, the Gentiles would soon be run out of the country, the liberal schools and newspapers suppressed, and a reign of terror inaugurated that would cost the United States millions of money and lives before the abolition of polygamy could be accomplished, while now a very little legislation, coupled with determination on the part of the Government would soon stop the evil from spreading, and place it in the way of complete annihilation.

It is not exaggeration to say that the system of persecution which compelled the Mormon women to submit to polygamy would again be adopted in case Utah were invested with the powers of State sovereignty, for there exists in Utah to-day as complete a system for teaching and preaching the abomination to the young girls. In every little settlement there is a female organization called the "Relief Society," which was instituted and is maintained by the orders of the priesthood. Here the young girls are brought every week, and the vile doctrine continually dinned into their ears. The same old story is ever repeated, that they can never obtain salvation except they enter it. They are also taught that polygamy is practiced all over the world in some form or other, that the Mormon system of plurality is the only pure and true one, and that all others are sinful.

A young girl of sixteen who had been born

and raised in the Salt Lake Valley, seemed completely astounded when informed by a Gentile whose acquaintance she casually made, that a man in New York or Massachusetts who married more than one wife would be sent to the penitentiary. Then these children are asked if they would not prefer to have their husbands live in the pure relations of celestial marriage, owning their wives and acknowledging their children, rather than to know or suspect that they were living in sin. A Mormon woman said not long ago, to a Gentile visitor: "What is the difference between our husbands having plural wives, and your husbands keeping mistresses?" The lady was equal to the occasion and quickly replied: "There is no difference at all, for the practices are identical; polygamy and prostitution are one and the same thing. But there is this distinction, while you extol the one as a saintly practice, we condemn the other as a sinful one."

The Mormons claim that the origin of the "Relief Society" was in pursuance of a direct revelation from God to Joseph Smith, and what is called the "Young Ladies' Association" was a revelation to Brigham Young. A member of the latter's household thus discourses in regard to this revelation :—

"After the Gentiles began to come to Utah, the young girls, getting their eyes opened a little, began to have doubts regarding the religious principles of polygamy, because they had seen so much of its unhappiness and its evil results. Some of them thought that to possess the love and devotion of a sinner, and to be well supported by him, might be preferable to neglect and poverty with the fraction of a Saint. Occasionally a maiden would be found bold enough to express her opinions, and declare that she would have a husband to herself, or have none. The president was quick to see that these ideas must be crushed immediately, or the young people would soon be on the road to apostasy. So he said to the elder women: 'Sisters, something must be done to counteract these infernal Gentile influences, and stop this feeling of rebellion against our holy practices. Organize societies, bring the young girls more in contact with you, mothers in Israel, and instruct them in the faith.' And so, the first of these societies was organized in our own household, (for I was a member of the family at the time), not to assist the poor and suffering, but to teach the young girls subjection to the dominant power. No woman has ever been permitted to hold office in one of these societies, except those who will carry out the plans of the Mormon theocracy."

And what shall be said of women who allow themselves to be the tools of a designing priesthood! They are either fanatics or hypocrites, and as such, unfit to be leaders and teachers of woman. God knows there are enough influences in this sorrowful world to render women's lives a dreary waste, without their own sex being the instruments to lure them to destruction. Of this class of women, more will be said hereafter.

CHAPTER IV.

Classes of Mormon Women.

Apostates.—Anti-Polygamous Mormons.—Full Believers.—Courage of the Apostates.

THE women of Mormonism—(in this general classification are included all who have ever been identified with the church)—may be divided into two classes, first and plural wives. Each of these classes may be again subdivided, and distinguished as, first, apostates, that is, those who have withdrawn entirely from the Mormon church; second, those who have not yet severed their connection with it, and who believe in all its doctrines with the exception of polygamy; and third, those who believe in the institution as a divine ordinance, or pretend they do.

The apostate element is, of course, very much in the minority, but it counts among its ranks many noble women who have burst from their trammels under innumerable difficulties,—women who have suffered untold martyrdom for the sake of a false god. It is our intention to say but little about this class, preferring to let them speak for themselves. In the stories which follow, there is nothing exaggerated nor set down in malice. Indeed, exaggeration

Mrs. SARAH A. COOKE.
President of the Woman's National Anti-Polygamy Society.

is impossible, since language is inadequate to half unveil the horrors of this loathsome object called celestial marriage. These pages are simple, truthful relations of how women have been beguiled and deluded; how their hearts have been crushed, their womanly feelings outraged, their homes desecrated, and they made almost physical, mental, and moral wrecks.

We can scarcely give too high a tribute to the courage of the apostate Mormon women. It may be thought a very easy matter to leave the church; but when it is remembered that leaving the church meant the entire breaking away from all old friendships, complete ostracism from all old associations, and perhaps starvation for their children, it will be seen that it required more moral strength than is possessed by every woman to cross the line that proclaimed her an outcast. Women, whose lives had been as pure and innocent as their yearling babe's, have had their reputations sullied and their characters assailed in every imaginable manner; others have been sent out like Hagar into the wilderness, with, alas, no angel near to comfort them, while every one was warned not to take them in. Many have laid life's burden down, too grievous to be longer borne; but to those who carried it bravely through to the end, we can safely say, "Verily, verily, ye shall have your reward."

CHAPTER V.

Woman's Consent.

A First Wife's Story.—Counseled to Humble His Wife.—"Wives Have no Rights in this Territory."—A Mother's Reason for Going to Utah.—The New House.—The Baby.—Persecutions.—Husband Persuaded.—Death of the Baby.—Wife Reluctantly Consents.—Consequences.—A Death-Bed Scene.—Escape

THE following stories of first wives will show how women have been, and still are, coerced into giving consent for their husbands to take other women, and also illustrate the beauties of that system which its votaries declare brings so much happiness, and is so ennobling to the female sex.

A FIRST WIFE'S STORY.

"Many friends who have heard me complain of the sorrows I have endured in polygamy, censure me deeply for having given my consent for my husband to take another wife. They say I could easily have prevented it if I had been determined and threatened him with Gentile law, as it is only a few years, comparatively speaking, since he went into plurality. I will relate the facts just as they are, and people can see for themselves how utterly impossible it would have been for me to have acted any differently.

"My husband was doing well in his business, and had frequently been counseled by various members of the priesthood, to avail himself of his privilege, and add to his family. It may not, perhaps, be understood by the Gentiles, that when a man shows signs of being prosperous, he is not given any peace until he has bound himself in the chains of polygamy. He is then a much greater slave to the priesthood, and not so likely to apostatize.

"One day my husband announced to me that he had determined to live his religion, and take another wife. In one way I was not much surprised, for I knew the influences that had been brought to bear upon him continually for months, influences which could not be ignored without the possibilities of utter ruin. Besides, I had seen that blighting shadow destroy the peace of too many homes not to fear that it might also cast its baleful influence over mine; yet still I hoped that it might pass me by. We had lived together happily for fifteen years, and seven children had been born to us, four of whom were living. One of these children was a dearly loved, I may say, an idolized, little girl, who had been an invalid from her birth, and whom I had cherished like a delicate, rare, hot-house flower; another was a babe in arms; the rest were two stout hearty little boys, not old enough to do anything to help themselves.

"When he told me of his intention to go into polygamy, he also said that he had been counseled to marry a certain woman. I had many reasons to regard this woman with special aversion. A year or two previous she had been a servant in my family, and in addition to a very high temper, she had annoyed and disgusted me by her efforts to attract the attention of my husband. He did not seem to notice her in the least at that time, and made no objections when I discharged her for an unkind action toward my little girl, whom she appeared to dislike extremely; and why, I never could imagine, for she was as sweet and gentle a little creature as ever lived. Subsequently, I heard that he had been advised by the church authorities to marry this woman, on purpose to humble me, because I was suspected of having more spirit and independence than was befitting a Mormon woman.

"Well, it is no use repeating what I said to him. I knew that it would be in vain, for the decree had gone forth. It was like a drowning man clutching at a straw when I wept and prayed him to avert the disaster a little longer, if not altogether, and not to ruin our happy home. I reminded him of what we had been to each other for fifteen long years, and how I had forsaken all my friends for him; how I had tried to be an exemplary wife and a good mother to our children.

"'It is well that you think of your children,' was his reply, 'for if you will not do your duty and consent for me to do mine, by living up to the privileges of a Latter-day Saint, they shall have neither food, clothing, nor shelter of my providing during the coming winter.'

"Gentile ladies who read this will perhaps think that my husband was a brute. On the contrary, he had been one of the best of husbands, and had never given me a rough word in fifteen years of married life, until he considered himself forced to 'bring me to my senses,' as the Mormons would say. None but those who have lived and suffered in it, can imagine the tyranny of Mormonism.

"But what could I do? Could I see my innocent children, who had always been tenderly cared for, go hungry, naked, and homeless? I was not strong enough to do all my own household work, and I had a three months' old baby at my breast. I could not go out and earn their food and clothes. I could not bring myself to see them suffer, as I knew they must do, for I knew him well enough to be assured that he would carry out his threat; so I said, 'Well, if you must take another wife, do so, but let it be any other woman in the world rather than the one you have named. You know how hateful she was to May, and how could I tolerate any one in the house that would be unkind to her? Choose any other woman in the city, and I will try to make the best of it.'

"He answered, 'She it must be, and none other, and there need not be any trouble. You will keep your side of the house and mind your children, and I will make her keep hers.'

"'Henry,' I said, 'the day that woman enters this house will be the last day of domestic happiness for us.'

"'I cannot help it, Mary,' he replied, 'I am determined to live my religion; and if you know when you are well off, you will not make any fuss, but act like a sensible woman. There is nothing to prevent my leaving you without a penny, if I like, for you know that women, especially first wives, have no rights in this Territory, not even the right of dower. Do as you ought, and I will pledge myself that neither you nor the children shall ever want for anything; but make a fool of yourself, and you may go where you like, and do the best you can for them.'

"Again I ask, what could I do? Nothing. So I consented, went to the Endowment House, and gave as wife to my husband the woman that I most hated and despised of all women in the world. I saw her enter my house and take my place in the heart of the man for whom I had given up all I had held dear in this life. I know that, as a rule, the Gentile ladies consider the Mormon women weak, miserable creatures to bear what they do, but the sacrifices that many of us have made for our children will prove that we are not different from other women, at least in the matter of a mother's love.

"I could tell you much more, but to what purpose? I could tell you how that woman's influence awakened and fostered all that was evil in my nature, how we together changed my kind, tender husband into a perfect brute, how the strong arm that had defended me for fifteen years came to be lifted against me, and how the death blow came to my little angel child in trying to save her mother from it, as she thought. But I ask again, to what purpose? It will not avail me anything, for there is neither law, justice, nor mercy for women in this Territory. It was not my intention to give any history of my sufferings in polygamy, I simply wanted to tell how I was coerced into giving my consent for my husband to enter it; and I will say this much, that Satan himself could not devise any worse tortures than women experience in the infernal system called 'Celestial Marriage.'"

Here is the experience of another first wife on the very same point, giving consent for her husband to take another wife:—

"A Gentile lady remarked not long ago in the presence of several women who had been Mormons, that she had no patience with first wives who gave consent for their husbands to take other women. They deserved to suffer for being so weak, and if they had been determined they might have prevented it. This lady had been in Utah a few months, and thought she knew all the workings of Mormonism; but when she has lived here seven or eight years, perhaps she will discover that she had not then found out the real inner machinery of polygamy. It takes a person who has lived in it, and suffered in it, to understand what it is. And it takes one who has been a Mormon herself to fully comprehend the pressure, the organized system of tyranny that is brought to bear upon people to compel them to submit to the dictates of the priesthood.

"Years ago, a woman had no choice but to submit

or die; it would have been happier for many if the latter had been their fate, but they had ties that bound them to earth,—their little children,—so they lived on, suffering eternal torments every day of their lives. It is not quite so bad now, perhaps, for women can leave their husbands more easily, and if they have any friends they can get away from Utah without being murdered by 'Indians' in the mountains or on the plains. But in another respect it is worse, for now men will marry other women without asking the consent of their wives, which was deemed necessary some years ago.

"I will relate my own experience, and then let any candid person decide if I could have done otherwise than give consent for my husband to take a plural wife. What I have suffered through the doctrine of polygamy cannot be half told.

"My husband and I emigrated to Utah nearly twenty years ago. We had been married about three years, and had been converted to Mormonism by a traveling missionary in New York State some three months previous. We had been in haste to gather to Zion, not so much to be with God's people, for we had many friends from whom it was hard to part, and besides, rumors had reached us that the promised land was not exactly as the missionaries represented, but because my health was rather delicate, and a change was deemed beneficial. We had heard of the glorious climate of these valleys, and their health-giving properties, and were anxious to secure their benefits. As I said, we had been married three years; but no little child had been sent to sanctify our union, and the Mormon missionary had assured us that this blessing would be ours if we would leave wicked Babylon, and cast our lot with the Saints of God.

"We did not have very much of this world's goods, but my husband was a superior mechanic, besides having a good knowledge of book-keeping, acquired in leisure hours, and I was an excellent needle-woman, consequently we had no fears of not being able to make a living in any place. We sold our little home, and the proceeds were more than sufficient to defray comfortably the expenses of the journey, and leave a surplus for our maintenance until my husband should be able to get into some business. The missionary offered to take charge of George's extra funds, but he was not sufficiently blinded or bigoted to trust the elder so implicitly. Besides, in those days he was very independent, and thought he was fully able to take care of himself and everything belonging to him. A course of Mormon dietetics somewhat modified this characteristic, but for years it was prominent enough to cause both of us many troubles and heart-aches. I often think that if we had been 'blood-atoned' in the days of our early love, and buried together side by side in one grave, we should have escaped many sorrows, and been more glad to meet each other in the resurrection day than we shall be now. But regrets are vain, and what is done can never be undone.

"We had heard in our New York home that

polygamy was practiced among the Saints, but we were assured by the elder that it was entirely optional with the people themselves, and that if a man's religious convictions did not prompt him to enter it, or if a wife thought she was not fitted to carry out the principles of the celestial doctrine, there was no compulsion whatever employed. Of course, he depicted in glowing colors the advantages of the system when lived aright, that the women who embraced it were perfectly happy in this life, and assured of the highest bliss in the world to come. I did not trouble myself very much about the matter after he stated so positively that polygamy was not compulsory, for I was sure that George would never enter it against my wishes, and I was so anxious to get to Utah that I was willing to assume almost any risk. I was not a fanatic or a religious enthusiast by any means, but I had an irresistible longing to experience the joys of motherhood, and I had faith in a change of climate to accomplish this much-desired end.

"In due time we arrived in Utah, after a pleasant journey across the plains, and my husband was not long in obtaining steady employment. Of course, we experienced a measure of regret and sorrow at leaving our old home, and severing so many old ties, but the anticipations for the future soon overbalanced these, and our first year in Zion was one of peace and contentment. We had secured a lot, and intended to build a little home very soon, and in my limited way I was making preparations to adorn it with articles of taste, if not elegance. George was fond of seeing things look pretty around him, and our old home had been as tastefully furnished as our means would permit. And what rendered us still happier, was the fact that my fond hopes were to be realized, and the next spring, God willing, a baby of my own should be folded to my breast.

"Ah me! I grow almost insane when I look back upon those days, and recall the memory of what my husband and I were to each other. Our marriage had been one of pure affection, and the knowledge of this coming pledge of our love drew us even more closely together, and made earth seem almost a Paradise. I used to stand sometimes by my open door and gaze on the lovely valley, bathed in the evening sunlight, and then over the snow-capped mountains, and think that God could not make a lovelier spot than my mountain home. But I lived to see the day when I cursed those mountains for being my prison walls, and almost cursed God for allowing them to exist.

"I need not tell any mother the delight and rapture I felt when I held a lovely baby boy in my arms; and George was no less rejoiced. Everything in our past lives seemed nothing when compared with this event; and from the number of congratulations we received, it also seemed as if the entire city was rejoicing too.

"When our boy was about six months old, the shadow first began to gather around our lives, and it was in this wise. We had a neighbor, a polygamist with two wives, who had lived pretty peaceably together up to that time. But dissensions began to arise, and before long their quarrels were the theme of the neighborhood. One day the two women had a severe altercation in the front door-yard, which the husband undertook to stop, and all three used a great deal of language which, to say the least, was very unbecoming to Saints. My husband spoke his opinion very frankly in regard to an institution which produced such results, and within the space of an hour it was carried to the bishop of the ward, who came down that very evening to remonstrate with George, whom he accused of a leaning toward apostasy. George, being high spirited, and unaccustomed to any dictation or reproof, quietly informed the bishop that he had best mind his own concerns, for he should entertain any opinions he chose about polygamy or any other doctrine. The bishop went directly and reported to the church authorities, and from that moment our doom was sealed. From that moment began a series of persecutions which never ceased until my happiness was wrecked forever.

"We had always been in the habit of going regularly to meeting, paying tithes promptly, and outwardly conforming to all the observances of the Mormon faith. But soon George received an intimation that he was not living up to his privileges as a Saint, and unless he wanted to make trouble for himself, he had better speak more respectfully of the divine ordinance. But, as I said before, he was an independent man and would not be dictated to;

but he discovered after awhile that in Zion the least said was soonest mended, and a man who thought for himself had best also keep those thoughts to himself.

"I could not recount the number of mean and petty persecutions to which we were subjected. We were not threatened openly, because George was making money, and was very liberal in contributing whenever he was called on, consequently he was in good standing. But he could never go to a meeting of the Seventies, or even a Sunday ward meeting, without polygamy being hurled at him in some way or other. I was very quiet, because I had so much confidence in him; and so long as I felt sure that he would not go into it, I judged it best not to make matters worse by talking myself. But there came a time when all this was changed. One evening we had a visit from a friend whom we both honored and respected, and who said that he had come to talk seriously with George. I believe he was honest in his intentions, and firmly thought he had our best interests at heart; but oh, how I hate and despise the very sight of that man!

"He told us that if George did not change his course, he would either be sent on a three-years' mission, or pay the penalty of his indiscretion and disobedience to the law of God. He gave us the particulars of one case, which had happened only a few months previous. We knew the man was missing, but nothing more. I had then lived in Zion long enough to know what going on a mission portended. For me, destitution, or hard labor to keep soul and body together, exposure to all manner of insult from other Saints in my husband's absence, and persecution and slander if I remained true to him. For him, it meant a three-years' absence from wife and boy whom he tenderly loved, and *liberty*, if not *strict private orders* to make entanglements with any number of women he pleased. I had known more than one missionary to return with young girls as wives,—men whom their wives had trusted as much as I did my husband.

"I had learned a great deal the last six months we had lived in Salt Lake City. Before that, we had been so thoroughly engrossed with our own affairs as to pay little attention to what was going on around us. Also, he had been purposely kept in ignorance of evil deeds that were transpiring almost every day. I had learned, too, what was meant by 'paying the penalty,'—a lonely, unmarked grave somewhere on the outskirts of the city, or a ghastly corpse left in some secluded locality to be the prey of wild animals. We listened to our friend, and were impressed by his sincerity, and he gave us unmistakable tokens that he had not come of his own accord, but had been commissioned from head-quarters. When he was leaving he said, 'Think of what I have been telling you, brother and sister M——, for it would be a pity if that fine little fellow there should wake up some morning and find himself fatherless, and perhaps motherless too.'

"I was silent during the interview, but the mo-

NEW RESIDENCE OF THE LATE BRIGHAM YOUNG.

MAYOR LITTLE'S RESIDENCE.

GREAT SALT LAKE. (BLACK ROCK BATHING RESORT.)

ment he was gone, I could not restrain my feelings any longer, and I burst into tears, exclaiming, 'O George, let us get away from this dreadful place! I cannot consent to your embracing that dreadful doctrine, and yet I feel it is true, what brother B. has said, that you will either be blood-atoned or sent on a mission.' He soothed me as well as he could, assured me I need not fear he would break my heart by taking another woman, and that perhaps all would yet come right in the end.

"We agreed, however, that for the present he should be very cautious in expressing his views, and not say anything more against polygamy openly.

"From that day forward an almost unaccountable change came over him. Formerly, he used to talk of polygamy with loathing; now he would say sometimes that it was a good enough doctrine for some people if it was lived aright, but it would never do for him. I know that he was continually pursued by some of the elders, acting under instructions, and when they found that he no longer talked against it, they followed up what they thought a decided advantage. After six months more of this persecution, he became almost maddened, and told me that he believed the best thing for all of us would be to submit. He assured me that matters could not remain in this way much longer, and both our lives were at stake if he did not take another wife. He furthermore assured me that it would never make the slightest difference in our relations. He loved me, and only me; but if I did not give my consent, he could not answer for the consequences.

"At first, I was angry, indignant, and would not listen to the thing for a moment. Afterward, I wept, pleaded, and prayed him rather to let us die together if there was no other way of escape, and our baby with us, than to thus pollute and disgrace our household. Oh, the agony of those never to be forgotten days! Oh, the martyrdom I suffered, in having my heart crucified over and over again! I got to such a pitch of frenzy and despair that I almost cursed my darling boy, who was commencing to toddle after me and lisp my name, as the author of this misfortune. God forgive me, for I knew not what I did!

"While I was in that state of anguish, our boy was taken ill suddenly, and though apparently in perfect health one morning, on the next his little helpless form lay ready for the grave. I can never trust myself to speak of this occurrence. Mothers will comprehend my feelings, and to others my grief is too sacred to be even mentioned. If it were not absolutely necessary, I would not relate what follows; but how can these evils be remedied unless their infamy is exposed? While my husband and myself stood weeping over the cold and senseless form of our idolized little one, a certain member of the Mormon priesthood entered the chamber, and said to me, 'Sister M., *this dispensation of Providence is not mysterious to us who can see clearly; it is only a punishment for your pertinacity in not permitting brother G. to do his duty and live his religion. And mark my words, you will never have another child as long as you oppose the will of the Lord.'* We were both so completely bowed down with sorrow that we neither understood fully his brutality, nor had power to resent it.

"George said subsequently that if he had only been himself, that man would never have left the house alive. But as it was, his words sunk into my heart, because he was considered a just and good man, and I was tortured, almost consumed, with doubt and fear. Friends urged me to seek the consolation of religion in my sorrow. Every influence possible was brought to bear upon me. I went constantly to the meeting-house, where polygamy was dinned forever in my ears, and the wickedness of opposing the celestial ordinance fully set forth. My physical strength gave way. In mind I became almost an imbecile. And as the months sped by, and gave me no signs or hopes of maternity, I began to think that I was cursed of God, and was only expiating my own sin. Then, when the mother love grew again so strong as to be almost uncontrollable, when day and night were haunted by visions of the child who had gone from me forever, and whom I so ardently yearned to replace, in a period of unusual weakness of mind and body, I took the fatal step, I gave consent for my husband to share my place with another.

"I was not allowed to relent. No time was given

me to reconsider. A girl had long been picked out for him. They were married in the Endowment House, and he took her back to her mother until a home could be provided for her. He had enough respect for me not to bring her to my house, and I know that in his heart he regretted the deed as soon as it was done. But this infernal doctrine will destroy all that is good in the best men. They can learn to look unmoved upon sorrows that would awaken pity in the heart of Satan himself. Men who would not allow the wind to blow roughly on their wives, will learn to see them hungry and naked without a pang, and their children the same. Sometimes, when I sit and meditate upon the atrocities that have been perpetrated in the name of God and religion, I wish I had the tongue of an angel, that I might go forth to the world and proclaim the truth as it is.

"I ask now if I was not excusable, if not justified, in giving consent for my husband to go into polygamy. I might perhaps have held out a little longer, but in all probability the end would have been the same. I yielded in a time of weakness, and whether or not I deserved to suffer as my Gentile friend declared, I have been richly repaid for it all the same.

"After George had married, he did not return to my lonely home for several days. He was afraid to meet the storm of grief and indignation which he knew I could not repress. And when he did come, I felt as if I could have torn him in pieces. I wanted to kill him with my own hand, and then

I could have fallen dead at his feet. He was not my own husband any longer, the life of my life, and soul of my soul. Another had come between us and severed the mystic bond that had made us ONE. He could never be to me again on earth what he had been before.

"The girl he married had been brought up in a polygamous family, and of course had been taught to consider the institution a religious one, although her faith had been somewhat weakened by the scenes of strife and discord to which she had been a daily witness almost all her life.

"Though she did me, unwittingly perhaps, the most grievous wrong that one woman can do another, yet I will not be unjust to her. She was naturally good tempered, and never deliberately set to work to torture or annoy me, as I have known too many plural wives to do. Still I hated her with a more than mortal hatred, for had she not come between me and my all in this world?

"As soon as possible a house was built for her quite near my own, and it was as handsomely fitted up as his means would permit. I was not stinted in any comforts, had all I desired, and for awhile George was as kind and attentive to me as before. He returned punctually when the week was over, and always professed that he was delighted to get back to me, his *wife* and his only love. While he was absent I did nothing but weep and mourn, and if by chance a neighbor ventured in, I could not refrain from speaking my mind freely about the abominable institution. When he was with me I tried to be as much like my olden self as possible, for I could not blame him entirely, knowing as I did that he had been almost forced into it. But the specter had come between us, and could not but make his ghastly presence perceptible sooner or later.

"After awhile George would leave the house immediately after supper, almost every evening, saying that he had a little business out, and must also look in upon Emma a few moments, as she was not at all well, and perhaps he would tell me not to wait up for him, as he might be late. Of course I rebelled, for during all our married life previous to his entering polygamy, he had scarcely spent an evening away from home unless I accompanied him. But my remonstrances were in vain. His answer would be, 'Mary, you know that, as I have married Emma, it is only my duty to do what is right by her, and she is now in a condition to demand my care and attention, while you are strong and well, and do not need me at all.' Then, when I would reproach him with having lost his love for me, which only a few short months ago he had assured me was strong as ever, he would reply impatiently, 'Don't be a fool, Mary; of course I love you, and always shall, but I cannot neglect Emma just to gratify your whims. Do be reasonable and look upon things in their proper light. I provide for you and am as kind to you as I ever was; but you ought to see, yourself, that at present, my place is by Emma's side instead of yours.' Think of it, you happy wives, especially you who may be childless, what a *religion*, that drags your husband away from you to the side of another woman who has the expectation of being a mother by him! Think of a *religion* that has so benumbed the moral and intellectual faculties of a wife, that she immolates herself on such a foul altar, in hopes that the coveted boon may be bestowed upon her. When I think upon it, I only wonder that those in the outside world, calling themselves disciples of the loving and tender Christ who was the friend of woman, do not come with fire and sword, and sweep the monster from the face of the earth, that commits such atrocities in his dear name.

"I was alone, in my lonely, childless house, I will no longer call it a *home*, when the tidings were brought to me that a son was born to my husband's second wife. Oh, the unutterable anguish of that long, dreary night! I walked the floor until the dim light of early morning, when my tottering limbs refused to bear me any longer, and I fell to the floor, where I lay for hours in a semi-unconscious state. There was feasting and rejoicing in the other house, while a darkness, worse than that of death, lay over mine.

"Another year, and still another went by, and the reward for which I had bartered my happiness had not been vouchsafed to me. A little daughter had been added to the other household, and I was drinking in its fullness the bitter cup, for my husband no longer made any pretense of staying with me. His *home* was with his other wife and her children. I have no doubt but she made it pleasanter for him than I did, with my tears and reproaches; and while fondling her children, he forgot all about the little boy who was sleeping on the dreary hillside alone.

"Soon after her second child was born, I determined not to live in that unnatural manner any longer. I would make him choose between us, and if she were his choice, I would go entirely away from him and live out my own life. I felt convinced that I could not exist another year in that way, and retain my senses; and perhaps if we were separated forever I could live out the measure of my days, not in happiness, that never could be, but without the intense suffering which I now experienced every day and hour. I could easily have died; but pride, if nothing else, should keep me alive, at least until I had severed all relations with him.

"I will relate here an incident which occurred about this time, not that it has any bearing on my own story, but because it illustrates so well the demoralizing influences of the infamous system.

"A man with two wives lived only a short distance from my house. He was a brute by instinct, and polygamy had made him even more brutal. He was one of those who were not contented with breaking their wives' hearts, but tried to break their heads also. At times, their home was like the infernal regions, an abode of strife and discord; and yet, the first wife, perhaps in memory of their youth, was as patient and forbearing as a woman could possibly be. But now, this man lay dying, and I was summoned with some other neighbors to render a little assistance. If I could live to be a thousand years old, I never should forget the horrible scene which transpired in that chamber of death. Several persons were present, among them the second wife, when the first wife attempted to enter the room. The second tried to prevent her, but another woman assisted her, and both together forced open the door. I knew this woman as the first wife of a certain man, and that her life had been ruined on account of polygamy; and, strange to say, her husband and his other wife were also in the room. When she had effected an entrance, she turned to the second wife of the dying man, and said in thrilling tones, 'This is his *wife*, and she has a *right* to be here, which you have not.' Then looking at her own husband's second wife, she said, 'I want you to remember that if my husband ever lies dying, and *you* try to prevent me from entering the room, I will *hurl* you, yes, *hurl* you out of the house!'

"In the meantime the poor old wife of the dying man stood by the bedside weeping. 'Why do you weep?' said the woman, who appeared almost like an avenging angel; 'you should rather laugh, for you are now free from your misery. There lies the man who wrecked your happiness, and ruined your life, powerless to harm you any more!' Then, touching the hand of the man already cold with approaching death, she exclaimed, 'THANK GOD, THIS CAN NEVER STRIKE A WOMAN AGAIN!' Nearly all the occupants of the room left in horror, frightened at the appearance of this awful woman. I said to her, 'Sister H——, what has come over you, you act as if you were crazy?' She grasped my hand, and replied, 'Sister M——, I am almost wild when I think what this infernal doctrine of polygamy has done for us poor women!'

"As my principal object in unveiling the past was to explain how I was beguiled into polygamy, I will not say much in regard to how I came out of it, except that I was the victim of all manner of slanderous tales; but for that I was partially prepared, and knew that I should have to live them down. When I first told my husband of my decision, he was violently angry; but when he saw that I was not to be moved, he told me to go where I liked, that he should remain with his *wife and children*. In accordance with instructions from some of the priesthood, he sold the roof over my head, and in the darkness of evening, I went forth, with only a little bundle containing a change of clothing in my hand,—went forth from the home where I had seen so much happiness, and afterward so much misery. I went to sister H——, the first wife alluded to before, and asked shelter for the night, which was willingly granted. I remained with her a few days, and then I was fortunate enough to obtain a situation as needle-woman in a family that were themselves inclined to apostasy, but whose wealth and position kept them from the persecution that would have been dealt unsparingly to poorer people.

"Since then, I have been in a measure prospered. Yet still my life has been a lonely and desolate one. But he who ruined my happiness, did not in the end encompass his own. He took more wives, and many children were born to him, but the most of them died in childhood, and those who were spared did not prove either a comfort or a blessing. Lonely as my lot is, I would not exchange it for his.

"Not long ago, I met him in the street face to face. We had not spoken together for ten long years. I was about to pass, but he stopped me, and said, 'Mary, I do not wonder that you do not wish to speak to me, after the way I treated you. But I only want to say this, I hope that just punishment will be meted out to those who separated us.'

"I drew my veil over my face to hide my tears as I answered him, 'We were to blame ourselves, and this cursed libel on the name of religion, polygamy!'

"We have not met since, and as I said once before in the course of this narrative, I feel as if I could not even look on his face in the resurrection day."

CHAPTER VI.

A First Wife's Revenge.

Both Fanatic and Fool.—A Husband's Promise.—The Husband Ensnared.—Happiness of Polygamous Families.—Sickness.—The Vow.—English Mollie.—The Third Wife.—A Religious Enthusiast.

IN the ensuing narrative of a first wife we design to show the evil effect of the system on those living in it, and who may have once advocated it from a conscientious motive. It was originally published under the title of "What Polygamy has done for Women:"—

"Since reading some articles in the *Anti-Polygamy Standard* on the evil effects of polygamy, I have been considering a great deal, and at last have come to the conclusion that it is my duty to relate my experience on this point, and tell what the dreadful system has done for me. It is a very difficult task for a woman to write herself down either a fanatic or a fool, and I have been both; yet still, I appreciate the fact that the horrors of the system can never be fully ventilated or truly told, unless we women who have been mixed up with it are willing to put our shoulders to the wheel, and help on the good work by exposing its iniquities to the world. No other consideration on earth could induce me to acknowledge what a dupe, and afterward what a virago I was, except the hope that it may, perhaps, have some influence in preventing another woman from sharing the same fate. I wish only that the *Standard* could be placed in the hands of every young girl in this Territory. Hundreds of them would gladly read it, and profit by its teachings, if it were placed within their reach.

"My husband and self became converted to Mormonism in an Eastern State through the preaching of a traveling missionary. We were both enthusiastic converts, and speedily removed to Zion, bringing with us two little ones and a fair share of this world's goods. While on the plains, we heard of the doctrine of polygamy; but I was in such an abnormal state of mind, being so completely infatuated with the new religion, that I received the announcement of the revelation with comparatively little astonishment. I was so convinced that the Saints were God's chosen people that it seemed impossible to me that they could err in anything, even though their practices should be entirely at variance with all the ideas I had held hitherto in regard to these subjects. I remember one old lady making the remark that it (polygamy) must be a dreadful cross for the women to bear, and I answered her, 'Whom the Lord loveth he chasteneth.' But this was before the cross was given me to carry myself. My sentiments in regard to the Lord having anything to do with it underwent a decided change after I had personal experience of the doctrine in my own family.

"Of course, after we had been in Zion for awhile, my husband was admonished to 'live his religion.' When I found the cross likely to come home to me, although I began to feel very different about it, I had still sufficient faith in the system as a divine principle, not to violently oppose my husband. I told him it would break my heart to see another supersede me in his affections; but that I loved him too well to peril his future glory, and prevent his exaltation in the next world, consequently I would sacrifice my own feelings, and not oppose him, if he would promise me solemnly that I should always be first in his esteem and regard. This he readily did, and I went with him to the Endowment House, and gave him as wife a young girl, a daughter of one of the high priests who had been chosen for him. It is only justice to say, that however my feelings were wounded by his conduct in after days, there was no courtship or love-making before they were sealed. He was simply told by the priesthood that she would make a suitable wife for him, and he obeyed counsel. He used frequently to say to me that it would make but little difference to him whom he should take as second, that he should do it only from religious conviction in order to secure future exaltation, and that I should always retain the first place in his heart.

"It may seem incredible to outsiders that the priesthood should take it upon themselves to order men to marry certain girls, and that they should obey; but any one who has ever been a Mormon knows that this is a very common occurrence. Polygamists who have large families, if they are men high in authority, will often thrust two of their daughters on some man at the same time, and it is very seldom that he will dare refuse; others again, will, like Jacob of old, make the best of a Leah, in order to win a Rachel.

"While we were in the Endowment House, at the very altar, a realization of what I had done,—given my husband to another woman,—seemed to rush over me, and after one moment of agony that is indescribable, I fainted at his feet. He seemed also to realize the situation; but it was too late for regrets, and the consequences had to be borne as well as we could.

"The young bride was brought home to my house, and became one of our family, no provision for separate housekeeping being made for her. I tried to feel kindly toward her; for after I had consented to the marriage, I was woman enough to try and treat her well; although, at times, the very sight of her at my table, or sitting in my little sewing-room with my husband at her side, almost drove me wild with jealousy, even before I perceived that she was using all her arts, and every means at her command, to win his affections from me. She was a true daughter of her father,—a man who stepped on hearts as if they were stones,—and, little by little, I discovered how she was ensnaring my husband, getting him so completely in her power, and under her control, that he seemed to have no thoughts for any one but her. In less than six months, her influence over him became so strong that he did her bidding as if he were a mere child, while wife and little ones were totally neglected. When he entered the house, he would rush off to her apartment, unmindful of me, or the children whom he had always met with a smile and a kiss. I cannot describe the change that came over our home in those few months; and when I found that I, his true and loyal wife, who had left home, friends, and kindred to follow him to the promised land, was being neglected and almost totally discarded for a girl whose name we did not even know one short year before, I became nearly insane with grief and remorse. I suffered the bitterest kind of remorse, for in reality I was more to blame in the outset than he; and I could not disguise from myself the fact that I had dug a grave, and buried my happiness with my own hands.

"Of course, I made matters worse constantly by my tears and reproaches; for, after awhile, it became impossible for me to control myself. The house was a perfect hell, as every polygamous household is. No matter what the advocates of polygamy may say to the contrary, I affirm here, and I wish it could be circulated all over the United States, that I have never known a polygamist family, and I have been intimate with many from the highest in authority down, where hatred and discord did not exist. I have known families who were extolled as models of respectability and exemplary conduct, where the most disgraceful quarrels were of daily occurrence, and I have also known instances where the wives have scarcely risen from their knees after family devotions, before they would begin to quarrel, and call each other by the lowest kind of epithets. And what is more, I defy any man or woman in this Territory, to cite one instance of a polygamous household where there is anything approaching harmony,—where there is not bickering, constant jealousy and heart-aches, even where the semblance of good relations is most rigidly observed.

"I could name one family that has been frequently held up as a model of purity, loveliness, and piety, the polygamous wives and daughters being designated as 'tabernacles, wherein dwelt holy spirits,' and I know for a fact that one of those plural wives tried to poison another whom she thought was the recipient of too much attention from the husband. It is now no secret, but a matter of common talk, that more than one of those lovely and pious daughters are so lost to even the outward forms of decency that their best friends have abandoned all hope of their reformation. When I look back and think of what I have known to happen, as well as personally suffered, I become almost desperate, and am ready to exclaim, 'Can there be a God, when such a system is permitted to grow and flourish in what is called a *Christian* land!'

"I have been digressing from my narrative, but

my readers must bear with me, and permit me to have my own way in telling my story. I am entirely unaccustomed to writing for the press, and must relate facts and occurrences in my own simple language and manner, trusting that truth will atone for the many other deficiencies.

"I told how I could not longer control myself when I saw my husband so devoted to Louise, and what exasperated me still more was the fact that she knew how to use my folly to her own advantage.

"No matter how enraged I was, she was always cool; but her calm and often silent scorn was far more difficult to endure than rage would have been. One day, after a scene which was more than usually tempestuous on my part, she said to me, 'Sister Sarah, it seems as if you ought to be able to control your temper by this time. Can you not see that your fury only makes brother B. love me the more?' I was so maddened by that word *love*, that I threw the glass I was wiping at her head, shattering it, and inflicting quite a severe flesh wound upon her forehead. If I had been sure that the blow would have killed her, it would have been all the same, for I was too enraged to think of consequences.

"This episode angered my husband so much that he threatened to provide a separate home for Louise, and also to leave me entirely. I did not care, and told him so; and I presume he would have done it at once, if I had not fallen ill suddenly, the result of grief and excitement. Whether to avoid scandal,

Hon. ELI H. MURRAY,
Governor of Utah.

or whether he still felt some of the old affection for me, I do not know; but he certainly gave me every care and attention, and nursed me as tenderly as if there had never been any estrangement between us. Sometimes she would share his night watches by my bedside, and when she could not be present in the room, she managed that another person should, if possible, so as not to allow me any opportunity of talking with him alone, fearing lest I should regain my old influence over him.

"One night, when they thought I was asleep,—I always feigned to be asleep, if I were not really so, when she was in the room,—they were talking about me and my illness, and my husband said, 'We ought not to blame Sarah too much; it certainly must be a great trial to her, for she loved me devotedly.' 'That may be so,' she replied, 'but, William, you know that I love you just as well as she ever has; yes, better, for she is colder hearted naturally than I am. I know that I should die if you should ever turn against me, or take another whom you would love more than you do me.' I felt as if I could spring from my bed, and choke her, but I controlled myself, and waited for his reply. 'You need never fear that, Louise,' he said, 'I shall never care for any one but you.'

"Strange to relate, I lay there quietly, not giving any sign that I had heard one word. I suppose my feelings were in part paralyzed by grief, but still I experienced a thousand deaths in those few moments. Whatever of love and esteem there was remaining for my husband, seemed to be struck dead as it were by one blow, and I lay awake the rest of that long, wearisome night, pondering and planning what I could do to render them as miserable and unhappy as they had made me. I made a vow which I only kept too well, that he *should* care for another besides her, and that I would live to see her experience the same torments I had gone through, which had killed all that was lovable or womanly in my nature, and had left me but a wreck of my former self, in body, mind, and soul.

"I laid my plans well, and was not in particular haste in trying to put them into execution. After my recovery, my husband abandoned the idea of furnishing another home for Louise, and we lived on together as before. But Louise and I seemed to have changed places and dispositions. I became so indifferent to him that his attentions to her no longer annoyed me or gave me pain. Consequently, she did not have the satisfaction of seeing me get into a temper, and this of itself seemed to irritate her beyond measure. I used to go about my work, apparently so intent on my own affairs that I did not care to notice either of them, while all the time I was thinking what a glorious revenge I should have some day on both of them. Louise was no housekeeper, in fact, she greatly disliked domestic labor of any kind, so I exerted myself more than ever to always have everything neat and comfortable. I always had as good meals as possible, for William was something of an epicure in his way, and enjoyed the good things of this life. He was an excellent provider, so far as materials for cooking were concerned, and I always made the best of them.

"I wish I could adequately express my thoughts and feelings at this period of our lives. I did not feel jealous at William's devotion to Louise, for love was dead; I hated her, and nearly hated him, and treated them both with supreme indifference; yet, when lying awake as I often did for hours during the night, thinking of my position as an unloved and unloving wife, and of the happy years we had spent together before this unhappiness came, my heart would become as tender as a child's, and I would shed many bitter tears. Then, when I thought of the woman who occupied the place that was rightfully mine, I would banish all regret, fight it out by myself, and the next morning would be again the hardened, heartless woman, whose main object in life was to secure revenge.

"It may be thought strange that I have not spoken of my children. During those dark days, they were a great comfort to me, and a great sorrow too, for the poor innocents had to bear the consequences of their parents' transgression. The place they called home was that only in name, and the scenes to which they were daily witnesses, were enough to ruin any children. But I am thankful for one thing, that all this had the effect of making them despise polygamy, so that they were never entangled in its meshes.

"Louise had been sealed to my husband for nearly

two years before she had a child, and when a little girl was born, it seemed to me that she was not over pleased. She was naturally indolent, and her training had not remedied that defect; consequently, any labor or responsibility was irksome to her, and the idea of having a child to care for was not what she desired, and was far from being agreeable. She had been treated like a spoiled, petted child by William, and since she had lived in my family, she had spent the most of her time in dressing and making herself captivating to my husband; but that could not last forever.

"During her illness, my family cares and nursing her in addition, were too much for me, and William told me to get some help. An emigration was expected in that very evening, and I went to the tithing yard to secure a girl. I found a young English girl about sixteen years old, as fresh and pretty as a picture, and strong and willing to work. She was a very good Saint too; and, as I soon discovered, was not in the least averse to living her religion, and securing future exaltation by plurality.

"English Mollie, as the children named her, had been in the house only a few days, when William remarked what a bright, pretty girl she was, and so smart for her age. This remark set me thinking that perhaps the way was opened for that revenge I was so longing for, and before long I had my plan all perfected. Women who have never been placed in a similar position will probably say that I was a very wicked, designing wretch. Well, if I was, it was polygamy that made me so, and I fearlessly assert that the system is responsible for the ruin of more women than can ever be estimated, or even imagined.

"My plan was, that English Mollie should be my husband's third wife, and I felt sure there would be no difficulty in accomplishing it. William had very soon forgotten his promises to me, and I imagined that he would not be any more faithful to Louise. My first step was to insist upon a separate home for her. I pleaded my inability to care for such a large family any longer, and I was so determined that I soon carried this point, and a few weeks found Louise in another home, a little cottage not far from us. English Mollie went with her to assist in getting settled, but came back to me in the course of a few days.

"In a very short time the trouble began, as I had foreseen that it would. William would come to my house complaining that he could not get a meal fit to eat, that the house was always untidy, the baby crying continually, and things generally in a muddle. He wanted Mollie to go back again, when I told him plainly that there was only one condition upon which I would permit her to return, that she should be sealed to him first. He seemed a little surprised at the proposal, but did not object. After a man has taken the first plural wife, he can take twenty without any compunctions of conscience. But he was afraid that Louise would never consent, and perhaps Mollie would not be willing. I answered him that it was not necessary to inform Louise about it, that she would get over it as I had; and as for Mollie, I would undertake to get her consent. I told him that as Louise was such a poor manager, it was absolutely necessary to have some one to keep things in order, and Mollie had grown very competent even in the short time she had been under my tuition.

"When I found him quite willing to be sealed to Mollie, I consented for her to go there again, in order to straighten up matters, but I extorted a solemn promise from him not to inform Louise of his matrimonial intentions for the present. Mollie also was pledged to secrecy,—it had taken just ten minutes for me to convince her that it was her duty to enter polygamy,—and we arranged that the marriage should not take place for a few months, or until Mollie should have time to get ready some wedding garments, which I had promised to assist her in making.

"Mollie had been at the cottage about two weeks when she came to my house one evening, saying that Louise had sent her away, ordering her never to return again. It seems that William and she had been indulging in a little surreptitious love-making, and Louise had discovered them. She was very indignant, and in a day or two came down to me, almost boiling over with rage at 'Mollie's brazen conduct,' as she expressed it. I apparently agreed with her, in order to throw her off her guard, and said that Mollie was only to remain in my house until she could find another home. I also said that she had another home in view, but I did *not* say where that home was.

"On account of the circumstances, we hastened the preparations, and in about two weeks we had everything ready. I went with them to the Endowment House, and then invited them home with me to remain two or three days until he could furnish her rooms at the cottage. I told William that he had better place her in charge at once, and Louise would come to her senses after awhile, as I had.

"After returning from the Endowment House, I sent word to Louise to come and take supper with me, as I had company I would like her to meet. She declined because the baby was so cross, but would come later in the evening. When she came in, we were all seated in the parlor, and I shall never forget the satisfaction, I may say exultation, I felt as I said: 'Louise, allow me to present brother B. and his *third wife.* They were married to-day, and will come and live with you next week.'

"She turned scarlet, then pale as death, and I thought she was going to faint. But instead, she broke into a terrible passion of rage, which frightened all the rest, and brought in some of the neighbors to see what was the matter. But I was not frightened, and I went up to her and said, 'Louise, you must not indulge in so much temper, you must control yourself; don't you know it will only make brother B. love Mollie all the better?' At these words she burst into tears and said: 'I can see it all now; this is your work, and you have done it for revenge!'

"'You are not far out of the way,' was my reply, and now you will have an opportunity of knowing what you made me suffer when you stole my husband's heart. You will also know what it is to be an unloved and neglected wife.' She left my house cursing me, and calling down on my head the vengeance of Heaven for having been the instrument of so much deception being practiced on her.

"To tell of the dreadful life they led afterward, and how Mollie succeeded in obtaining the mastery over him, so that Louise was completely ignored, the sufferings of the latter, who had really loved William, and her sorrowful death some years later, would more than fill a large volume. He was a just man, so far as providing for his families in accordance with his means, so she did not want for temporal comforts; but she literally died of a broken heart, when she found it impossible to win him back. It did not matter to me how devoted he was to Mollie, so long as he provided for my children, for my love for him was buried too deep ever to be resurrected on earth.

"Women of America, honored, loved, and loving wives, see what the awful system of polygamy has done for me! I was a religious enthusiast. I was a devoted wife, would almost have sacrificed my own hopes of heaven to add to my husband's happiness. I was accounted an amiable woman, and would not have wronged the meanest or lowest of my sex. But polygamy has not only robbed me of my earthly happiness, it has also deprived me of all future hope, for I have no faith in any religion whatever. It made me the meanest kind of a deceiver in carrying out a plan of revenge, and caused me to glory in the sufferings of another woman. It made me so unwomanly as to pick out another wife for my husband, when I felt in my own soul that polygamy was no more ordered by God than it was in accordance with the laws of man, and I did it simply to make another woman unhappy. It has made me lose all love for the husband of my youth, and the father of my children, and left me a cold, calculating, heartless woman, only enduring his presence for the sake of the material comforts provided for me. It has taken from me all that I held dear in this world, and left me no hope for the world to come.

"Women of America, can you hesitate when your assistance is implored for the overthrow of this vile system which renders women a shame and a disgrace to their sex?"

We omit the latter portion of this woman's story, relating how she became an apostate, because it is almost identical with those of other women who have broken the chains of Mormonism. They all have about the same experience to undergo,—slander, persecution, and social ostracism from the Mormons. The only difference between the present and the past is, that now they have not quite so much difficulty in obtaining employment, as there are more Gentiles in the Territory, and consequently, less absolute dependence on those who dare not disobey counsel in their treatment of the unfortunates who have laid themselves under the ban of the priesthood. Still, she is a brave woman who even to-day severs her connection with Mormonism, unless she has means to leave Utah immediately, and place herself beyond the reach of all Mormon influences.

CHAPTER VII.

A Victim of Pious Words.

Married to a Missionary.—The Awakening.—Tempted to Murder Her Own Children.—Apostasy.—More Demon than Woman.

THE next narrative is one of a second wife, and is designed to show the deception that is practiced upon innocent and unsuspecting young girls in order to lure them into plural marriage. And we have no hesitancy in saying that the same arts are employed at the present time for the same purpose, with perhaps this exception, polygamy is not so strenuously denied by the missionaries abroad as it was in former years. They will, however, represent themselves as single men, and marry young girls under circumstances precisely similar, to those narrated in the following case :—

"I have been requested by some of the ladies of the Anti-Polygamy Society to tell how I became a polygamous wife, and why I continued living in that unlawful relation, when I did not believe in the institution as a divine ordinance, and hated the system with my whole soul. My story is not an uncommon one, and can easily find many a parallel in the history of Mormonism.

"I was born in England, and belonged to a respectable family of the middle class. My father was a successful tradesman, and to me, an only child, the best educational advantages were afforded. In fact, I received what is termed in that country a finished education. When I was about sixteen years old, my parents became converts to Mormonism. I had always been religiously inclined, and the Mormon doctrines, as there preached, seemed to me so simple, beautiful, and good, that it was not long before I became an enthusiastic votary of the new religion. I had heard that the Saints in America practiced polygamy, but I did not trouble myself much about it, as I did not anticipate leaving my own country. Besides, the missionaries always denied it, and said the report was only a wicked invention of their enemies to injure the reputation of the Saints in the outside world. Subsequently, when I was sought in marriage by a missionary, my parents inquired into the matter very particularly, but were positively assured by him that no such thing as polygamy existed. We were married, and lived happily for two years, when he was recalled to Utah, and I, of course, accompanied him to the promised land. I left my childhood's home, and bade farewell to my parents with many tears and regrets, yet with many bright hopes and anticipations for a happy future in Zion. They were on the declining side of life, and could not bear to sever themselves from all old ties and associations, but they gave up me, their dearest treasure, and bade me 'God speed' with their last blessing.

"The shock I received may be imagined when upon arriving in Salt Lake City, my husband brought me *home* to a house, where another woman was installed as mistress, his first wife, who was the mother of several children. They told me afterward that for several days I raved like a mad woman, then came a long period of unconsciousness. When I recovered from the attack of brain fever, and realized how shamefully I had been duped, I became a changed creature. Although my husband was always kind and tender, and provided well for my temporal wants, and his first wife was not especially disagreeable, I could not forget the miserable deception he had practiced upon me, and the very name of religion became hateful and obnoxious.

"After my health became somewhat restored, I besought my husband to permit me to return to England, where, in the love and sympathy of my parents, I might find some consolation for the terrible sufferings I had endured in my brief absence from them. For some time he objected, but at last he told me that I might go, since I was so unhappy; but I must leave my babes with him, one scarcely sixteen months old, the other, not nearly so many weeks. I pleaded, oh so earnestly, against this cruel stipulation, but he was inexorable. I could not abandon my children, so for their sakes, I remained and bore my sufferings with all the fortitude I could summon to my aid.

"Will any mother believe me, when I say that often I was tempted to give the little innocents something that would make them sleep their last long slumber, thus purchasing freedom from a life at which my nature revolted, and which my conscience told me was as sinful as it was degrading to my womanhood? But it is true, and I marvel now that I resisted the temptation as well as I did. Upon learning the true state of affairs, my father made preparations to come to Utah after me, but he died suddenly before his intentions could be fulfilled, and my broken-hearted mother was not long in following him to the grave. If I had only known how short a time they were to live, I should have spared them the knowledge of the bitter truth.

"From that time until his death, my husband was kind and affectionate to me, and considerate enough of my feelings never to mention the word religion in private in connection with polygamy. In his public talks, for he was a member of the priesthood, he used sometimes to exhort the people to live up to their religious privileges. We lived on quietly for years, no one suspecting or knowing of my disaffection, but one trusted friend, who would not betray me for her own life. In those days, it was a terrible crime for a woman to disbelieve any portion of the Mormon creed, especially plurality, and if known she was subjected to all manner of persecution. My husband loved me well enough to shield me from the consequences which must inevitably ensue, should my true feelings become known to those in authority. Though he deceived me so outrageously, yet he would not betray me; and

I must do him the justice to say, that apart from his delusion, he was one of the best and truest-hearted men that ever lived.

"After he died I gradually withdrew myself and family from all Mormon influences, devoting myself entirely to my children, whom I taught secretly to abhor the very name of Mormonism. I was in very comfortable circumstances, because what my dear parents left had come to me, consequently I did not need to labor for a support. But I was obliged for years to use the utmost caution in teaching what was contrary to Mormon doctrine, and I tremble now, when I look back and think of my temerity in doing as I did. The same course has caused more than one woman, and her children also, to be blood-atoned. But I succeeded in rearing my children as I desired in that particular. If I had not, I would a thousand times rather have laid them in their graves.

"As for me, I am sometimes at a loss how to define myself. Often I think I am more demon than human. I have two lovely and interesting daughters, both honored wives and mothers, (the rest of my children, thank God, died in babyhood, and in heaven, if there is one, there will be no slurs cast upon their birth), and, although I was so heartlessly beguiled into the system, sometimes I can scarcely help regarding them as children of shame. Before I came to Utah, I was a trustful, true-hearted girl, and in religious fervor almost a devotee. Now, I am but a poor, miserable apology for a woman. I have no belief in anything; no confidence in humanity, no faith in religion, no hope in God! I am simply a wreck, like thousands of other women, whose lives have been blasted under this cruel system.

"This, ladies, is my story. Take it, if you will and tell the women of America what polygamy has done for

'ONE WOMAN.'"

CHAPTER VIII.

A Slave to the First Wife.

Sorrows of Plural Wives.—An Elder's Importunities.—An Unwilling Consent.—Slavery.—A Disappointed Lover.—Escape from Home.—Tracked.—Driven Back.—Shameful Neglect.—Leaving Home a Second Time.—Lying Justified.—A Husband's Treachery.—Doubts and Apostasy.

WE now present another story of a second wife, which illustrates still another phase of the "divine ordinance," and shows the motives that sometimes induce first wives to give other women to their husbands. This young girl was very sweet and amiable naturally, and the woman who treated her so harshly was never considered as either cruel or vindictive, until polygamy developed, or perhaps engendered, these evil qualities. There is a great deal of truth in the remark once made by an old Mormon, "My wife was a perfect angel until I took a second, and then she became a perfect demon."

"The majority of people have the idea that in polygamy the grievances are all on the side of the first wife, and that the other women spend the most of their time in planning how to annoy her and make her miserable. Let me relate my story, and people will see that the plural wives also have their sorrows, and are deserving of commiseration and sympathy too. It will also be seen that the first wives are not always so averse to their husbands' going into polygamy as outsiders often think. In my own experience, I have known more than one first wife to choose a second wife for her husband.

"I came to Utah a number of years ago, when I was about eighteen years of age. There were quite a number of Saints going from our town, and my parents allowed me to go with a neighbor's family, because I was in rather delicate health, and one of the elders told my mother that the climate of Zion would soon restore me to perfect strength. The rest of the family and my parents were to follow in the course of a year or two, and in the meantime I was to be partially in charge of the elder and his wife, who promised to find me a good situation. I was an excellent needle-woman, having lived for years in a nobleman's family as nurse-maid, and latterly as seamstress; but my failing health had obliged me to leave my place and return home.

"After we had started on the journey, I found that the fact of the elder's having a wife did not prevent him from offering me what I thought were decided insults, and, what astonished me still more, his wife did not resent his attentions to me. I knew very well that the Saints in Utah practiced polygamy, but I never had any thought of entering it, for

I had a sweetheart in England who was to emigrate later on with my own family.

"Soon after arriving in Salt Lake City I was taken down with intermittent or mountain fever, and was very ill for many weeks. The elder and his wife were very kind to me, and nursed me as if I had been a sister. But as soon as I was able to be around a little, they both commenced to talk polygamy to me, told me it was my duty to enter it, not only to repay them for their kindness, but also as the means of saving my soul. I objected very strongly, told them I could not marry at all, because they knew very well that I was engaged before I left England, and I had no idea of giving up my own lover for another woman's husband. But the more I objected, the more they urged me, and at last, being weak from recent illness, and being entirely penniless and a stranger, without a friend in the place, (my neighbor's family from England having gone to one of the settlements), I consented. What made me yield was the threat that if I persisted in refusing, I should be turned out of doors, and the Saints all told that I was a bad character. As I said before, I was very weak and nervous, not at all able to shift for myself, and under these circumstances consent was wrung from me. They both promised that I should always be well cared for, and be treated in the family as an equal in every respect.

"If I had not consented, I presume that I should have been turned out of doors, perhaps in the night, for such things used to be of frequent occurrence in early days. After I had become a plural wife, I learned of one instance where a young girl refused to become the fourth wife of a certain bishop, and she was sent away from the house at midnight. Of course the neighbors missed her, and inquiries were made, but no one seemed to know what had become of her. A few days afterward it was rumored that her body had been found in the Jordan river, and in relation to that fact, a good Mormon remarked in our own house, that 'Dead people tell no tales.'

"But to return to my own story. Before many months had passed I found out that she, at least, never had any intention of keeping the promise that I should be well treated, and that she urged him to marry me simply because she wanted a servant. I believe that he would have been kind to me, if he had not been so completely under her influence. He was naturally a peaceful man, and did as she desired him in order to avoid having trouble with her.

"I had been married to him but three months, when a younger sister of his told me that Polly supposed the president (Brigham Young) would make him go into polygamy some day, and she wanted him to marry me because I would make a good '*nigger*,' for she meant the second wife to be nothing but a 'nigger' who would know her place, and keep it, too. She told me, also, that it was arranged between them before they left England that he should marry me when we reached the valley, and that I should be entirely under her control and direction. She was willing he should be exalted in heaven; but she was also determined to be recompensed for it on earth.

"For three years she did with me just as she pleased. I was as much of a slave as any negro who ever lived. I could not begin to tell the privations I endured. Sometimes I was without food, except a little dry bread, for two or three days together, often without fire in the winter, and in addition, I had scorn and insults to bear from the first wife. She would often call me by names that decency will not let me repeat, and if the husband attempted to take my part, she would turn on him too. He sometimes promised to leave her entirely and take me away, but he never could shake off her influence long enough to think or act for himself.

"I did all the household work for the family, and when there was nothing else to be done in the house, washing and ironing and fine-sewing were taken in, which I did, and she put the pay in her pocket. I had no friends in whom I could confide, because she always took good care that I should not leave the house except in her company, so I never had the chance of making any acquaintances of my own.

"I threatened to leave the house once, and she told me that I would be glad enough to come back again, for she had informed every one that I was only an outcast whom they had picked up in the streets of Liverpool, and were trying to reform. I presume she would never have gained so complete a mastery over me, if my intellect had not been seriously weakened by the fever. I never should have gone into polygamy if I had been entirely in my right mind.

"The young man to whom I was promised, had been my sweetheart from the time we were village children together, and we were very much attached to each other. If I had been perfectly myself, I know I could not have been false to him. When he heard what I had done, he went to Australia instead of coming to America, and I never heard anything more from him.

"My first child was born dead. I was in labor two days, and had no assistance whatever until a kind neighbor who learned my situation, came and did what she could for me. My husband's first wife said she was glad the little —— was dead, for if I had a child to take care of, I should not be fit for anything else. She said, also, what I myself believe now, that there was no place for polygamous children in this world; but for all that, I shed many tears over the little girl whose face I had only looked on for a moment before she was taken away from me forever.

"For shame's sake, they gave me pretty good care for a week or two, because the neighbors were beginning to talk about the way I was treated. After that, things went on in the same old way again. Three weeks after my illness, I was doing all the work, besides some extra washing. I cannot express the suffering of both mind and body I endured all through that winter. I believe I should have taken my own life if I had not been sustained by the thought that my parents would soon be here to rescue and protect me.

"But when spring came, instead of having my anticipations realized, I was doomed to disappointment. My father, who was a carpenter by trade, had been seriously injured by falling from a scaffolding, and of course the family could not emigrate until he should recover. This news almost drove me wild, and in desperation I left the house secretly, and made my way to the residence of a Mrs. W., a Gentile lady whom I knew by name, and who, I had heard a neighbor say, was in need of a nurse and seamstress. I had nothing with me but one change of clothing.

"She happened to be at home, and in my despair I told her the whole story of my wrongs, and begged permission to remain at once. She said I could stay for the present, and if she found my story true, she would befriend me. I do not know what inquiries she made, but she kept me on from day to day, and week to week, and seemed well satisfied with me. I never left the house, for fear of being discovered, and I had asked my fellow-servants not to mention the circumstances under which I had come there. I have reason, however, to think that one girl, a good Mormon, betrayed me; for when I had been in the house about three months, I was called down stairs one evening, and there in the kitchen was my husband talking to my mistress.

"You may imagine how I felt; but he spoke

very kindly, promised faithfully that I should be well treated if I would return home with him, and said that if the first wife did not do right by me, he would complain to the president.

"I did not want to go back, because I thought I could save enough from my wages to keep me comfortable until I could work again, and my kind mistress told him that as long as I wished to remain under her roof, she would retain and protect me.

"He appeared very sorry; said it was Polly who had tracked me; that she would make a dreadful row, and perhaps it would be better for all of us if I would go home quietly. But I refused, and he left the house, and I heard nothing more for a few days, when my mistress told me with tears in her eyes that I must go home, as her husband had been warned by the church authorities that it would be the worse for him if he kept me in the house.

"There was not much chance of getting justice in those days, even in a Gentile court, and he did not care to involve himself in difficulties for a perfect stranger, and a polygamous wife at that, although he felt very sorry for my situation. People may think that this is exaggeration; but thousands in Salt Lake City can bear witness to the fact that there was a time when the Gentiles could not protect Mormon women, except at the risk of their own lives.

"I went back with my husband that same evening. I suppose some people will say I was very foolish to do it. But I was without a friend in the city, turned out of the only place of shelter, and expecting to be a mother again. I might, perhaps, have gone to the Jordan and drowned myself, or lain down in the streets and died; but that would have been poor consolation for my parents on their arrival, and in all my suffering I had thoughts of them.

"My husband was out of town on business when my second child was born. The same neighbor who had been with me in my first trial, kindly assisted me, and made me and my baby boy comfortable before she left us. It had been arranged before my husband left that an experienced midwife should attend me; but as he was absent, his first wife refused to allow her to be sent for, saying I could get along very well without such a fuss being made over me; *it was all nonsense treating polygamous women as if they were first wives.*

"And to their shame be it said, many of the first wives look upon the plural women as if they were more like animals than human kind, and think that they and their children need not be better housed nor fed than the horse in the stable or the ox in the yard. I suppose it is only natural for a first wife to be jealous of the second, and look upon her as a usurper of her rights; but if she professes to believe that polygamy is a divine institution, she ought certainly to allow the second wife to have her rights also.

"Those who preach polygamy always say that the wives are all equal in the sight of both God and man; but in many cases, plural wives are treated as if they were on a level with those women in the outside world who lead lives of shame. I do not wonder that Gentiles sometimes consider the polygamous women as no better than sinful creatures; for in many instances the first wives have set them the example.

"After my neighbor had rendered us comfortable, she was prevented from coming again for about twenty-four hours, and during that time the first wife never came near me. *I was left those twenty-four hours entirely alone, without so much as a drop of water to moisten my lips. My poor baby wailed all through that long night. I was unable to rise and get him anything to satisfy his hunger, and nature had not yet provided anything for him.*

"We were both so nearly dead when my friend came again, that the first wife was really frightened, and did all she could for our restoration. Sister A. told her that if we died, she would proclaim her as a murderess before the whole city. If this part of my story is doubted, I can mention more than one responsible person in the city who can substantiate my statements on oath.

"When my husband returned, he was very indignant at the way I had been treated, and assured me that anything like it should never happen again. But I knew better, and made up my mind quietly, without saying a word to any one, that as soon as I was able I would come out of polygamy if it should cost me my life. Rather than live any longer to be treated worse than a dog, I would die like a dog in the streets, if I could do no better.

"After awhile I confided my intention to sister A., with whom I had become quite friendly, and she promised to aid me all in her power. When my baby was six weeks old, I left home and went to sister A.'s house, simply leaving a few lines for my husband, telling him that I had left the family forever, and would kill myself and child rather than return. He came directly after me, but my mind was firmly made up, and was not to be changed.

"Sister A. talked very plainly to him; said their treatment of me had become town talk, and even if he had not been cruel to me himself, he had not controlled his first wife as he should. She ended by telling him that a man who could not govern one wife had no business to be a polygamist, for the true doctrine was that a husband should keep *all* his wives in subjection.

"Through the influence of sister A., who was universally loved for her kindness of heart, I obtained some sewing to do in the house; and my old mistress, Mrs. W., was also very kind to me, although she did not dare employ me in her family. She gave me work at home, however, and paid me so liberally that I was able to pay sister A. for my board, and was saving a little besides for a rainy day. My baby was growing to be a fine, healthy fellow, and I was beginning to feel almost like a young girl again, when sister A.'s husband told me one evening,—she had not the heart to tell me herself,—that I must find another home, for his reputation as a Saint was becoming very much compromised by harboring an apostate.

"I replied I was not an apostate. I had not abandoned Mormonism, nor had I any intention of so doing. I had only left a house where I had been ill-treated,—yes, shamefully abused,—and without any cause whatever.

"He said he felt very sorry for me; that as far as he could see I had behaved like a good woman since I had been in their house, but there were many ugly stories afloat about me, and for the sake of his own family he felt obliged to tell me that I must look for another home.

"And then it transpired that the first wife had been circulating some outrageous stories about me,—that I was not a good woman, had a very passionate temper, was almost everything wicked, and worse than all, I was a vile apostate, and ought to suffer the most severe punishment for my sins. I had been kept so much in the background that people knew but very little about me; and as an evil word flies quicker than a good one, there were many people who were ready to believe all she said, and consequently I found myself in a pretty bad situation.

"But I determined not to lose courage, for I was expecting my parents in a very short time, and although I should be obliged to leave sister A.'s house, yet she promised to still befriend me. She procured me a lodging with a friend of hers in another part of the city,—a woman whose husband was absent somewhere in the settlement with another wife.

"An emigration had just come in, and we three agreed to say that I was one of the new-comers, so as to put the first wife off the track. In my girlhood I should have thought it very wrong to tell what now seemed a justifiable falsehood, but I had found since I came to Utah that the Saints did not stop at telling what was not true when there seemed to be good occasion for it. They falsified whenever it pleased them to do so. I never was so horrified in all my life as when I heard President Young say on the stand that nowhere could be found greater or smoother liars than among the Mormon people. That was really the first thing that shook my faith in the principles of Mormonism.

"Another circumstance occurred about that time which weakened my faith still more, and which probably had great effect in causing my final apostasy. There lived a short distance from us a high Mormon who had only one wife, and who had, at her entreaties, managed to keep out of polygamy, although he was reputed quite wealthy. But all at once the wife imagined that he was paying altogether too much attention to her servant-girl, whom she discharged immediately.

"Shortly after, the husband became very anxious about the health of his wife, she being near her confinement, and he suggested that she should take her other child and stay with her mother until her trial was over. Not suspecting any treachery, she acceded to his desires and left him at home, as he said that he could shift for himself very well for a few weeks. Her mother lived in an extreme part of the city, but he seemed very attentive, coming to see her almost every day.

"When her child was about a week old, a talkative neighbor revealed the fact that her husband had been sealed to the girl she had discharged some two or three weeks previous. The wife would not believe it, and was very indignant, but the old lady insisted it was true, and added rather tauntingly, 'When you go home you will see that she is already mistress in the house.'

"Almost maddened with grief and excitement, the poor woman rose from her bed and went home, where she found it to be just as the old lady had said. The girl told her insultingly that she was a servant no longer, but as much of a lady as she was now. The injured wife fell fainting at the feet of her treacherous husband, was taken to bed, never regained consciousness, and in two days was carried to her grave, the victim of a husband's perfidy.

"Though I personally had no reason to feel any sympathy for first wives, yet this occurrence set me thinking that a system which was productive of so much sorrow and evil as even my own limited experience had seen, could not have been ordered by God.

"When once I began to have doubts regarding

the divine origin of polygamy, it was not long until I disbelieved other portions of the Mormon creed, and when my parents arrived, about two months after I had left sister A., they were both grieved and shocked to find that I was on the high road to apostasy.

"Even after I had related all my wrongs and sorrows, as well as what I had seen others suffer, they said: 'Never mind, daughter; though you had the misfortune to fall in with those who were wolves among the sheep, yet you must not let that shake your faith in holy revelation and the Latter-day prophets.'

"I did not say much, because I had been brought up to be respectful, and to pay much deference to my elders; but I hoped and felt sure that their eyes would be opened before they had been in Zion twelve months.

"I was not mistaken; and although we had a very hard time to get along for awhile, yet by keeping quiet, and not giving any publicity to our real sentiments, we escaped much trouble that might have fallen to our lot. After the Gentiles began to come in, we had no trouble in getting plenty of work, and we soon had a comfortable home again.

"I am married now, and have a husband of my own,—one whose kindness has atoned for some of those dark days of my past life,—but I can never repress a shudder when I think of what I endured in polygamy, and it is hard for me not to wish that the woman who was the cause of it all may yet receive the punishment which she so richly deserves."

CHAPTER IX.

Evidence vs. Statements.

Incident of the Endowment House.—Statement of a Mormon Bishop.—Testimony of a Victim.—Result of a Second Marriage.—Testimony of the United States District Attorney for Utah.

WE could present a large number of similar "heart histories" of apostate women, bearing on the same points which the foregoing stories have illustrated; but we think enough have been given to prove that from the earliest days of polygamy, the majority of victims sacrificed on its unclean altars have been unwilling ones.

Every wife who retains one spark of womanly feeling, or one trace of a true woman's nature, cannot help but curse the day when her home was desecrated by polygamy; and among those from whom a verbal consent has been wrung, by means that would disgrace savages, the same feeling exists.

There is a lady living at present in Salt Lake City, (and one of the best and most lovable of women she is, too), who was induced by methods which we dare not even mention, to make the last and most cruel sacrifice which this barbarous faith demands of woman,—that of placing the hand of the new bride in that of her husband. On their way to the Endowment House, she said to him: "I am going to lie to you, lie to the President, and lie to God, for I must say I *consent* to this marriage, when I had rather die a thousand deaths than have it take place."

Of course, polygamy was not "*forced*" upon this wife, nor upon thousands of others who have felt as she did; and yet the advocates of the doctrine will state unblushingly that it is never enforced in any case, but is the voluntary choice of all who are living in it.

In the year 1881 a certain Mormon bishop was interviewed in the East by the reporter of a prominent metropolitan newspaper. In the course of his remarks he made the following statements:—

"The polygamous system is the only natural one, and the time rapidly approaches when it will be the most conspicuous and beneficent of American institutions. It will be the grand characteristic feature of American society. Our women are contented with it,—nay, more, they are the most ardent defenders of it to be found in Utah. If the question were put to a vote to-morrow, nine-tenths of the women of Utah would vote to perpetuate polygamy."

This man is the representative of a class whose tyranny has enslaved thousands of victims who are living to-day in Utah Territory, and who envy the dead. In hundreds of homes, the aged wife, deserted by just such a man as this, who once

Mrs. A. G. PADDOCK,
Salt Lake City, Utah.

swore to love and cherish her until death should part them, sits solitary by the ashes of her desolate hearth, while the husband of her youth, sealed to women with fresher and fairer faces, gives scarcely a thought to her existence.

In hundreds of other homes, the feeble mother of half a dozen little ones, toils from morning till night to earn bread for her family, while the father of her children spends all that he has upon another wife who happens to be the favorite of the hour. And it is more probable than not that this same husband will never lose an opportunity of proclaiming to the world that "polygamy is not an outgrowth of lust, but is strictly a religious institution."

In contradistinction to the statements of this bishop, listen to those of a woman who has lived and suffered in polygamy:—

"If the American people could only realize all that Mormonism and polygamy mean to humanity! It renders man coarse, tyrannical, brutal, and heartless. It deals death to all sentiments of true manhood. It enslaves and ruins woman. It crucifies every God-given feeling of her nature. She is taught that to love her husband as her heart prompts her to do, and to feel the natural jealousy that comes from seeing her husband marry another woman, is wicked, and springs from her innate depravity; that she must crush out and annihilate all such feelings, and submit to whatever her husband and the Mormon church dictate. It brings thousands of children into being with the brand of illegitimacy upon them, whose birthright is hatred and wickedness. They are brought forth in sorrow and in tears. They are cradled in misery and iniquity. They grow up hating their fathers, as well as the plural wives and children. And at last they come to feel that if their parents live in that unlicensed manner, they, too have a right to follow their own evil inclinations. I solemnly aver that Mormon polygamy brings no good to man, woman, or child; but on the contrary it brings them darkness, destruction, and despair."

We recall the face of one woman,—a first wife,—and yet we need not say we recall it, for it haunts us continually. It is only four months since her husband was sealed to a new wife; but those months have done the work of two-score years. Her face, which was fair and youthful less than a year ago, looks now like that of one enduring the torments of a lost soul. The hollow eyes, the bloodless cheeks and lips, tell that she is dying by inches, and dying, too, in the midst of tortures compared with which the rack would be a bed of roses.

Can those who can never even imagine themselves in her place, ask why she submits to such a fate? Let us ask you in return, how a wife in Utah Territory can prevent her husband from marrying two, ten, or twenty women, if he chooses? There have been many instances where women, aware of their husbands' intention to take another wife, have gone to the United States Court to ask help to prevent the marriage, but they have always been told that nothing could be done. And then, when the marriages have taken place, there is absolutely no way of proving the felony, or punishing the law-breakers.

The District Attorney of Utah, in a recent letter to the press, said: "Do you remember that the other twin relic, American slavery, which, thank God, is no more, set up the same cry of 'Let us alone'? And oh, to the shame of this great nation it must be written, for years and years we did let it alone, until the bitter wail of 5,000,000 souls went up to God, and this nation was drenched in blood. To-day, not millions, but thousands of burdened souls, who have experienced the beastly practice, polygamy,—souls whose light has nearly gone out in this world, and whose faith in mankind is weak, if not extinct,—are praying for the hour when they may be disenthralled from a slavery which has been a living death to them.

"If every Congressman could hear the experience of some of the legal wives of Utah related by themselves, and hear the earnest prayers that are often spoken aloud, but oftener prayed in secret, there would be no need of any lobby at the Capitol to urge that laws be passed that would eventually stamp out this relic of barbarism."

CHAPTER X.

Still in the Toils.

Help of the Nation Needed.—Timidity of the Women Still in the Church.—Their Despair.—An Infatuated Wife.—A Sad Story.—Wives without Legal Rights.—The Third Wife.

YOU have heard the stories of some who have had the courage to come out from these abominations. Now listen to the appeals of those whom circumstances prevent from breaking their shackles, but who would gladly be free, would our Government but vouchsafe to them assistance and protection.

The saying, "Who would be free, themselves must strike the blow," is undoubtedly true in the majority of cases; yet the questions seem pertinent, Are all those in bondage so circumstanced that they can or will "strike the blow"? and if freedom is not to be theirs, except through their own courage and resistance, must they forever remain in fetters?

Had the abolition of slavery in the South depended entirely on the slaves' striking for freedom, they would have remained in bondage until this day. There are thousands of women who abhor polygamy in their inmost hearts, who feel that they have been deeply wronged and deceived, who appreciate the degrading bondage in which they are held, yet who, from the force of existing circumstances, cannot, unaided, strike the blow that is to procure their liberation. Help must come from a mightier arm than theirs. The blow must be dealt with the entire might of the nation!

The second class of the women of Mormonism,—those who are still in the church, and who, perhaps, believe in all the tenets of that creed except polygamy,—are entitled to heartfelt sympathy and commiseration from every true woman in the land.

Some of these, the majority, no doubt, have been entangled in its vile meshes; and they hate, yes, loathe, the system, but remain in it for the sake of bread for their children. The life of these women is a perpetual lie, and an outrage against every womanly feeling. They are obliged to deceive others constantly, and sometimes try to reconcile matters by deceiving themselves, but are continually doing all sorts of things against their better nature. They would greatly rejoice if polygamy was abolished; but they will not, or dare not, lift one finger in aid of their own deliverance.

Taking all things into consideration, perhaps they are not to be censured as much as people might imagine. They are very timid, because so many years of tyranny and oppression have robbed them of power to act or think for themselves, even in vindication of their own rights.

Nine-tenths of the women who have been Mormons have completely sunk their own identity in that of their masters. And though some of them are, in a great measure, unwilling slaves, they are securely bound, hand and foot, body and soul, and show no greater desire to burst their shackles than do the degraded few who pretend that they love their chains and would not accept freedom if offered to them.

Another reason is, they deem the attempt hopeless, and do not anticipate or look forward to anything better than the miserable existence they are now dragging out. They have long been taught that human law is powerless to interfere with the divine institution, and this assertion is verified in the repeated failures of Congress to enact efficient statutes.

If they should take an open position against polygamy, the limited support given them by their husbands would be withdrawn, and the church-vials of slander and detraction poured forth upon their defenseless heads. A polygamist usually provides shelter, flour, and perhaps fuel for his families, (other things they must obtain themselves), and a mother with little children will hesitate before taking a step that will deprive her even of these.

The Mormon emissaries abroad invariably lay much stress upon the point that the polygamists "support their wives and acknowledge their children." We assert, and challenge a contradiction of the assertion, that not more than one polygamist in ten furnishes his families with more than flour and fuel, and that not one in a hundred furnishes anything approaching an adequate support.

If these women had only the least idea, or the faintest hope, that the overthrow of the Mormon theocracy would ever be accomplished, some of them would no doubt come out and join the Anti-Polygamy ranks. But they have no faith whatever in Congress, and if the truth must be told, very little respect for a Government that cannot or will not enforce its own laws.

So they go on, bearing their burdens as best they may. If they have been in any manner instrumental in the husbands' entering polygamy, they are the more backward in openly condemning it. They are angry with themselves, and are often willing to acknowledge that they have been foolish; but they will not identify themselves with any movement for the suppression of the system that has ruined their happiness.

An incident illustrative of this point came under our notice not long ago. We accidentally became acquainted with a woman who told us her story frankly. She had once been a fanatical Mormon; and at a time when several of her neighbors were taking plural wives, she urged her husband to do the same, in order to give him future exaltation.

"One woman," she said, "as ignorant and superstitious as myself, taunted me because my husband did not have any prospects of a future kingdom, and so I never gave him any rest until he went into polygamy.

"And yet it was a severe trial to me. When the time came, I had a terrible struggle with myself before I could go to the Endowment House with them. But I was so infatuated, or rather fanatical, that I really thought I was doing God service, by subduing my own feelings and conquering the flesh, in giving my husband to another, and thus preparing a glorious future for us both.

"I had not been ignorant of the evil effects of the system in other families; but when I saw the same things occurring in my own, when I found myself in part supplanted by another woman, when discord and wrangling began to disturb the harmony of the household, I began to have my doubts regarding the divinity of the ordinance. I soon felt convinced that an institution which was productive of so much unhappiness could not be from God, and that no amount of bliss or exaltation in the next world could repay women for the misery and degradation they endure in this.

"And now," she continued, "I see my folly. The money which should go to support my children, is given to the second wife, and I am obliged to work hard from morning till night, and sometimes until nearly morning again, to provide necessaries for them. My husband is a good man, but of course he must also do something for his other family; and how can a laboring man support so many in any kind of comfort? Yes, I have seen the evils of polygamy, and almost wish I had buried my husband before he entered it."

"If you do not now believe in it as a religious principle, why are you not honest? Why not come out openly and join the Anti-Polygamy Movement?" we inquired.

"Because," she answered, "I caused my husband to go into it, and I must now bear the consequences of my own folly. If I should do anything of that kind, he would leave me entirely, for he is still a good Mormon, and for that, so am I. Though he is in polygamy, he is the husband of my youth, and I love him yet, for he is as good as any man could be under the circumstances. It was my fault that both of our lives have been in a measure ruined, and I will bear the consequences to the end, or until the United States Government will make provision for women to come out of polygamy peaceably and honorably."

Now, here was a woman who hated polygamy, was fully conscious of all its evils, did not believe in it as a religious ordinance, and yet could not under any circumstances be induced to join the movement for its suppression. And this woman is only one of thousands in Utah, whose very existence is torture, and to whom eternity means only a continuation of that tyranny and suffering which has already crushed the womanhood out of them.

Can any woman, loving and beloved, in the shelter of a pure uncontaminated home, read the following narrative of a first wife, and not lift up her voice in denunciation of that terrible demon which crushes women's hearts beneath its iron heel, and then laughs at the despairing agony of their tortured souls? Can any Christian woman, who believes in the truth of the sentence, "God is Love," read the ensuing pages and not realize that she is personally called upon to use all her influence for the extermination of a monster that permits such atrocities to be perpetrated in the name of GOD and RELIGION?—

"I should like to tell, through your pages, the sad story of my life, if you will permit me to do so without betraying my identity. I do not wish to do that, because I am still a Mormon, at least I am bound to the Mormon church by innumerable ties of kindred, and by the friendships and associations of many years, and at my time of life I should find it hard to break them. As to my identity, I suppose it does not much matter any way, for it may be merged in that of hundreds of other Mormon women in Utah, whose history is perhaps even more pitiable than mine, who, though their hearts are broken, still live on.

"More than twenty-five years ago, when I was a bright-eyed, round-cheeked girl of eighteen, I gave my hand in marriage to the only man I ever loved. Ah! if I could only then have looked down the long vista of troubled years to the cruel end! But I could not; what young girl can, as she stands upon the threshold of that awful mystery which marriage makes a reality?

"For more than twenty years I bore the burden of motherhood. The little ones came thick and fast, but, with a patience that love makes possible, I bore the oft-repeated pangs of maternity, and as I laid each new-born baby in my husband's arms, and saw his smile of pleasure that another jewel had been added to his crown, I thanked my God that I could thus give evidence of the love I bore him. From out the very depths of unearthly agony, I gave his children being, and then through the long, tedious nights that followed the birth of each new life, I lay with my babe at my breast, nursing away my health and strength, while my husband slept peacefully beside me, dreamlessly indifferent to my broken slumber and weary unrest. Or if he gave it one thought, it was to satisfy his conscience with the assurance that 'Woman is formed for the burdens she is to bear.'

"O men! men! do you not know that in the next life, at the judgment-seat of God, you must answer for the lives of the women you have murdered through your ungoverned lust, because might on the one hand, and some form of marriage on the other, have made you the masters? Does the reality of a woman's life-long love and devotion weigh nothing against the expected joys of a possible heaven hereafter? It seems not, in our creed at least; for like Henry the Eighth, the Mormon policy is, 'Sacrifice the mothers if it must be, but give us children.' Yes, and it might be added, 'Give us children to grow up without any home ties or associations, without any fatherly love, care, or tenderness; to be nursed in sorrow, reared in poverty and wretchedness; and when they reach maturity, to curse the parents who entailed upon them such a heritage of sin and misery!'

"Thus, during all these years, I bore children to my husband, watched over and tended them in infancy and illness, taught them to be pure and good, worked and toiled that house and little ones might be always bright and sweet for my husband's home-coming. With a patient energy born of love, I struggled to make home the fairest and dearest spot on earth to which my husband's and children's hearts should always turn with a thrill of pride, and a feeling of sweet restfulness. Upon the altar of his desires I sacrificed my will. I saw myself grow worn and haggard, old before my time. I saw the roses fade from my cheeks, and the gold of my hair turn gray; and if, as I watched these signs of approaching unloveliness, a fear crept into my heart, I stifled it with the trust that they might only render me more dear to the man in whose service I had received them.

"At last the burden of maternity was lifted from my tired shoulders; the children were no longer little ones, but were fast approaching man's estate and blooming girlhood, and I felt I might now begin to enjoy that perfect rest and quiet which many years of servitude and devotion had won me. At last, after the weariness and turmoil, would come the sweet peace for which I had so often longed, and which would now be made doubly dear to me by my husband's love and tenderness.

"But alas for the security of Mormon wifehood! The dark shadow which forever clouds our lives with an unspoken fear, may at any moment assume the tangible shape of a demon, and shatter at one blow all our hopes of happiness. And it came to me. At last the fear was to become for me an awful, living reality.

"It came one bright morning when I was so placidly happy,—when my heart and life seemed in accord with nature's sunshine and gladness. I was alone in my cosy sitting-room; it was very quiet and very pleasant there. My hands had dropped the piece of sewing with which they had been busy, and lay idly folded on my lap; an unspoken prayer of gratitude was in my heart. My trials were over, my toil was ended; for the strong arms of my brave boys and sweet girls were busy even then lifting the burdens.

"The door opened softly, and my husband came in. Although always a good, kind husband, his manner this morning seemed full of unusual warmth and tenderness. As he sat down beside me and took my poor, worn hands in both his own, he essayed to talk with a degree of cheerfulness which he evidently did not feel; for even as he smiled, a look of sadness and trouble was on his face,—a look, perhaps, of pity for the victim about to be sacrificed upon the altar of an unmerciful faith.

"Then gently, oh, so gently, he dealt the blow which left, in place of a heart, the dull, aching thing I have since carried in my bosom. I had been to him a good and faithful wife, and we had been very happy together, he said, but I was no longer young. I could give him no more children, and he felt it a duty which he owed to God to take another and a younger woman, that the measure of our glory might be full in the celestial kingdom.

"Much more he said, but the words were empty air. I felt only the awful, cruel reality. This was the man for whose sake agony had been a joy, servitude a pleasure, and sacrifices as nothing. This was my reward, *as it may be the reward of any faithful Mormon wife.* The reward which a hellish, diabolical creed makes possible.

"I did not cry out, I did not faint, I did not even weep in the extremity of my awful pain. I only felt the consciousness that by one swift stroke of the hand that should have shielded me, my life-long love was turned to bitter loathing; the fruit of a life's devotion had turned to ashes on my thirsting lips. My trust in a God who could thus scourge me was shaken, and my faith in a creed that demanded it was smitten. I was passive under the blow, for struggle as I might, it would avail me nothing.

"And then, the wish was in *his* heart. Since I could no longer serve him, it was his desire that I should stand aside, and give to a younger and perhaps fairer woman, my place as sovereign wife and mother.

"And did not my own and his religion sanction his right to make this demand, and teach me to obey it? I could have rebelled surely, but this would have brought only discord and contention to the only dear ones left me now, my children. My burdens had been many, and this last one, though heavier than all, I would bear in silence for their dear sakes.

"For the completion of my misery I had not long to wait. The fair young wife was soon found and brought home. For her so young and fair, deserving a better fate, I wept the tears I could not weep for myself. Bound like me by the fetters of an unmerciful creed, she had usurped in good faith the place of a dethroned wife and mother.

"'How long, oh, how long, in this land of boasted freedom, shall such things be possible?' is the dumb cry wrung from many a tortured heart in Utah. How long shall woman be weighed down with fetters that are forged by man's brutality and lust? How long shall woman be obliged to smother the holiest instincts of womanhood, and taught that to degenerate into mere child-bearers is fulfilling God's purpose? How long shall a lustful and unscrupulous priesthood hold a rod of iron upon our souls in the name of God and religion? Toward the noble men and women who, like yourselves, are making earnest efforts in our behalf, the hearts of hundreds of Mormon wives go out daily with a prayer of gratitude and thanksgiving. Though our lips seem dumb, we give you a silent God-speed. Speed, oh, speed the day when our chains are broken and we are free! Come soon as it may, for such as I it will be too late; but for our pure unsullied daughters we may yet hope deliverance is possible."

The woman who penned the above sketch is still considered a good Mormon. As she says, it would be very difficult for her, at her time of life, to bear the consequences that would inevitably ensue if she attempted to rebel against her fate. Her husband would probably turn her out of doors without a dollar, and several of her children are yet too young to care for themselves. The law could not give her any redress, for since a polygamous legislature, in order to break down the distinction between lawful wife and concubine, abolished the right of dower in the Territory, a wife has no claim whatever on the estate of her husband, either living or dead. Should she sue for a divorce, asking alimony, he could transfer every cent of his property to the second wife, and swear he had nothing in the world. Consequently it is not to be wondered at, that first wives are timid about openly condemning polygamy, and this particular case is only one of thousands.

Another argument which is very successful in preventing the plural wives from coming out of polygamy, is this: They are told that, as the system is not legalized outside of the Mormon church, it is regarded in the world in the same light as the social evil, and the plural wives are considered as fallen women. What aid or protection is ever extended to women who have once deviated from the path of virtue, even if they are desirous of leading pure lives again? Leave the church if you please, but of course you cannot expect the Saints to recognize apostates, and you need not think or hope that the

Gentiles will associate with women whom they deem no better than prostitutes. One single incident will illustrate with what success this argument is employed.

A certain prominent Mormon married for his third wife a young girl of sixteen who had been born and brought up in Mormonism. She was just an innocent child, and entered polygamy with the purest of motives, fully believing that she was doing God service, and securing her own future happiness. But after seeing the inner workings of the system, and experiencing its horrors for a few years, she became convinced that instead of being from God, it was only a device of man to pander to his own base passions. So she determined to leave her husband. She told him her convictions, and said: "It would be sin for me to live with you any longer, for I do not now believe in polygamy as a religious principle. I am willing to work for my own living; but cannot you, out of your abundance, do something for the support of your and my children?" He absolutely refused to settle anything upon the little ones, or give her anything for their support. Being a determined and plucky woman, she thought she would try to compel him to do what was only right and just in the matter. So she went to one of the heads of the church, and laid the case before him. It was rather a bold step for a woman to tell a Mormon high-priest that she disbelieved in polygamy, but she was a woman who would dare anything for the sake of her children. He listened to her story, then looked her full in the face and said: "Sister H., you know that, in the church, you are a *wife*, honored and respected, and your children are perfectly legitimate. Outside of it, you will be nothing *but a common woman. A Latter-day Saint could not conscientiously contribute to the support of the children of a prostitute.* Do you not think you had better remain where you are?"

It may easily be perceived that this mode of reasoning exerts a great influence over women who have not the courage to face the world as "those who have been living in sin." This statement, however, is a little exaggerated by the Mormons, for not all the Gentiles, by any means, regard the polygamous wives as fallen women. Still, it must be admitted that there is a measure of truth in it, and that outsiders, as a rule, look upon this class of women as very much their inferiors socially. So they say to themselves, We had better stay in the church, where we are regarded as wives, than come out of it, and be treated as common women,—we and our children thrown on the world, helpless and despised. If there was a law, legalizing the offspring of plural wives, and compelling the husband to provide for them in accordance with his means, we believe hundreds of plural women would not live another day in polygamy.

CHAPTER XI.

Fanaticism.

Degradation of the Fanatics.—Joseph Smith's Holiness.—Brigham Young's Opinion of Joseph.—Mormonism Justifies Lying for the Truth.—No Cross, no Crown.—One Man the Husband of Three Generations.—The Mormon Elder and His Wives.—Advice of a Mormon Woman.

THE third class of the women of Mormonism, those who believe, or pretend they believe, in polygamy as a divine ordinance, are the most degraded of all the women of Mormonism. This class may be divided into fanatics and hypocrites.

The fanatics are degraded, because they sacrifice reason, modesty, happiness, and all a true woman holds dear, to a false principle. Of course, the majority of these are totally uneducated, and mostly from the lower walks of European society, but one meets occasionally among them a woman whose birth and early training should have rendered her proof against such superstition and bigotry.

If you try to reason with them, and talk to them of the unhappiness existing in polygamy, and its evil effects, they will answer you that the flesh must be mortified, and the more a woman sacrifices in this world, the greater will be her reward in the next.

It is hard for a woman to share the affections of her husband with others, they will admit, but they will add that it is only for a little time, and the glory she will obtain in the hereafter will compensate her a thousand-fold for the trials she has endured in this life.

In regard to the many evils of polygamous life, and the utter wretchedness and misery which invariably accompany it, they will tell you that these things exist because the divine principle is not carried out as God intended it should be. If polygamy is practiced properly, there is no need of unhappiness; but should a principle be condemned because some people do not understand it, or know how to carry it out in a proper manner?

A husband should certainly treat all his wives alike, and not show any favoritism, and it is the duty of the wives to bear and forbear with each other. But if they fail to do this, is that a competent argument against the fact that God revealed the principles of polygamy to Joseph Smith? If men and women are weak or rebellious, and fail to do God's will, is that to prove that he has never revealed his will to men?

If you attempt to question the authority of Joseph Smith as a prophet, or venture to intimate that he was not the kind of person whom a pure and holy God would choose as a medium by which to reveal his will to men, you will be indignantly assured that Joseph was a God-like character himself, notwithstanding a mass of indisputable facts existing to the contrary.

We heard one of these women assert, and she was apparently honest in her convictions, that all the reports about Joseph's immorality were fabricated by his enemies, that his life was as pure as that of Christ Jesus, and she added pathetically, "Jesus was crucified on Calvary, and Joseph was martyred at Carthage."

Not without a little hesitation, we inquired, "Do you consider that Brigham Young was also a prophet of the Lord?"

"Yes, certainly," was the immediate reply. "The mantle of Joseph descended on brother Brigham."

"Then how do you account for the very poor opinion entertained by Brigham of his predecessor? We have read in one of his published sermons reported by your own church stenographer, a statement to the effect that 'Joseph was anything but a saint; that his virtues were few, his vices many, among the least of which were gambling, drinking, horse-racing, and seducing women.'"

Of course, she could not give a satisfactory reply, as she could not reconcile the statement of Brigham Young with her own belief in the purity of Joseph Smith, neither did she wish to admit that she had any doubts of Brigham's veracity. So she quickly changed the subject, saying, "Let us talk of something else. You outsiders cannot comprehend the depths of our religion, and if you could, you are too prejudiced to do it justice, or judge it fairly."

This woman had been born and bred in New England, and had received a fair education; but she was so thoroughly imbued with the truth of Mormonism and polygamy, and so blindly, fanatically attached to them, that she frequently declared she would willingly die for them.

At another time we said to her, "Why have your leading and representative Mormons on certain occasions denied the existence of polygamy? Why did John Taylor, and even Joseph Smith himself, deny it? If, as you assert, your religion requires a sacrifice of all things, even to life itself, and polygamy is an essential part of that religion, why did not these and others die, if need be, in openly defending it, instead of cowardly denying it in order to shield their craven heads?"

"But our religion teaches us that it is justifiable, under certain circumstances, to lie for the truth," was the ready answer.

"Lie for the truth! Does not that idea strike you as being rather absurd?" we asked.

"Not absurd at all. There are numerous instances in the Bible where deception, and if necessary, even out-and-out falsifying, were practiced and apparently approved. We Mormons believe the Bible, and our faith is founded upon that book. Search the Scriptures, and you find them full of Mormonism, including our doctrine of celestial marriage, which you Gentiles term polygamy."

It is entirely useless to try to reason with these women, to endeavor to convince them that they are liable to misinterpret sacred writ, for they claim to have received through Joseph Smith the gospel in all its fullness, by which it is impossible to err. If, for the sake of argument, you grant that polygamy may have been practiced by the ancient Israelites by God's sanction, but attempt to show them that the system is not in accordance with the civilization of our day, and that its evil effects are sufficient condemnation of its practice, they will still assert that the *principle* is a divine one.

They are willing to admit that polygamy has its sorrows and evils. They even acknowledge that some men enter it from wrong motives, from lust instead of religion. But they insist that all the misery is produced by a wrong mode of practice; and they are too ignorant or too bigoted to see that the system itself is responsible for all its effects.

The entire burden of their song is, that the cross must be borne in order that the crown may be won. Is it not enough to make a woman almost ashamed of herself to see so many of them deliberately rejecting the pure teachings of Christ, and holding with so much tenacity to the degrading doctrines of a loose, immoral, *soi disant* prophet, of whom even his best friends were compelled to admit that he was a rake and a libertine?

Numberless illustrations of the bigotry and fanaticism of this class of women might be given, but a few incidents will be sufficient. Our readers may think some of them exaggerated, for it is difficult to even imagine that women who are wives and mothers can sink to such depths of depravity, through blind devotion to a false doctrine.

The following was related by the wife of a noted United States explorer to a Gentile lady of Salt Lake City, who will vouch for its genuineness. There are cases well known in the annals of polygamy where three generations of women have been married to one man; but we trust, for the credit of our sex, that the circumstances attending the marriages have been different from those in the instance under consideration.

"While traveling in Southern Utah, we came to a small settlement where we were detained a day or two by inclement weather. We found shelter in the humble but neat and hospitable home of a monogamist Saint, whose family hated polygamy, and through whose influence we were permitted a glance at some of the beastliness that characterizes the peculiar institution.

"Only a short distance from the dwelling of my friendly entertainers, there stood a miserable adobe hut, I could not conscientiously call it a house, where lived a Saint with three wives, all of whom had families. My hostess made some neighborly errand an excuse for paying them a visit, and permitted me to accompany her; but before going she made me acquainted with the relationship existing between the three women who were living with, and had borne children to, the same man.

"The first and second women were sisters, and the latter had been a widow with one child when she married her sister's husband. When this child had grown to be about sixteen years old, her stepfather had also married her, but not succeeding in winning the husband entirely away from her mother and aunt, she left and became sealed to another man as plural wife. She had two children by him; then he died, and she returned to her first husband bringing her children with her, the eldest of whom at the time I am speaking of, was a girl about fifteen years old, and my informant stated for a fact, that the old wretch had thoughts of marrying her too.

"When we entered the hut, the scene that met my eyes totally beggars description. Imagine one low, smoky, filthy room serving as living room and sleeping apartment for three women and their offspring, some of the latter almost grown up, the majority, however, being little children. I could never have even dreamed of such dirt, rags, and squalor existing in a Christian country. I had seen nothing equal to it among the Digger Indians; in fact, the latter were quite civilized in comparison.

"But the worst of my story is yet to come. The young girl of whom my hostess had spoken as a probable bride of her grandfather, was sitting in a corner sobbing and crying bitterly. Upon inquiring the cause of her distress, we were told quite frankly that her grandmother had given her a severe castigation for speaking disrespectfully of polygamy, and declaring that she would never become the wife of her mother's and grandmother's husband.

"After we left the house, I could not restrain my indignation, and I said, 'What a lovely religion this is, to make such beasts out of human creatures!'

"'It is not religion, but the lack of it, that makes them beasts,' quietly rejoined my hostess, 'and you will find many cases as bad as this one if you travel far in Utah. There is a man in this very settlement who has for plural wives his own half-sister and her mother, and their house has only two small rooms.' As my friend had predicted, I found more families like these as we traveled farther south. No one who has not been through the country can form the slightest idea of the degradation existing among the people of Southern Utah.

"But the sequel to this 'o'er true tale' is still more horrible. I hesitate to tell it, and only do so to show how Mormonism blunts the moral sense of its votaries. About a year afterward, we had occasion to pass through that settlement again, and for a day we were guests of our former hostess. She told me that the young girl was really sealed to her grandfather, being literally forced into it by her own mother and grandmother, *under circumstances so revolting that delicacy would not allow me to repeat them, even to one of my own sex.*

"The grandmother was determined that the child should become a polygamic wife in order to save her soul, and excused her conduct by saying that she would not like to see her own flesh and blood go to perdition, that brother B. was as good a husband as she would be likely to find, and it was better for her to marry among her own family than to go among strangers.

"Even in that polygamic community, the excitement was so great that there was talk of lynching the degraded trio, the man and the two elder women; but the feeling soon passed over, and was eventually forgotten, or only remembered as an episode of the 'peculiar institution.'"

Another incident, which is too well known to hundreds of persons in Utah for any one to attempt its contradiction, will illustrate this astounding fanaticism which is so characteristic of this class of women.

A certain elder was sent to England to have charge of the British Conference of Latter-day Saints, and though he left two wives in Salt Lake City, yet this trifling fact did not prevent him from paying devoted attention to a number of young girls. It seems he had obtained permission from Brigham Young to marry while he was abroad, but at the same time he was instructed to represent himself as a single man, so as not to become liable for bigamy under English law, in case he should find a new affinity.

In a very short time, he married a young English girl, and he informed his wives in Utah of the event, taking good care however to conceal from his new wife the existence of the two other Mrs. C.'s in Utah. These received the tidings with resignation, for they expected nothing different, and were consequently prepared for it. They had seen too many missionaries make additions to their kingdom in the same manner to be in the least surprised to hear that their husband had gone and done likewise.

When this good elder had been married about two years to this English girl, his first wife went to the Eastern States on a visit to her relatives. Her health was exceedingly impaired,—the result of mental suffering, though she would not own it, even to herself,—and she was recommended to take a sea voyage, whereupon she immediately wrote to her husband, asking permission to join him in Liverpool, where he was then stationed.

He accorded her the desired permission upon one condition, that she would temporarily abrogate her rights as a wife, and allow herself to pass as his sister. He was willing to give her the benefit of the change in climate, but he stipulated in return that she should shield him from the consequences of his transgression. If his English wife should by any means become possessed of the truth, she would undoubtedly hand him over to the officers of the law, and thus avenge her wrongs. We venture to assert that not one wife in ten thousand would have entered into so degrading a compact, but she was so anxious to take the voyage on account of her failing health, that she agreed to do as he desired.

On her arrival in Liverpool, she found that her husband was so infatuated with his new love, that he scarcely noticed her at all, and many were the comments of the Saints at his indifference to, and neglect of, the "sister" who had come such a distance across the ocean to visit her brother. The poor woman was almost bowed to the earth with grief, and she soon regretted having taken the journey; but there was no way of escape from the trial. She had no means of returning until her husband's mission was ended, which would not be for two years at the least.

Our saintly elder, almost entirely ignoring the existence of his legal wife, traveled all over Europe with his English bride, introducing her everywhere as Mrs. C., while the poor "sister" remained in Liverpool, dependent upon the bounty of the charitable Saints. The despised and neglected wife had not even been supplied by him with the merest necessaries of life, but every luxury of dress and adornment was lavished upon the concubine.

But notwithstanding all the neglect she experienced, and the cruel treatment she endured, though she had lost both love for and faith in her husband, yet her devotion and loyalty to her religion never wavered one particle.

"You would not have found me enduring such treatment," remarked a friend to her, after she had returned to Utah and the facts had become known. "I would not have lived in poverty and seclusion, and known that he was running round the country with her, squandering money on her as if she had been a princess,— money, too, that was squeezed out of the poor deluded Saints. I would soon have had him landed in Old Bailey."

"I could have done that, I suppose," responded the poor, heart-broken wife, "but it would not have availed me anything, and it would have brought so much discredit and scandal upon the church. I was tempted more than once to take such a step, but was always restrained by the thought that my religion required me to sacrifice everything for its sake, even to life itself. There can be no denying the fact that polygamy is a dreadful ordeal, and involves the most terrible sacrifices; but, 'No cross, no crown.'"

We never hear the word "*cross*" employed in Utah without wishing that we had the tongue of an angel, and could proclaim to these poor misguided creatures *the* Cross that was borne and raised for the sins of the whole world. But, alas! their infatuation is so deep seated that we fear they would not believe, even if "one from the dead" should come to them. Truly, if, as Mrs. Browning says, "Earth's fanatics make heaven's saints," these women will not go without their dearly won reward.

One more illustration of this fanaticism before passing to the hypocrites of Mormonism.

A certain good Mormon, whose intelligent, lovely, and exemplary wife had exercised her influence successfully in keeping him out of polygamy for a number of years, at last came to the determination that he must live his religion. The poor wife, who was to have the sanctity of her home thus invaded, went to a certain representative woman in the church for sympathy in that sorrow which to her was far worse than death.

This woman is perfectly insane on the subject of polygamy, though otherwise said to be amiable and intelligent. She listened to the poor wife's tale of woe, condoled with her, said she presumed it was hard to give up her husband, or share his affections with another, but reminded her that it was for his future exaltation, and urged her to bear the cross bravely, and she should be duly rewarded.

"Oh, I cannot bear it," wailed the poor grief-stricken wife. "We have been so happy together. I shall die if he takes another. I cannot live and have another woman come between us."

"Die, then," responded the female apostle of polygamy. "*There are hundreds of better women than you lying up in that graveyard, who have died from the same cause!*"

Women of America, do not the words of this votary of polygamy prove that the cruel system is a foe to every household in the land?

CHAPTER XII.

Tools of the Priesthood.

Remarkable Statement.—Polygamy Instilled into the Young.—Apostates Become Infidels or Spiritualists.—No Sympathy for the Tools.—A Young Girl's Statement.—Attempts to Keep a Young Lady from Apostatizing.—Corruption Fund.—Woman to the Rescue.

HE very worst class of women of Mormonism, and those who do the most injury, are the hypocrites,—women who are too intelligent to believe that there ever was a revelation on polygamy, and who cannot close their eyes to the evil effects of the system.

Some of these women were brought into Mormonism at an early age by their parents. Others were born in it, and in some cases were forced by circumstances to marry in polygamy. They are degraded; and being themselves shameless, they are continually endeavoring to drag others down to their own level.

It may perhaps seem a very harsh and uncharitable judgment to say that the earth holds no viler of their sex than some of these women, but it is, nevertheless, only too true.

A young girl who had been brought up in the polygamous household of one of the highest Mormon

Hon. JAMES B. McKEAN,
Late Chief Justice of Utah.

dignitaries, and who was familiar with the domestic life of all the principal apostles, and who knew certain of these women thoroughly and the part they were constantly playing in the polygamous tragedy, made these remarks in regard to them: "*I can only compare these women to those dreadful characters that they say exist in the outside world, and whose business it is to lure young girls to destruction. They are nothing but tools of the priesthood; and while professing to be working for the elevation of women, they are in reality doing nothing but seeking for new victims to gratify the base passions of their infamous masters.*"

We have before alluded to an organization of women which exists in this Territory under the name of the "Female Relief Society." This association was not formed for the purpose of relieving the poor and needy; for do not all the Mormon emissaries abroad, declare that there are no paupers in Zion, no poverty or misery among this industrious, thrifty, and godly people? But it will be seen that there were other and more potent reasons for the existence of these Societies.

None understand better than the Mormon autocrats the importance of thorough and perfect organization. It is by means of their organization that such a complete system of espionage is kept over the Mormon people, and the policy of the church so rigidly enforced. It is this complete organization that has made the Mormon power as "absolute a despotism over its own people as ever existed upon earth."

The "Relief Society" was organized by the command of the head of the Mormon church, and a branch exists in every settlement throughout Utah, no matter how small or remote. We are told by Mormons that it also extends into all surrounding Territories. This Society has two principal objects, the propagation of polygamy, and the gathering of tithes for replenishing the church treasury, especially for the purpose of corrupting members of Congress, and subsidizing the national press.

At the meetings of these Societies, which are held regularly, the main topics of discussion,—for they make a show of free thought and free speech,—are the principles of polygamy, subservience to husbands, and implicit obedience to the holy priesthood.

Does any person ask why polygamy is on the increase to-day in Utah, notwithstanding the counteracting influences brought to bear against it by the establishment of Christian churches and schools, and why young and ignorant girls are every day entering into the unlawful relation? The reason is obvious: Because this female organization is constantly at work, carrying out the plans of a licentious and tyrannical priesthood.

The young girls are brought to these meetings every week, and the principles of polygamy thoroughly and systematically inculcated. With such a belief impressed upon the plastic hearts and minds of children, what is the natural result? When they are fourteen or sixteen years of age, and are told that they must be sealed to brother

So-and-So, and that thus their eternal happiness and glory will be assured, they go to the Endowment House and become the plural wives of the brothers selected, almost without hesitation.

If they stop to think or reason at all, it will be in this wise: "Polygamy must be right. We are taught that it is. There is a great deal of unhappiness in it, but if our religion is worth anything at all, it is worth making sacrifices for."

Others again will say to themselves, "We may as well marry in polygamy, for we shall have to live in it any way. If we become first wives, our husbands will be sure to take others after awhile; and as plural ones, we stand as good a chance of comfort in this world, and we shall be better off in the next." And so the young girl will take a step that not only ruins her happiness on earth, but too frequently causes her to lose faith in both God and man.

The majority of people who leave the Mormon church, become either spiritualists or infidels. And it is not strange that they do. They have seen such atrocities committed in the name of God and religion, that when once free from Mormon trammels, they appear to hate their very names. "Don't talk to us of God or religion," is a very frequent remark of apostate Mormons, "we have had enough of that for both time and eternity!"

The *motive power* of the female polygamic organization is the class of women of which we have been treating.

Were it not for certain of these women the organization could *not live a year*. But they make a semi-annual tour of the Territory, visiting every settlement, and holding, as it were, revival meetings, expounding the beauties and glories of a polygamous life, and exhorting the sisters to be faithful followers of the "new and everlasting covenant of marriage."

Of course these women are called the most noted in the Church, and are regarded very highly by the priesthood for their inestimable services in propagating the peculiar doctrine and in continually furnishing new victims to be sacrificed on the altar of that insatiable monster, polygamy.

For the fanatics, we must have a little sympathy and commiseration. They are deserving of real pity, for they should be regarded as partially insane. People whose infatuation completely overpowers their reason can scarcely be declared in a normal intellectual condition.

But what sentiments shall good women entertain for others who are described as "endowed by the Creator with more than the poet's soul, gifts that are not of mere religious training or growth, but have come down from the ages; who are inspired by the mystic memories of the past,—daughters of Judah's royal house, possessing fine sentiment, richness of fancy, quick sympathy, rare enthusiasm, and deathless devotion,—genius which God wills them to manifest for the great world's good, whose lives are devoted to labors for the benefit and elevation of woman?" What sentiments, we repeat, shall be entertained for these, who, were but one tithe of what is said about them true, would walk as sisters to the gods? And yet, they are hailed by the ignorant and deluded dupes of Mormonism as the "early exponents, by precept and example, of the new and everlasting covenant of marriage, and as leaders in the self-sacrifice at first necessary to establish its principles."

What sentiments shall be entertained for women possessing these *noble qualities and God-like attributes*, and who can permit themselves to be styled, "honored wives of our revered and martyred prophet, Joseph Smith,"—who can announce themselves exponents of a faith that is alike dishonoring and degrading to womanhood; a faith that makes a beast of man and a slave of woman; a faith that renders marriage a by-word, and imprints a mark of shame on the brows of innocent children; a faith that entails untold wrongs and misery upon generation after generation; a system which is characterized by shameless indecencies, fearful brutalities, and almost incredible beastliness?

Did God endow women with the divine gift of genius, that they should openly advocate a system which permits a man to marry a woman and her two daughters and live with them, raising families, and only one room? a system that permits a man to marry the children of his own brother? a system that sets at defiance all law, order, morality, and decency? Verily, this may be called the "Divine *curse* of genius!"

A certain young girl who had been allured into polygamy through the instrumentality of one of these women, said not very long ago, "The names of some representative women of Mormonism should be handed down to posterity, branded with eternal infamy, for the part they have had in the ruin of young girls and women. They are responsible for the destruction of more girls, during the half century that they have been tools of the priesthood, than all the bad women of the United States put together. Hundreds of young girls have been destroyed every year, body and soul, through the direct influence of these creatures. Hundreds of women are lying in unwept graves, murdered by polygamy, who embraced the doctrine through the teaching of these women. Women, did I say? No, they are not women, they are not human, they are *ghouls!*"

Another young lady who apostatized lately, the daughter of a very high Mormon dignitary, said that when it was known that she was becoming weak in the faith, a number of the sisters—leading Mormon women—came to expostulate with her, and get her back into the fold. They did not want her to apostatize *because she knew too much*, and as she was fearless enough to express her opinions very freely in regard to the degrading institution and its upholders, they were afraid that her revelations would cause a shaking among the dry bones.

But it was the "ministrations" of two of these women that was the last straw in the camel's load. Her eyes had been opened by the wholesale perjury and falsehood she had seen committed by the leaders in order to conceal their crimes and iniquities, but she was scarcely prepared for the consummate hypocrisy displayed by these "priestesses."

In reference to one of them, she said: "The idea of that woman talking *religion* to me, prating about the faith of my father, and the pure doctrines of this holy church, when she knew that I was well aware of the fact *that she had deceived one husband, and lived as plural wife to Joseph Smith, before she had become the concubine of my own father.* When she spoke of my father, I said to her, 'I loved my father, because he was good to me; but I cannot disguise this truth which you know very well, that polygamy made him a cruel tyrant who broke the hearts of many women. You know also that polygamy destroyed the life of your only daughter; and yet whenever you hear of a young girl who is intelligent or independent enough to think for herself, you can never rest until you get her bound in these chains.'

"But what angered and disgusted me the most," continued this young lady in speaking of the interview, "was the fact that I knew so well that they did not believe one word they were saying, and the only motive they had in pleading with me to remain in the church was, they were afraid that if I apostatized I would ventilate some of the wrongs and impositions of Mormonism. And I had more than one fact in my keeping regarding themselves which did not redound much to their credit, and, if exposed, would not add to their reputations as true wives or virtuous women. And yet they can talk by the hour in the Relief Society about the pure doctrines of Mormonism,—doctrines that rob women of purity, modesty, womanliness, and all that a true woman can hold dear in this life."

But preaching polygamy is not the only way in which these infamous women assist in maintaining the power of the Mormon theocracy. Two sources of that power are, the keeping of the people in ignorance and in poverty. This last condition is maintained not only by forced contributions, called tithing, for the support of the church, but by the unestimated amount of corruption money that is annually wrung from the poor, to cement more firmly the chains that bind the wrists of justice. Some idea of the amount of the corruption fund required annually, may be imagined by simply quoting some of their own statements. Brigham Young said frequently in public that he could and would buy every member of Congress in the United States, if necessary, in order to defeat legislation against this people.

A former delegate from this Territory openly boasted that he owned a good man in every bureau in each department in Washington.

In the early part of 1881, at the time that Gov. Murray of Utah issued the certificate of election to

Hon. A. G. Campbell and denied it to George Q. Cannon, when it looked as if the sentiment of the country would soon force the Mormon question to a climax, it was currently reported throughout the Territory, that Cannon telegraphed from Washington to Salt Lake City, that he would need the sum of $800,000 to insure him success, should there be an extra session and a contest ensue; and no sooner was the news received than a system of extortion was commenced to compel the Saints to contribute to this fund. There was manifested a disposition among some to let Cannon take care of himself, and a reluctance, if not a positive determination among the poorer classes not to allow themselves to be bled for this enormous sum.

But a Mormon cannot remain a Mormon and not comply with the demands of the church, however unjust they may be. And as soon as the mandate had gone forth that this money must be raised, the Relief Societies commenced their work of levying on the poor.

"These ghouls," said one outspoken woman, "will divest the poorest class of people of every available egg and ounce of butter, under penalty of excommunication. They will do more than that, they will even take the bread out of the children's mouths to cast it to the dogs. 'Corruption fund' is truly an appropriate name for this money, which is fairly squeezed out of the body and blood of these poor, misguided people."

We could pursue this subject still further, but it is heart sickening and repulsive. It is bad enough to know that men with untamed passions and lust for power will subjugate women and hold them at their mercy; but to see women prostituting talents, capacity, and energy to the service of these vile masters is more than enough to make a woman curse her sex, and wish that she had been anything else than a woman. Is it not sufficient to make the women of the country rise *en masse* and demand the immediate abolition of a system which renders WOMAN only a term of reproach and dishonor?

Women of America, we have shown you how woman is most cruelly wronged under this infamous system, and is it not fitting that woman should be the most active in working for its suppression? The victims of polygamy are women, and is it not meet that women should take the initiative measures that will lead to its complete abolition?

And do you wonder now, that we whose lot has been cast in the midst of this deluded people, who have seen the hypocrisy and brutality of the Mormon leaders, who have learned the workings of this infamous system, who have listened to these tales of tyranny and outrage from the lips of the women themselves, who have seen their hopeless, dejected countenances, from which the light of hope and faith has forever fled, who have heard them declare that they had no trust in either humanity or God,—do you wonder that we sometimes think that our Christianity is but a mockery, and the boasted freedom of our nation a by-word of shame and reproach, so long as there exists in our country such a class as the "Women of Mormonism?"

CHAPTER XIII.

An Earnest Appeal.

Quotation from the *Deseret News.*—Joseph Smith's Widows.—Changed Views.—Smith's Denunciation of Polygamy.—Married or Single.—Controversy with God.—Polygamy Binding upon All or None.—No Plural Marriage.

THE following was published in a little different form, but substantially the same, in the columns of the *Anti-Polygamy Standard.* It was addressed to those Mormon women, collectively, who are public advocates of the doctrine of polygamy, and whose teachings have been potent in influencing hundreds of women to sacrifice themselves upon this cruel altar. Of course, the appeal never elicited any reply or explanation. None could be truthfully given without convicting a number of these sisters of falsehood, as any unprejudiced reader can see for himself by comparing the *historical facts* quoted below from their own church records.

Writing to the *Deseret News*, the Mormon church organ, under date Oct. 17, 1879, Eliza R. Snow says:—

"It may be asked, Why defend plurality of wives, since the United States Government forbids its practice? The action of the executors of this Government can neither change nor annihilate a fundamental truth; and this action, in preventing the practice of plural marriage, shoulders a heavier responsibility than any nation has ever assumed, with one exception,—that of the ancient Jews. If the Government can afford it, we can. The controversy is with God, not us."

This was signed "Eliza R. Snow, a wife of Joseph Smith, the prophet."

On the occasion of a woman's meeting at the Theater in Salt Lake City in the fall of 1878, for the purpose of justifying the doctrine of plural marriage, and of protesting against the right of the United States Government to interfere with its practice, Mrs. Zina D. Jacobs, (generally known as Mrs. Zina Young,) proclaimed herself as one of the widows of the prophet Smith. At that same meeting, Miss Eliza R. Snow and Mrs. Phebe Woodruff declared that they *knew* polygamy was a divine ordinance, and its practice a direct command from God. Miss Snow further said that she looked with sympathy and commiseration upon the misguided Gentile women who were opposing the sacred institution. "They are trying to measure arms with the Almighty," she exclaimed, "and they know not what they do. We believe in the principle of plural marriage as sacredly as we believe in any other institution which God has revealed."

We will not question the sincerity of these "priestesses of polygamy," but we would like to ask them how they have happened to change their minds so completely; for in early days they assumed a very different attitude upon this question. Some of us, workers in the Anti-Polygamy cause, were good Mormons in the days before polygamy was a principle of the Latter-day faith. Some of us were in Nauvoo when Joseph Smith and John C. Bennett were deceiving any number of sisters, and when "spiritual wifery" was first concocted as a means of allaying the scandal which had grown to such alarming proportions, that there were threats from the most devout Mormons, of cleaning out the entire iniquitous nest. But worse than all, the scandal was not confined to Nauvoo, but had also gained credence in the outside world.

However, the prophet was a man of sagacity equal to the occasion, and he immediately came out in an article, which can be found in Vol. 3 of *Times and Seasons*, the Mormon church official organ, denouncing the "secret wife" system as the manufacture of John C. Bennett, who thus perpetrated a foul and infamous slander upon an innocent people.

Elder Hyrum Brown was excommunicated for preaching polygamy in Michigan, and certificates were published, numerously signed, setting forth that the Latter-day church and the people of Nauvoo know of no other system of marriage than that contained in the "Book of Doctrines and Covenants," which, of course, was monogamic.

And some of us remember the indignation manifested by these very sisters who are now so positive of the divinity of polygamy, that such a "foul slander should have been perpetrated upon the innocent Mormons." Some of these sisters who now announce themselves as widows of the martyred prophet, then testified publicly that polygamy did not exist, as witness the following, which we copy from *Times and Seasons* of 1843:—

"We, the undersigned, members of the Ladies' Relief Society, and *married females*, do certify and declare that we know of no system of marriage being practiced in the church of Jesus Christ of Latter-day Saints, save the one contained in the 'Book of Doctrines and Covenants;' and we give this certificate to the public to show that J. C. Bennett's 'secret wife' system is a disclosure of his own make." This is signed by Eliza R. Snow, Phebe Woodruff, and fifteen others.

Both of these sisters now call themselves widows of Joseph Smith, who was killed in 1844, only one year subsequent to the time when they testified that the "secret wife" system was a disclosure of J. C. Bennett's own make. We should be gratified if they would explain these conflicting statements, and tell us why they *then* denied so solemnly the existence of what they *now* declare they *know* to be a divine institution, revealed by God. And furthermore, we should be glad if sister Eliza would tell us to whom she was married at the time of that denial, for she publicly avowed herself to be a "married female," and we knew her as Miss Eliza R. Snow, a single woman.

If she was married to Joseph Smith at that time, as a plural wife, then she signed her name to what she must have known was a falsehood; and if she was not married to the prophet, then she publicly acknowledges herself to be an impostor in now claiming to be his widow.

It is these glaring discrepancies that make us doubt their ability to lead the masses of the Mormon women, of whom they are the acknowledged head and teachers, in the paths of truth and virtue. It is these which make us think, even at the risk of being deemed uncharitable, that they are more culpable than " blind leaders of the blind."

But, in regard to the declaration of E. R. Snow that "the controversy is with God, not us," we would say:—

Be that as it may, we of the Anti-Polygamy cause, in behalf of ourselves, and in the interest of the innocent women,—yes, of all women, innocent or guilty,—and of the girls in this Territory, "with charity to all, and with malice toward none,"—we have a controversy with E. R. Snow, and Mrs. Jacobs, and Mrs. Woodruff, and with any other polygamous person who publicly proclaims adherence to and belief in polygamy. We desire to know fully and explicitly upon what such belief and adherence is based.

Come, and let us reason awhile together upon this all-important subject. If polygamy is good for you, why would it not be good for us? and if it is a blessing and benefit for one, it should be a benefit and blessing for all. If there be any obligation to accept, or any condemnation in rejecting polygamy, we stand ready, in desire at least, to share in your glory, present and prospective, through accepting it; and on the other hand, to be made partakers of the "condemnation" which you tell us, and tell your non-polygamous Mormon sisters, must follow the rejection of the doctrine.

If polygamy is right, and especially if it be a command of God, then it is our duty to look upon it in that light, and to yield obedience to it. If it is wrong, and especially if, upon full and fair canvassing of the whole matter, it becomes evident that upon no valid claim can it be regarded as the command of God, then it is your duty and that of all others to regard it accordingly, and to turn away from it.

Is there anything to prevent us from seeing eye to eye in this matter? Is there a beam in our eye, and but a mote in yours, or vice versa? Let us pluck out from our eyes every beam and every mote, and then we shall see with clearness.

We have reflected long, written much, conversed and corresponded with many on this vexed question. Peaceably or forcibly it must be settled—it will be settled. But harsh measures—force—cannot eradicate an idea when once that idea has taken root in the mind of man or woman. The Divine Spirit only, co-operating with human reason and science, has power to do that.

It is useless to enter into any argument respecting

the origin of polygamy. That is not a matter of obscurity, but of plain historic record, so well authenticated that it would be as foolish to question it as it would be to question whether or not the battle of Waterloo ever occurred.

Of course, the advocates of the system persistently ignore this historical record; but that is no evidence of its incorrectness, as there are people living in Utah to-day, whose word is as worthy of confidence as that of the polygamy advocates can be, whose personal experience will fully corroborate and sustain the historical fact.

In the quotation at the head of this article, E. R. Snow says,—and we are quite pleased to agree with her in this,—"The action of the Government can neither change nor annihilate a fundamental truth." That proposition is so plain as to require no argument, no defense. But when she adds that "this nation, in preventing the practice of plural marriage, shoulders a responsibility heavier than any other nation has ever assumed,—with one exception, that of the ancient Jews,"—as Christian wives and mothers, as lovers of our sex and of our country, we call upon her to indicate more clearly than she seems inclined to do, in what this awful responsibility consists.

And first, that E. R. Snow may learn where we stand, and where we claim the country stands upon this matter, we hold there can in reality be no such thing under our, or any other, civilized Government as "plural marriage." Marriage is the union of *one* man with *one* woman. Any arrangement aside from this is not of the nature of marriage at all.

And if, leaving our country and time, she insists upon "fundamental truth,"—upon the fundamental basis of marriage,—we need only cite our first parents. They certainly were *one pair*,—one man and one woman,—that was God's original ordaining. That, we claim, may fairly be esteemed "fundamental."

Now, if E. R. Snow, or any other person, claims that a union of the sexes upon any other basis is marriage, it must be made clear beyond all controversy or doubt, that that basis which is to supersede the original or "fundamental" ordaining of the sexual relation, is not of man and his lusts, but of God and his love.

Although man changes, God is the same, yesterday, to-day, and forever. Although our views of truth may change or enlarge, truth itself is forever unchangeable, forever the same. What seemed a truth yesterday, may not seem a truth to-day. But God is God, and truth is truth. And we perfectly agree with her, that any Government would assume a very great responsibility in presuming to interfere with the "fundamental" law of marriage.

Eliza R. Snow, Mrs. Jacobs, and others, we mildly and in all sincerity and charity of soul suggest to you, that before leaving this checkered scene of mortal life,—and your time, our time, may be short,—you could not possibly do a better or a nobler thing than to come out boldly and frankly,

AN EARNEST APPEAL. 163

and tell us, and especially your non-polygamous Mormon sisters, just what influences and agencies were brought to bear upon you to induce you to accept polygamy as having the sanction of God.

You must wander back to days and years long past, but let us know whether you were flattered, cajoled, or intimidated into the acceptance of that from which your naturally clear sense, and all your womanly feelings and instincts, must have revolted. And may the all-loving Father sustain your souls to make the crowning sacrifice for Truth's sake.

CHAPTER XIV.

Open Letter to the Mormon Women.

Anti-Polygamists Animated Only by Love of Humanity.—A Revelation Cannot Release from Allegiance to Law.—Fruits of Polygamy.—Geo. Q. Cannon's Four Wives.—Ann Eliza Young's Suit.—Letter from Ann Eliza Young.—Woman in Utah and Other Sections.

LETTER NUMBER ONE.

BELIEVING that there are many Mormon women who conscientiously accept polygamy as a part of their religion, and who submit to all it imposes because they think that God requires such submission, or, perhaps, as one of their number has said, because they *fear it may be true* that God requires it, we feel that it is due to them, as well as to ourselves, to make a statement of our position in the Anti-Polygamy Movement.

In the first place, we desire you to understand fully and distinctly that we have been impelled to the work we have undertaken only by a common love of humanity, and we feel we should be criminally culpable, did we not exert our utmost influence to impede a system which can only result in an accumulation of evil and misfortune, and which has already brought sorrow and shame into so many households in this Territory. We are confident that this and succeeding generations will be benefited by our efforts, and we believe that many Mormon women, in their secret hearts, wish us complete and glorious success.

We are not, as has been frequently asserted by some of your leaders, "banded together to destroy the most sacred ties between man and woman; to make children bastards, and trample upon the holiest affections of the human heart." We should indeed regret that any sorrow should come to you through our action, for we are all sisters by virtue of our common womanhood, and we know that of all sorrows, that is the greatest which opens our eyes to the fact that we have been cherishing idols of clay, and have raised false gods and have fallen down to worship them. No sorrow that we are able to avert shall come to the Mormon women. We do not wish, as your leaders claim, to misrepresent our own sex in regard to the holy relations of wife and mother, and our only desire is to accomplish good for the poor, persecuted women of Utah, as you call yourselves.

We concede to all the right to the free exercise of their religion. Our country is a land of civil and religious liberty; but while our nation is one of freedom, it is by common consent governed by law. Now, if you are what is always claimed for you, loyal American citizens, devoted to the maintenance of law, you must admit that no assumed revelation can exempt any one from obedience to that law; for, if one has a right to obey a revelation which he pretends to have had, another may do the same, and thus any crime may be justified. If some of us should come to you and say we had received a revelation from Heaven commanding us to murder you or your dear children, would you submit quietly? Would you not claim the protection of the law?

The revelation on polygamy is as directly opposed to our law as a revelation to practice wholesale murder would be. Neither was it an institution of the primitive Mormon church; and if, as you assume, truth cannot change,—God is the same yesterday, to-day, and forever,—will you enlighten us how his mind has changed in this one particular case?

But the best way to judge of the good or evil of any system, is by its effects. Can any of you honestly and truthfully say that one single good has resulted from the practice of polygamy? On the contrary, can any of you deny that its consequences have been a long train of evils, some of which we cannot even hint at and preserve our self-respect? Can you deny that it has planted sorrows which have blasted ten thousand lives, and whose influences will be felt upon generations yet unborn?

Do not thousands of you feel, though you dare not say so, that there never was such a mockery of God, such a blasphemy, as to call this accursed institution of polygamy a religious principle? If you would only reflect seriously for a few moments and let the scales fall from your eyes, you could not help seeing that the system was founded by the most transparent fraud of the century, and its supports are superstition, ignorance, falsehood, and lust.

It has been well said that the civilization of any people can be measured by the respect and tenderness bestowed upon woman. Tried by this standard, what degree of civilization has been attained by the Mormon people? We appeal to any Mormon woman who knows the practical workings of polygamy to answer this question. In the polygamous households of your neighbors and friends, is woman honored? Is she treated with tenderness or respect? Is her life made happy by her husband's care, and by his consideration for her feelings and her wishes? On the contrary, are you not told that you have no right to expect your husband to love you, and that it is enough honor for you to be allowed to bear children to a Saint? Is this fulfilling God's purpose toward woman on earth, to be obliged to smother the holiest instincts of womanhood, and to degenerate into mere child-bearers, *as you know you have degenerated?* And do the men of your faith, these *Saints*, treat the mothers of their children as *wives*, respecting them as such, and demanding the same respect from others?

When George Q. Cannon made his public answer to G. R. Maxwell, who contested his seat in Congress, he said, "I deny that I am living with four wives." What did this mean? George Q. Cannon was certainly living at that time with four women, all of whom had borne him children, and he lives with them to this day. If they are not his wives, what are they? Will any of you undertake to explain this to us?

Only a few days ago, the brother of George Q. Cannon was a witness in the case of Cannon vs. Campbell, the Utah contestant for Delegate to Congress. This brother declared upon oath that he did not know George Q. Cannon was living in polygamy, and that he knew the name of no woman who claimed to be a wife of George Q. Cannon, except one, and that one was Elizabeth Hoagland, his first wife. You know that there is scarcely a Mormon child in Salt Lake City who does not know the four women who are called George Q. Cannon's wives, also their children.

When Ann Eliza Young commenced her suit for divorce, Brigham Young's answer to her plea, as made in court, was in substance, that she was not his wife, because he had been lawfully married to Mary Ann Angell many years before, and his wife, the said Mary Ann Angell, was still living and undivorced. Can you not see plainly the position in which this answer places all but the first wife?

Will you tell us now who it is that "would destroy the most sacred ties between man and woman, make children bastards, and trample upon the holiest affections of the human heart"? When George Q. Cannon denied that he had four wives, what status did he assign to those plural wives, and also to their children? When Brigham Young said Ann

Eliza was not his wife, did he not tacitly avow that neither of his other plural wives were married to him, and that in consequence their children were illegitimate?

If you would only lift your eyes and look through the mists of superstition which envelop you, you would see that the fetters which weigh you down were forged by man's brutality, and not laid upon you by a just and merciful God. Can you not see how you have been ensnared, and have you not been deluded long enough? Will you not listen to the voices of your own hearts, and break the chains which not only bind you, but which divorce from your hearts all the holier instincts of womanhood? Will you not, we most earnestly entreat, join hands with us, bravely and fearlessly, in the cause of purity, happiness, and justice to yourselves?

Non-Mormon Women.

LETTER NUMBER TWO.

Ever since my escape from the dark prison-house of polygamous slavery into the light of freedom and Christianity, one thought has been in my mind. If I could only show to every woman the contrast between the lives of women in Utah and those in all other parts of this great land; if I could make the women of Utah understand what a glorious sense of freedom one feels, who, breaking away from the gloom, the slavery, the misery of an existence under the teachings of the Mormon priesthood, comes into the society, the civilization, which is based upon Christianity, which protects the family and honors womanhood; if the women of Utah could only see and feel, even a little of the wonderful difference between the two cases, as I soon began to see and feel it after my deliverance,—then it seems to me they would make every effort, run almost any risk, to break their chains and find true liberty.

When I first began to travel, and go into the houses of this country, I was filled with new sensations, to see the respect and courtesy shown by husbands to wives,—the affectionate solicitude for their comfort, the glad welcome given after separation, the pride which husbands seemed to feel in their wives. It was all so wonderful and new to me! How many, many times did tears spring to my eyes, at witnessing so often the tender partings of husbands and wives when only leaving each other for a few days, or the joyous greetings after a few days' separation.

And what touched me most of all was the anxious and unceasing care which frail or sick wives received from their husbands. Such things are of daily occurrence. People do not notice them, they are so much a matter of course. But such devotion is unknown to the women of Utah, except it be to the reigning favorite. And every Mormon woman knows how certain it is that this favoritism will be transient, hence she is ever pervaded with a feeling of insecurity.

Is it strange that thoughts unutterably sad were

aroused, that my mind went back to scenes of everyday occurrence where polygamy holds sway? Obedience to the tenets of Brigham Young and his fellow tyrants produces no such tender care of women as that I have spoken of.

He used to whine in coarse, contemptuous mockery when women came to him with their hearts overladen with miseries growing out of polygamy, and send them away without one word of comfort. I am not speaking of his wives; they soon learned not to go to him for sympathy.

But hundreds, yes, thousands, of women yet living in Utah can testify that Mormon teaching withers and destroys those sentiments which lead a true man to show respect and courtesy to his wife, to care for her though her health may fail and her beauty wane.

How my heart ached, and still aches, to think that the sister-women I had left behind were robbed of such blessings by the cunning falsehoods of coarse and evil men! How rich in love and happiness were the lives of women everywhere in the United States, except in the fair Territory of Utah! *There* they were barren of all that makes life dear to a true woman. Riches can be cheerfully dispensed with, privation and toil do not drive out happiness; but to have poverty of affection and sympathy—*that* despoils and ruins the life of woman.

And to have this evil result brought about under the pretense of religion and religious duty,—that is the saddest and most hopeless thing of all! That there are coarse and unfeeling men outside of Utah is most true; men who neglect their wives, who wrong them, who are cruel and wicked. But though husbands be unfaithful here, the wife is not forced to have her rival brought into her home, and in her very presence see her husband lavish upon the usurper the tokens of his affections.

The wife here is not told from the pulpit, by her religious teachers, that it is her duty to submit to this outrage upon her wifely love. On the contrary, the husband tries to conceal his misconduct. Discovery is the one thing he dreads. And if it becomes known, the wife receives the sympathy of all good people. She is not made to believe it a religious duty to bear such cruelty, and that the rebellion of her womanly nature against it is proof of her sinful nature. She is not compelled to go to the altar and place the hand of another woman,—perhaps the one she hates the most of all women in the world,—in the hand of her husband, thus stifling her truest instincts.

On the contrary, if she desires it, the law is prompt to unloose her hand from the clasp of him who has shown himself unworthy. Here, when the wife and mother grows old, she is not set aside as worthless, perhaps turned out of her home to give place to a younger and a fairer favorite. Here, every added wrinkle or silver hair awakens added devotion and more tender care. She is revered and loved for a life of devotion to her husband.

But in Utah, in polygamy, the harder and more

successfully she has worked to assist her husband to accumulate property, the more likely she is to have to yield her place to another. The old wife does not harmonize with the fine furniture and modern improvements of the new house; a younger and more lovely one must be taken to preside over the establishment.

It makes my soul burn with indignation when I dwell upon these outrages. Surely, never was the sacred name of religion so desecrated as now, when it is used to render possible such crimes!

My heart goes out with pitying tenderness to the women of Utah; and I pray that light may shine into their minds, that they may see the foulness of the accursed doctrines they have been taught, and that moral courage and strength may be given them to break the wicked chains which bind them to wretchedness.

I know, my sisters, that in your most secret thoughts you regard the family life which prevails outside of Utah as far brighter and happier than that which results from polygamy. I beg of you, do not think such thoughts to be wicked. They are not. Cherish them, strive to attain the freedom which from afar shines with the radiance of heaven. It is a heavenly radiance. It is God's assent to the deepest and truest yearnings of your womanhood. Not the good God, but false priests, have put upon you burdens too grievous to be borne. And if you will help yourselves, he will help you to escape from your bondage into sweet, pure liberty!

Mrs. Ann Eliza Young.

CHAPTER XV.

The Beauties of Polygamy.

A Saintly Husband.—A Wedding and a Funeral.—The Trio Victorious.—"It Rejoices Mother Beyond Measure."—"I Prefer to Scratch for Myself *Now.*"—"I am Heart-Broken."—The Black Eye.—An Eastern Lady.—Four Wives and Three Beds.—Sixteen Children Left.—Peculiar Consolation.—Would Visit His Sick Wife Next Sunday.—Would not Harmonize.—Arraignment of Polygamy by a Victim.

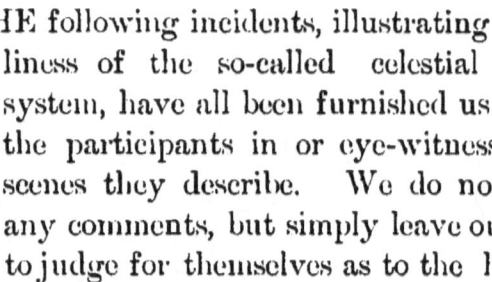HE following incidents, illustrating the loveliness of the so-called celestial marriage system, have all been furnished us either by the participants in or eye-witnesses of the scenes they describe. We do not venture any comments, but simply leave our readers to judge for themselves as to the holiness of this divine ordinance.

In a settlement not many miles from Salt Lake City, lives a bishop, who was the saintly husband of two wives; but being desirous of still higher celestial glory, he determined to add another to his kingdom, a young girl of seventeen years of age, whose salvation he wished to insure. He had a large family by each of his other wives, and his youngest child was several months older than the girl he intended making his third wife. She did not object, because the bishop was said to be a man of considerable means, and had the reputation of being good to his family.

During the courtship, which was brief, but exceedingly ardent, his legal wife was taken very ill. Notwithstanding that, the lover and bride elect repaired to Salt Lake City, and were sealed in the Endowment House.

When they returned home a grand feast was made in honor of the occasion. Neighbors and friends were bidden from near and far to do honor to the event. While the festivities were in progress, one blunt old lady remarked, "Brother B., does it not seem a little out of place to have this affair while sister Jane is so ill? What if she should die!" "Well, sister," was the reply of the tender husband, "it is rather rough on Jane that she can't join us; but we thought best to have the wedding now, because if Jane should die, you know we could n't have a party *right after a funeral.*"

The poor old lady died a few days afterward, and the husband of her youth, and the father of her ten children, was present neither at her death nor burial. He was on a wedding journey with his new wife. Her last words were: "An eternity of happiness could not recompense me for the tortures I have endured in this last week, to say nothing of what I went through before, in twenty-five years of polygamy."

The daughter of this woman said to the writer: "Polygamy is responsible for the death of my mother. When father commenced courting that girl, she fell ill, and she was struck with death on the evening of the wedding party." And yet there are people who profess to believe that this system has been ordered by God.

The next incident is a beautiful illustration of the holy and benign influences with which the celestial system surrounds the women, and shows how sweet and heavenly it renders their dispositions.

An elder who had three wives thought it his duty to take a fourth. The three women banded together, and determined to make it warm for their celestializing spouse, and his new affinity who was a stranger in Zion, having come in by a recent emigration. Their first act was to secrete all the eatables in an out-of-the-way place, so that when the bride and groom returned to the house after the long and fatiguing ceremonies at the Endowment House, there was no supper prepared for them, nor the slightest indications that they would receive any temporal refreshment whatever. There was absolutely nothing eatable to be found in the house, and neither Susan, Mary, nor Eliza could be coaxed or threatened to produce anything.

At last the baffled husband took his bride to the house of a compassionate neighbor, who regaled them with a comfortable meal, and with whom they spent a pleasant evening, not going home until nearly midnight. Upon arriving there, they found the doors securely barred, and no amount of knocking could get them opened. After vainly endeavor-

Miss LYDIA M. TICHENOR,
CHICAGO, ILL.

ing to obtain entrance, standing in the pouring rain for nearly half an hour, they repaired again to their hospitable neighbor, who provided them with a shelter for that night.

The next day the elder found another home for his young wife. There was a *scene* in that family, it may be well imagined; but the old man promised to forgive the indignity offered to himself and bride, if the other women would keep it quiet, in order to avoid a scandal in Zion. It did leak out, however, and one of the women said, in the hearing of the writer, that nothing in her life ever gave her as much satisfaction as the fact of those two standing at midnight in the pouring rain. And yet, ordinarily, this woman was very kind hearted, and has been known to do numberless humane and charitable deeds.

Another incident of the same order comes to us from a source whose reliability cannot be questioned.

A very prominent member of the Mormon priesthood, who had a large number of wives, had married a young girl with whom he was completely infatuated, and who embraced every occasion for exhibiting the power she had obtained over the old gentleman. His other wives were entirely neglected, and he was as devoted to his new favorite as a youthful lover is to the first object of his affections.

A girl companion of one of his first wife's children said to her one day: "Does it not grieve your mother to see your father paying so much attention to his new wife? I should think it would annoy her exceedingly. He is making himself the town talk on account of that girl."

"On the contrary," was the reply, "it affords her, as well as the other wives, the greatest delight. You know that Emma (another plural wife, and former favorite of the old man) has had everything her own way, and been father's pet and idol for years. You know how she has lorded it over the other women, making even my poor old mother stand aside, and how she has boasted that *she* should never be superseded in his affections. *But she is now getting her turn.* It rejoices mother beyond measure to know that she is now experiencing the tortures that she has made others suffer." And yet this old lady, who took such delight in the knowledge that the other "was getting her turn," was a lovely and amiable character when not controlled by the pious influences of the divine ordinance.

There was a certain good Saint living in Zion, who had three wives already, and about sixteen children, but he felt duty urging him to live his religion to a still greater extent, and to enlarge his kingdom still further; so he began to pay his addresses to a youthful companion of one of his daughters. Although born and reared in polygamy, she had no particular desire for celestializing, having seen enough of its effects. Consequently the old man's advances were not received with the warmth he desired.

One day, while endeavoring to gain her consent,

and speaking of the advantages of the divine ordinance, she met him with the question: "Brother M., you are not a rich man; you do not, or cannot, provide for the families you have already; how do you expect to support any more?"

"Oh," was the reply, "I have taken care of the old ones long enough; they must now do like the chickens, turn out and scratch for themselves."

"Then I suppose I should have to do the same thing after awhile," said the girl. "I prefer to scratch for myself *now.*"

The words of this Saint are characteristic of Mormon polygamy. When a man wants new wives, he can turn the old ones out to "scratch for themselves."

It is not often that casual observers will discern much of the heartaches and jealousy which invariably exist among women living in polygamy. The greatest pains are taken to preserve an appearance of decorum, and conceal the unpleasant features of the system from the gaze of strangers; but in spite of all efforts, they will sometimes come to the surface, so that even they who run may read.

We saw, not long ago, in the waiting-room of a railroad depot, a scene that was enough to have chilled the heart of any woman.

A man who had three wives was preparing to take a journey, accompanied by the legal wife and one of the plural women. The latter was dressed in gay attire, and was very busily coquetting around him, while making preparations for travel.

She seemed to be as happy as a bad woman can be while torturing some rival for a man's attentions.

Off in one corner, entirely alone, sat a lady dressed in plain garb, almost presenting the appearance of mourning. Her close watchfulness of all that was transpiring between the man and his concubine attracted general attention.

We knew the man and woman she was so closely watching, and it did not take even strangers long to discern the situation. Every feature of her countenance showed suffering and blasted hopes. Tears were coursing their way down the furrows in her faded cheeks, which had once been as fresh as rose-leaves. She was the first wife, who had been robbed of the affections of a once kind and loving husband.

His own passions and the counseling of the priesthood had driven him into polygamy, and this first wife was living such a life of torture that her every look and action said to the world, "I am heart-broken."

The long journey she was going to take with her recreant husband, had few if any bright prospects for her, while the happiness of the other woman seemed only to be inspired by jealousy and gratification in her success as a rival. And yet there are people who will assert positively that the women are happy and contented in polygamy!

The following anecdote was related at a meeting of the Anti-Polygamy Society, by one of its members, and the lady to whom it refers is the wife of one of those good brethren who delight in preaching about the divine ordinance, and who will inform credulous strangers that "nowhere on the earth is woman so highly honored and so tenderly cared for as among the Mormons."

"A neighbor of mine, the first wife of a prominent Mormon, living at present in Salt Lake City, came into my house some little time ago with her otherwise handsome and intelligent face sadly marred by a black eye. Being aware that the celestial order of marriage sometimes occasions peculiar occurrences in the household, we refrained from making any allusion to the disfigurement until she apologized for it, saying, 'This is one of the fruits of our holy religion.'

"We asked for an explanation, which was given in the following words: 'You know that my husband has lately married my servant girl, and they are billing and cooing like young turtle-doves. Nothing in the house is good enough for her, and I have so far forgotten my duties as a Mormon wife as to be unwilling to recognize her as the *entire* mistress of the house, which, as it happens, is mine, and not my husband's. It and everything in it was given me by my father. Yesterday she graciously informed me that if I behaved myself I might remain, otherwise she would turn me out of the house. Unfortunately I had the audacity to resent this remark, and was commencing to give her a dose of her own medicine by putting some of her things out of doors, when my husband came home. For this exhibition of a wrong spirit, he whipped me severely, leaving the marks you see, and upon leaving the room he remarked, 'I am determined to live my religion if it kills us all.'"

An Eastern lady who was visiting Zion a short time ago was captured, so to speak, by a female apostle of polygamy, who assured our Eastern friend that the women living in the celestial ordinance were perfectly happy; that they would not exchange their fraction of a saintly husband for the undivided affection of the best sinner that ever lived; that the children born in plurality were equal or superior to those of monogamic origin; and in short, that all the statements which have been published in regard to the beastliness and brutality of polygamy were base fabrications, invented by vile apostates or wicked Gentiles.

Our traveler would have left Zion with very vague and unsatisfactory ideas, as all she had read previously about the institution was so entirely at variance with what she heard from the polygamic sister, had she not met accidentally a member of the Anti-Polygamy Society, who exhibited to her gaze the other side of the picture.

She introduced her to some women whose happiness had been blasted, their lives blighted, and their homes ruined, by the infernal doctrine. Of course, much that she was told seemed incredible,—so incompatible with her ideas of modesty and decency, let alone religion,—especially the facts of consanguineous marriages, and two or more women living with the same man, and raising children to him in a house of one or two rooms.

We do not wonder that decent people cannot believe that such things exist in a Christian land. But an incident occurred not very long ago which illustrates this peculiar beauty of the polygamic system.

Three young men, pleasure seekers, left one of our cities for a fishing tour in one of the valleys of the mountains. After being out a few days, one of the number was taken ill, and as a severe storm was evidently approaching, they went to a small settlement near by, and asked for shelter in a small house on the outskirts of the place. They found that the house contained only one room, and that not very inviting, and from all appearances there were as many occupants for the three beds as Serepta Smith had when her house was invaded by church delegates, as related by Josiah Allen's wife, in one of her books.

Our tourists would fain have sought more comfortable quarters, but the invalid could go no further without endangering his life. One of them staid in the house to nurse his friend, while the other slept outside in their traveling wagon.

They soon discovered who were the occupants of the cabin, and they were indeed a saintly crew. A man, his *three wives and their families*, had been living there for a number of years. One of the women apologized for being just then a little more crowded than usual, *because that day the old man had brought home a young bride*, which rather contracted their accommodations for strangers.

If some of our Eastern doubters could step in and

spend the night in one of these hotels, we think their doubts would be set at rest forever in regard to the beauty of polygamy.

A life of only a few years in Utah is enough to give the observer, unless he deliberately closes his eyes and ears, a knowledge of things which, were it possible to fully portray them to the world, would shock and raise the indignation of all decent people.

A prominent member of the Anti-Polygamy Society is responsible for the following anecdote, which is a single illustration of how utterly destructive polygamy is to the sacred relation of family, and how the hydra-headed monster outrages all the holiest feelings of the human heart:—

"There is a neighbor of mine, a good elder, who lives his religion to the extent of having six wives. He bears the reputation of being a good man, a warm friend, and an obliging neighbor, and about as just in the treatment of his numerous families as it is possible to be. He does not pretend to support them all, for he is not rich by any means, but he tries to give them facilities for contributing to their own support.

"One wife has cows, and sells milk and butter. Another has a machine, and takes in sewing; while the daughters from the age of twelve and upwards have always helped to earn their own living.

"His legal wife is a superior woman, and her large family has been very well brought up, being exceptionally well behaved for Mormon children. She has taken great pains to instruct them herself,

A POLYGAMOUS FAMILY.
From a Photograph.

and worked very hard to afford them a few more educational advantages than are enjoyed by the majority of children in Utah.

"A short time ago, sickness and death visited the household, taking away two little ones belonging to the legal wife, and leaving the other parts of the family unscathed. It was not said of her, as I have known it to be in other instances, that the affliction was sent because she opposed the will of the Lord; for I have never known a woman in all my Mormon experience that was so patient in bearing the cross imposed by polygamy as was this lovely and devoted wife. And though sometimes the load was almost too heavy to be borne, yet she never complained or murmured, but strove to think that it was the will of her Heavenly Father that she should bear it.

"I had been the recipient of many neighborly kindnesses from both the elder and his wife, since I left the church, as well as in former days, but I was prevented by illness in my own household from going to see them during the days of their affliction. When I did go, the poor woman was so prostrated by sorrow and fatigue that she was unable to be seen.

"I offered a few words of condolence to her husband, asking him to convey my warmest sympathies to his heart-broken wife. He thanked me for my kindness, and then said, 'My poor wife is indeed bowed down to the earth with grief; but it is not so bad for me, for you know, Mrs. D., I still have *sixteen children by the other women!*'"

These lines will in all probability be read by many mothers of dearly loved children. Can one of you imagine yourself weeping over the cold form or the newly made grave of one of those idolized little ones, and think of your husband consoling himself with the idea that *your* loss does not affect him very much? *he* can soon forget it because there are so many more children left him by his other women!

Apropos of this same phase of the subject, there was a funeral in one of the principal towns in Utah a few months ago, the object of mourning being the only wife of a brother in the church. Five saintly polygamists officiated at the obsequies, and all exalted the principles of the Latter-day church, and particularly descanted upon the loveliness of polygamy. One old Saint, who was the husband of five wives, eulogized the departed sister and deplored the loss of the good brother in being obliged to part from the faithful companion of his youth, and then said: " We should sympathize with him more deeply than with many others, for he has lost his *only companion*. If I should lose one of *my* companions, I should still have several left to console and comfort me."

Oh, what a consolation to tender the bereaved heart in such an hour as this! But each of the other speakers went over the same ground, and gave no greater consolation than that the brother had been very foolish in not having several wives, so his loss would not now be that of the solitary one.

Another incident, which was related to us by the daughter of the woman in question, shows how impossible, under this cruel system, is that mutual sympathy and affection which should exist between husband and wife.

"My mother was quite ill at one time, and I being the eldest daughter took care of her. I did the best I could for her according to the suggestions of friends, for we were not permitted to call a doctor. Father used to spend a week in turn with each of his wives, and when mother was taken sick, which was quite suddenly, her week was just over, and he was in the next house staying with another woman.

"After a day or two, I became alarmed, and went in there, and told him I thought mother was very ill and needed more skillful attention than I was able to give her. I asked him if he would not come in and see her awhile. Before he could reply, the other woman answered me very sharply, saying mother had her turn the week before, and should be satisfied with what was right.

"Not noticing her remarks at all, I said, 'Father, mother feels very badly indeed this evening, and would like to see you particularly. Could you not come in and sit with her for half an hour? It would cheer her up, and do her so much good.'

"'I can't do it, Lucy,' he answered, 'because I have promised certain to go with Mary here to the ward-party to-night. You take good care of her, and if she is not feeling better in the morning, let me know, and I will have the bishop go in and lay hands on her. Tell her, I'll try to drop in on Sunday after meeting is over.'

"Mother might have died a half dozen times over before Sunday; and I was so indignant at his carelessness that had I been sure she would die the next minute I would neither have gone after him nor allowed him to be sent for. He did come in on Sunday, but fortunately mother was so much better by that time that she did not care to see him, and treated him very coolly.

"He always professed to think a great deal of mother, but could not pay her the slightest extra attention without getting into trouble with the other women. I tell you that polygamy is the most heartless and love-destroying system that could ever have been invented. I was brought up in it, but would rather, a thousand times, lay a daughter of my own in the grave than see her enter it."

The following is another illustration of the sweet unity and delightful family relations which are characteristic of the divine ordinance:—

A certain elder in Israel desired to build up a celestial kingdom after the divinely ordained plan, and married a young widow, against the wishes of his wife, who had no belief in polygamy. She did not possess that first requisite in a Mormon woman, "a submissive spirit;" and having no other method of redress, she sought revenge by the only means in her power—by tormenting her husband and his second wife in all possible ways.

He was determined that the two should live together, as he could not or would not build another house. But alas for the celestial doctrine! whatever advantages it might bring in the future, he soon found from sad experience that it gave no happiness here. There was no such thing as one moment's peace in the house. He had heard it said frequently by the high-priests, that if a man could not rule his earthly kingdom, he would never be fitted to be a king in the world to come. As he was very ambitious for regal honors, he was in great grief, and much perplexed, how to govern two unruly, contentious, and exasperated women.

After awhile he found that he must separate them. So he gave each her own apartments. This did not mend matters at all, but rather made them worse. For he could not divide his time between them to the satisfaction of either, or to his own convenience.

His business demanded his presence at his store at certain hours. It would suit Mary to have meals ready only at those hours, and perhaps Jane would take it into her head to be as contrary as Mary. Then, in addition, each one seemed angry and jealous when he was with the other, yet during her own time made him as miserable as possible with her jealousy and recriminations.

While he was with one, the other would frequently apply her ear to the key-hole of her rival's apartment, to discover what was passing. When the first wife was too busy to attend the key-hole herself, she would place there her little six-year-old daughter, and tell her to repeat what she had heard. Of course the child told the most ridiculous stories, which the mother affected to believe, and repeated to the husband when he next visited her. All this was the cause of the most bitter quarrels.

As soon as possible, the husband built a second house a few rods distant, in which he installed his second wife. But the two women could never come even within speaking distance of each other without having a quarrel, which often ended in personal violence, blows being exchanged, hair pulled, and dresses torn in the struggles. At last, after running away himself, and coming back on account of his children whom he dearly loved, he was obliged to divorce number two, when peace was again restored to his earthly home, although at the expense of his heavenly kingdom.

This incident shows how completely polygamy has demoralized the women, and rendered them fiendish in their dispositions. Both the women in question were good enough by themselves, and calculated to make loving, tender wives; but the accursed system brought, as it always does, the very worst passions to the surface, and made each of them a demon who found delight in tormenting her husband and torturing her rival.

These incidents could be multipled by hundreds, yes, by thousands, and yet the truth would not half be told. There are incidents of almost daily occurrence that could not be repeated, or if they could, would scarcely seem credible, they are so revolting to every sense of modesty and decency.

Before concluding this chapter on the "Beauties

of Polygamy," we submit the following arraignment of the system, by a lady who was a Mormon for nearly a score of years, had a large acquaintance with all classes of polygamous families, both rich and poor, and was in every way competent to pass judgment on the institution:—

"Mormon polygamy is characterized by deceit and treachery. Men will break, without the slightest compunction, the most solemn vows that man can pledge to woman. They will take other wives clandestinely, and then excuse their duplicity by saying they did it to avoid a row or a scandal; or they were afraid their wives would not consent to their taking more women; but when it was done, they could not help themselves, and would be obliged to submit and accept the situation. I could myself mention fifty instances of the meanest kind of treachery whose terrible results upon the innocent, trustful victims, are seen in the insane asylum, or the grave.

"Mormon polygamy is characterized by oppression and tyranny. The worst evils of negro slavery had no parallel with some of the evils of this nefarious doctrine. A Mormon not only counts himself the possessor and master of his women bodily, but he is also the self-constituted owner of their souls. I have known cases where men have kept their wives in a constant state of anxiety and torment, and rendered their lives more miserable than can be expressed, by the simple intimation, 'If *you* won't be submissive, I will get a woman who will!' It can easily be seen how this threat, hanging constantly over a woman's head, terrifies her, until womanhood is gone, and she consents to anything but the loss of her husband, and the breaking up of her already none too peaceful home.

"Then again there are men who will make a show of gaining the consent of their wives to take other women, but this is the manner in which it is done: A Saint becomes acquainted with a woman or girl that attracts his fancy, and he immediately is filled with the spirit of the Lord. It is wonderful how pious and devoted to religion a man becomes, and how eager he is to do his Master's bidding in such a case. He then informs his wife that duty urges him to live up to his privileges and build up his kingdom.

"If she objects, or is in any way opposed to this phase of duty, he will say, 'Do as you please, consent or not, it will make no difference to me; but if you do not, you may take your children and go where you please. You are probably aware that you have no rights at all in this Territory. But behave yourself, consent quietly and make no scandal, and I will continue to support you.'

"Cases have come to my own knowledge where first wives have invited young girls to tea, and entertained them to the best of their ability, all for the sake of getting from their husbands a few necessaries, a few yards of flannel, or two or three pairs of shoes for their little children; and perhaps that very same girl would soon be brought home as **wife number two.**

SALT LAKE CITY, LOOKING SOUTH-EAST. WAHSATCH MOUNTAINS IN THE BACKGROUND.

"Mormon polygamy is characterized by brutality. Incidents have come to the knowledge of almost every Gentile lady who has lived for any length of time in this Territory, and who has manifested the least interest in investigating the system, which prove that the most cold-blooded brutality and cruelty are everywhere characteristic of polygamy as it exists in Utah. The traditions of every settlement, of almost every household, could substantiate this assertion. The cemeteries of Utah are peopled with women who have died prematurely, and too often on account of physical violence. A woman's health, and even life, are not weighed in the balance against the polygamist's desires which he calls the will of the Lord.

"Mormon polygamy is characterized also by immorality and licentiousness. It is a notorious fact, and a refutation is challenged from any source, that the Mormon youth and children are precocious in wickedness to a remarkable degree, and are entirely lacking in that simplicity and innocence which is an attribute of children almost the world over. Some of these children, almost from infancy, develop the lowest and most depraved tastes, and are familiar with the vilest of practices.

"Such relations cannot help blunting the moral sense, and destroying every vestige of womanly modesty and refinement.

"How can a wife have those holy and tender feelings which should always be associated with the marriage tie, and which are inseparable from a true union, when she can speak, and to all appearances calmly, of her husband's having 'gone to stay with some of the other women'?

"What ideas of home love and home associations can children have who talk about 'father's week at the other house,' and who discuss freely which woman is his favorite, and why she is so, and which woman's children he is most indulgent to, and provides for the best?

"There are many good Mormons who pretend to have no doubt as to the divine origin of polygamy, who are free to admit that the experiment has proved a failure in this day and generation, and who acknowledge that the majority of men only enter it from licentious motives, and have no religious convictions whatever.

"During the twenty years that I was a Mormon, I have known a few men who embraced the system from pure motives; but a large majority went into it from pure wickedness. And I assert without any hesitation that polygamy is solely and entirely responsible for the corruption of our youth, the lax moral principle, the indecency and shameless practices that prevail all over Utah Territory."

But in the following chapter the results of the system upon the children of Mormonism will be dwelt upon more particularly.

CHAPTER XVI.

The Effects of Polygamy.

Affects Unborn Generations.—Young Girls.—Remarkable Statement.—Testimony of Stenhouse.—House of Correction.—An Apostle's Son.—A Bishop's Hopeful Heir.—Taylor's Refusal.—"Poor Boy."—Unfortunate Girl.—"Surprised that They Lived together so Long."—Fifty Children in the Cemetery.—Joseph Smith's Son.—"Queen of the Harem."

IN a previous chapter it was asserted that the Mormon children and youth are extraordinarily precocious in evil, and that they grow to manhood and womanhood without being taught the common decencies of life, to say nothing of its refinements. This is due to several causes, each and all of which have their origin in polygamy.

This phase of the subject is one that it is difficult to deal with, because every feature of it is so repugnant; yet it is one which needs to be exposed as fully as possible. If the wrongs and evils of polygamy affected only its present victims, there might be some excuse for letting it die a natural death; but it is entailing wrongs that will blast thousands of lives, and giving to a vast multitude of children still unborn a heritage of woe and crime. And it is no less for the sake of these unborn thousands than for its present victims that we plead for measures which shall tend to check the abomination.

It is a notorious fact that ninety per cent of these unholy alliances are contracted when the former wives are in that condition which most craves a husband's tender care and sympathy. It is not an uncommon occurrence for a wife to be near the hour of trial when the husband is off on a honeymoon with another woman. The inevitable mourning for the loss of her husband, the longing for his society, and hatred of the other wife, exercise the most deleterious influences upon the moral faculties of the children.

It sometimes happens that a wife under these circumstances will resort to the use of stimulants or potent drugs in order to drown her sorrows, and for the time being render her oblivious to her own grief, or the triumphs of her rival. Tastes and predilections are thus imbibed and acquired by children, which often result in their early ruin. That these are not mere baseless assertions can be proven by the history of some leading polygamous families in Utah,—families whose wealth and position, it might be thought, would keep them exempt from the vices of the poorer and more degraded classes.

One of the effects of polygamy is that young girls brought up in the system do not think it a possible thing for a wife to be the only mistress of a pure and happy home, and the only recipient of a true and honorable husband's devotion. They have been taught that a man who does not have plural wives must keep mistresses, and as they have always heard polygamy compared with the social evil, they soon learn to place the two systems on the same level. And as a consequence, girls who have seen the utter misery produced by the one system do not hesitate about embracing the other in preference. There is a certain noted woman in Salt Lake City, who declares that during her residence there, she has refused admission to hundreds of young Mormon girls who would lead voluntary lives of shame.

One of the reasons given by the apostles of polygamy for its acceptance is, that its practice will redeem the race from the many evils which are prevalent in modern society; that it respects the desires of every woman to be an honorable wife and mother, and leaves no unmarried element to go astray.

In a recent newspaper article, one of the Mormon leaders made the remarkable statement that the Mormons held chastity in man as a virtue that should be maintained as rigidly as in woman, and that it should be valued and cherished in both sexes as more precious than life itself. We repeat, a "remarkable statement," because none knew its falsity better than the man who made it; and it was made for the express purpose of deceiving those people who were inclined to favor legislation against Mormon polygamy. But let us see if the history of Mormonism will bear out any of these specious reasons given for the practice of the peculiar institution.

Stenhouse, who was a Mormon for twenty years

or more, and whose "Rocky Mountain Saints" is admitted by the most bigoted Mormons to be a true and impartial history of their sect, says, in speaking of the early days of Mormonism: "Even at this time a few of the new converts appear to have exhibited loose notions of morality. Of these, some charged with being adulterers and adulteresses were stated to have been turned away, and others were warned to beware and repent speedily."

He further says: "All through the history of the church, during the lifetime of Joseph Smith, may be noticed a disposition to free-loveism." These statements are very mild compared with those of other authors, but we do not think they prove very conclusively that this virtue was rigidly observed in the early days of the church.

To show that the morals of the Saints had not improved very radically in the days of the prophet Brigham, we will quote again from Stenhouse, in regard to the famous (or infamous) "Reformation" in Utah. It is recorded that "on one occasion, a public meeting was called at the Social Hall, which was very largely attended by the priesthood or male members only. Brigham Young, Heber C. Kimball, and others, addressed the elders. Brigham, in his speech, requested all present who had been unfaithful to their marriage vows to stand up. To the surprise of some, and the chagrin of the presidency, more than three-fourths stood on their feet. It is related that Brigham was as much appalled at this sight as was Macbeth when he beheld the woods of

Birnam marching on to Dunsinane. A bishop arose and asked if there was not some misunderstanding among the brethren concerning the question. He thought that perhaps the elders understood Brigham's inquiry to apply to their conduct before they had thrown off the works of the devil and embraced Mormonism; but upon Brigham's reiterating that he referred to sins committed since they had entered the church, the brethren to a man still stood up. Brigham had evoked a specter that he little expected. Of course, no women being present, the men only answered for themselves—the inference had to be imagined about the other sex."

Now, in order to prove that the status of morality is no higher at the present day, especially among the children and youth, we need only give the testimony of the Mormons themselves.

One of the church organs has made the depravity of the youth of this Territory, the subject of more than one leader during the past year, and has strongly recommended the establishment of a House of Correction, or some similar institution, where children might be placed for reformation. For whose children? it may be asked. Certainly not for those of the Gentiles; for there are comparatively very few families among the Gentile residents, the bulk of that class of the population being miners, and men who have no families.

It is a source of constant complaint among those who have children, that with all their care, they can scarcely prevent them from coming in contact with the accursed influences that surround the rising generation of Mormons. What some of these influences are may be imagined when it is known that the bishops of many settlements have been complaining to the priesthood that a large majority of the marriages contracted between young persons during the past few years have occurred under compulsion, because circumstances obliged the bride's honor to be vindicated.

The bishop of one settlement not very remote from Salt Lake is the authority for the statement that in one year more than twenty illegitimate children were born (outside of polygamy), and not one Gentile in the place. The Mormons are wont to say that it was the Gentiles who brought all social irregularities into Zion, but this instance is at least one refutation of that assertion.

Not many months ago, a son of that selfsame apostle who pays such high tribute to the virtue of this people, was compelled to leave his home in one of the Northern settlements of Utah for a flagrant breach of social decorum. He had a nice young wife, and a baby only a few months old; but this did not prevent him from indulging in celestializing propensities, and the worst of it was that he omitted going through the Endowment ceremonies with the young lady.

A still later case is that of a bishop's son,—and the facts have appeared in the local journals,—who has three wives, two of whom he married within a few weeks of each other, and both under compulsory cir-

cumstances. It was proved beyond a shadow of
doubt that the brutal instincts of this young Mormon,
came through his parents, and that every child
of theirs had been almost on a par with this one,
—showing how truly Mormon polygamy makes
beasts of nearly all who become entangled in its
folds.

A reputable female physician who had a very large
practice in Salt Lake City among what is called
the higher class of Mormons (they never employ
male physicians except in extreme cases), has made
the statement repeatedly, that a majority of her
patients were in need of her services when they had
been married six or seven months; and for a young
mother to have been married nine months was something
of a rarity.

Only a few weeks ago a certain Mormon asked
permission of John Taylor, the present head of the
church, to take another wife. To his credit be it
said, when he became acquainted with the circumstances,
he refused to allow the marriage to take
place, saying that polygamy should not be used
as a means of covering sin. But if he had been as discriminating
in every case of the same kind during
the past few years, the number of " waifs " thrown
on the world would be alarming.

But a tree is known by its fruits, and in lieu of
any more comments on the system, we submit the
following incontrovertible facts, known to thousands
of people at present living in Utah. We suppress
names, because there are members of each family

still living. *Persons* are nothing, but facts speak for themselves, and we leave any candid man or woman to judge from the effects of polygamy whether it should be crushed as a poisonous viper, or still be allowed to spread its venomous slime under the name of *Religion!*

The first wife of a prominent Mormon had several sons, one of whom evinced a most cruel, vindictive, and blood-thirsty disposition almost from his birth. From his earliest childhood, he seemed to take the greatest delight in torturing and then killing animals or birds; as he grew older he became a perfect terror in the neighborhood where his parents lived.

When people came to his mother to complain, or to demand satisfaction for some new depredatory act upon fowls or animals, or some cruelty perpetrated upon their children, she would shake her head sorrowfully and say, "Poor boy, it is not his fault, it is only his misfortune."

When asked for an explanation of her words, she declined to give it, but would repeat them over and over again, much to the disgust of her friends, who pronounced him to be, "without exception, the worst child they had ever seen or heard of." Neither the tears nor prayers of his mother, nor the punishments of his father, made any impression upon him. He grew steadily worse.

When he was about sixteen years old he went away from home, and for some time nothing was heard from him, until at last it was discovered that he was living with a band of desperadoes who were both robbers and murderers. More than once were his hands stained with the blood of a fellow-mortal. His own death occurred by being lynched by an infuriated mob for a peculiarly unprovoked and outrageous murder.

When his mother heard of his dreadful end, she shook her gray head sorrowfully, as she had done of old, and repeated the same words, " Poor boy, it was not his fault, only his misfortune. I knew it would end just as it has."

Shortly afterward, some friends came to condole with her, among whom was a person high in authority in the church. An eye-witness said that she should never forget the scene.

After a few sympathetic words had been said, the poor, half-crazed creature rose, and looking the elder straight in the face, said in thrilling tones:—

" You are responsible for the fate of my poor boy; you and the infernal doctrine of polygamy. It was *you* who persuaded my husband to take another wife, to live up to his privileges, as you termed it. We had lived happily until that time, but polygamy made our home like the abode of Satan. For months before the birth of that boy, I felt as if I wanted to kill his father's second wife, the woman who had destroyed our home and robbed me of my husband's love. Murder, and nothing but murder, was in my heart all the time. I never looked at her but I wanted to kill her. There were times when I would willingly have yielded up my own life, if I could have had the satisfaction of seeing her dead first, and by my hand. That poor, unfortunate boy has only paid the penalty of his father's sin and his mother's sorrow." Then raising her withered hand on high, she continued, "I pray God that the curse of an injured wife and a bereaved mother may follow you all the days of your life, for it was *you* who led my husband into polygamy."

Immediately after the publication of the foregoing incident in the *Anti-Polygamy Standard*, the following letter was received by the editor:—

"The article in the last number of your valuable paper entitled 'The Effects of Polygamy' recalled to my mind another incident illustrative of that same point, which occurred in a family of my own connections.

"The first wife fell into a state of despondency on account of her husband's neglect of her, and devotion to another woman, and nothing could arouse her from her constant condition of sadness and lethargy combined. Formerly the neatest and most active of women, she became the most careless and indolent. Her house, children, even habits of personal neatness, were entirely neglected; and she did scarcely anything but sit in a most careless undress, and silently bemoan the sad fate which had robbed her of a husband's love.

"After a period spent in the foregoing manner, a reaction came, defiance took the place of sorrow, and a restless, aimless energy succeeded apathy and despair.

"The child that was born soon after is a compound of all these elements. At times she will sit around, or lie in bed for days; will say she is ill, but will never permit any remedies to be given her. All she wants is to be let alone. Then, after that mood has passed, she will fly around and yet accomplish nothing, as some of the family say.

"Her energy can never be directed to any permanently useful or beneficial channel, and it scarcely ever lasts more than long enough to clear away the *debris* accumulated during her period of inactivity and despondency.

"The poor girl is of no earthly account to herself or to others. Who is to blame? I may answer in the words of your other correspondent, 'The unfortunate child is only paying the penalty of her father's crime and her mother's sorrow.'"

Instances of a similar nature might be multiplied almost without end.

A most striking illustration was made public during a divorce suit a year or two ago. Both the parties belonged to leading Mormon families. The husband sought a dissolution of the marriage tie on account of the furious and almost ungovernable temper of his wife. Her fits of passion were perfectly extraordinary. He deemed the lives of himself and of his children to be in constant danger.

She was not by any means an evil-disposed woman, and after her storms of passion were over, her penitence and remorse seemed so deep and sincere, that for a long time he hesitated about taking the final step, but at last he felt compelled to do it for the sake of his children.

Of course the affair was the subject of many and varied comments, but to those who knew her best, the sequel was not a matter of surprise.

Said one aged relative, who was still a member of the Mormon church: "I am only surprised that they lived together as long as they did. For that girl, though not wanting in many excellent qualities, had the temper of a demon; and, to tell the truth, it was hers honestly.

"Her mother was a second wife, and for some years had been the idol of the husband. But a new face charmed him, and he decided that he must live his religion to a still greater extent.

"As it often happens, the second wife made more objections to the third marriage than did the first; indeed, the latter was quite willing that the power of the second woman should be broken. She was naturally high tempered, but after the advent of number three, she used to have such terrible fits of passion as to frighten every one with whom she came in contact.

"The scenes that occurred in that household would put to blush the Prince of Darkness. It was not an uncommon event for the bishop of the ward, or men in higher authority, to be called in to calm her passion, and restore peace in the family.

"Before that girl was born, her father was heard to remark more than once, that it would be a happy circumstance for the child if it should be born dead.

He had seen enough of polygamous life, and could not close his eyes to its effect on children. And *I feel justified in saying that if he could have had his way, she would not have lived very long after her birth.* Shortly before he died, which was when she was about eight years old, he said, 'I am afraid that Mary will yet curse the day she was born.'"

This principle of the transmission of hereditary traits was acknowledged by Brigham Young himself to such an extent that he virtually discarded one of his wives, who possessed a very violent and ungovernable temper. She had only one child, and the prophet said plainly that he did "not intend to have any more of that breed raised."

Brigham Young, who certainly was very shrewd, and had the most practical ideas of life, is accredited with saying more than once that if he had his way he "would discriminate among the women, and not all the wives, by any means, should be mothers."

We shall say but little of the physical effects of polygamy on the children, although this is a very important phase of the subject. The rows of tiny mounds in the Mormon graveyards tell the tale briefly, but forcibly.

A noted polygamist in Salt Lake City was said before his death to have more than fifty children buried in the cemetery, who had died in early infancy. We might pursue this subject further, but our present mission is to deal with the moral phases of the question.

One very noted polygamous family in Utah furnished a number of pregnant illustrations of the deleterious effects of the system. The legal wife is a very elderly lady now, and has had a number of children, all of whom, so far as living, are quite advanced in life.

It is said, on pretty good authority, that she was a plural wife of the prophet Joseph, and her eldest son belonged to that worthy, though always bearing the name, and being generally recognized as the child, of her husband. Let us glance at the life-pages of that son.

From his earliest boyhood he indulged in nearly every kind of vice, and was frequently sent on missions, in order to effect a reformation, but he invariably returned worse than ever. He continually drank to excess, and besides being a "four-ply" polygamist, he had the well-merited reputation of trying to insult every woman he might happen to meet.

Shrewd and unprincipled in business affairs, in private life he was equally unreliable, and was held in just odium by the entire people of the Territory.

He met his death in a fitting manner, being shot by an incensed brother, for an attempt upon his sister's honor. He was in his usual state of beastly intoxication at the time, and the avenger shot him down like a dog.

Another cause was given for his death, but by command of his father, the matter was instantly hushed up, and few members even of his own family learned until months afterward how a swift Nemesis had overtaken him.

Rt. Rev. DANIEL S. TUTTLE.
Diocese of Utah.

His body was brought to Salt Lake City (he had been living in one of the settlements for the previous year), but was interred quietly and immediately, and was not permitted to be seen by a single person. This was in accordance with his father's instructions, and for obvious reasons.

His oldest daughter married in polygamy, but not until she had several "little affairs" with other gentlemen. It was well known that her married life was very unhappy.

The fact of her being a wife did not prevent her from enjoying the society of gentlemen, and forming other attachments. One of these proved unfortunate. The gentleman did not return her friendship, and in a fit of desperation she threw the life aside that had been only too full of vanity and vexation of spirit. She was found dead one morning, and a little vial which was clasped tightly in the ice-cold hand told the sad story.

The polygamist in question had perhaps twenty wives, none ever knew the exact number but himself, and it is doubtful if even a complete record is extant in the Utah Endowment House, as a number were sealed to him in the old Nauvoo days.

One of those plural wives, who was for a long time reigning favorite, was married to him when very young, and people who knew her at that time say she was a most beautiful girl. She held her position for many years as "Queen of the Harem," but her time also came to be displaced. Without doubt, she had been devotedly attached to her husband, and being also somewhat of an invalid, the blow struck her with greater force.

One day a small quantity of laudanum was administered to her to deaden an acute paroxysm. It lulled her bodily pain and soothed her mental anguish, and from that moment until the day of her death she used the deadly drug continually. For years she was a confirmed opium-eater, and made no efforts to control the habit which consumed her own life and exercised such a baneful influence upon the lives of others.

A member of the family says that the death-bed of this woman was horrible in the extreme. In a frenzy of despair and agony, before the last fatal dose was administered to "quiet her nerves," she had every one of her children called to her bedside, and made them swear a solemn oath that they would never go into polygamy, that they would then and there forever renounce the foul demon that had ruined her, body and soul.

They took the oath, and have kept it; but the fatal curse that wrecked their mother's life has followed more than one of them.

Two of the daughters are almost hopeless inebriates. Another is an equally hopeless opium-eater, and an outcast in every sense of the word. She is bright, intelligent, generous to a fault, and in her first youth was as lovely as her ill-fated mother. She evidently does not consider herself to blame for her frailties; for she asked a friend who was remonstrating with her on the course she was pursuing, if it was strange that a man who had so many wives should transmit to his daughters a *penchant* for numerous husbands.

Truly what is written in the sacred Word has been fulfilled in this man's family,—The sins of the fathers shall be visited on those of the third generation; for many instances may be cited where his children have escaped, but the curse has fallen on his grandchildren.

An old lady who is thoroughly acquainted with this family remarked, not long ago, that unless every law which governs hereditary transmission should be at fault, the next generation of this brood would furnish almost innumerable materials for the insane asylum and the scaffold.

Two plural wives of this man were driven insane by polygamy, one died a raving maniac, calling upon Heaven to curse her husband, and declaring that she was going to hell, sent there by polygamy. As yet, her children have shown no decided symptoms of her malady, but there are people who declare that the curse will not pass them by. Several other wives were sent to the grave broken-hearted, by neglect and ill-treatment; and one, at least so it is whispered, paid the penalty of unbelief in the divinity of Mormonism, with her life. A number of his children are already lying in drunkards' graves, and more will lie beside them before many years.

Many others have avowedly no faith in Mormonism, though not formally separated from the church. In belief they are either infidels or atheists, and their children will be launched on the world with no faith in God, heaven or hell, no sound, moral principles, and no respect for a Government which has permitted the continuation of that system which has made them, in a measure, outcasts from civilized society. This is a brief statement of some of the effects of polygamy in only *one* family in Utah.

We could fill volumes with facts of a similar nature regarding almost every single polygamous family of note in the Territory, and those whose social position does not bring them into so much prominence are much worse.

As people descend in the social scale, their family relations will bear less investigation; but we do not know that morality is any more outraged. The outward surroundings, however, appear more hideous, probably because vice is not so well concealed as in those who are favored by more fortunate circumstances. The effects of the system are precisely the same in all classes of society, and a general description of its results in one family or community will answer for the entire people.

Polygamy is utterly at variance with every known principle of law, order, or morality; and people who practice it as in Utah, if let alone will soon degenerate into mere brutes. Its effects are to destroy the moral and intellectual nature, and develop only the animal. It remains to be seen whether the American nation will permit such an institution to be perpetuated within its borders.

CHAPTER XVII.

A Heart History.

Wedding Anniversary.—Mormon Missionary.—His Visit.—The Shock.—The Old Home.—Invalid Sister.—The Mother's Advice.—The Journey to Zion.—Bishop Parker's Wives.—A Solemn Promise.—The New Home.—Obscene Sermons.—Mrs. Parker's Friendship.—Unwelcome Visitor.—"Murdered."

IT was Maggie Blake's wedding anniversary, and memory carried her back to her bridal day. In fancy she stood once more at the altar, listening to the words that bound her to the man she loved, until death should them part.

Tears had filled her eyes when those solemn vows were uttered, and she had whispered a prayer to the God above for help to faithfully keep them. Happy in the love of husband and child, the years had rolled peacefully by.

But to-night, as she stood on the little vine-wreathed porch awaiting her husband's return, a presentiment of a coming evil, a nameless something that she could not define, seemed to hang over her; and she sighed aloud while murmuring to herself the words of the poet:—

"Thy fate is the common fate of all.
Into each life some rain must fall."

Little dreamed this young wife how soon the shadows of grief would darken the sunlight of her happiness, and a cup of sorrow be held to her lips, from which she would drink to the lees, and whose bitterness would poison her young life for evermore.

The sound of her husband's footfall broke in upon her reverie, and she ran blithely down the walk to meet him.

"Well, little wife," were his first words, "I am late to-night, but business before pleasure, always. I stopped at Judge Vernon's to talk over the plan of his new house. I am to begin it immediately, and before it is finished there will be a good many hundred dollars in my pocket."

When Maggie attempted to scold him for thinking of money-making on his wedding-day, he laughingly answered that she must veil her eyes if she wished to feign anger; they were tell-tales, and showed her gratification too plainly. But when, after tea, he asked her to go with him to hear a missionary from Utah speak, although she consented she was greatly disappointed that he did not wish to spend *this* evening at home. "Ah!" she thought, "men do not think of these things, or if they do, they call them trifles, but it is the observance of such *trifles* that make the sum of woman's happiness."

A little later they entered the public hall of the village, where a large crowd had gathered to listen to the discourse on this new religion; some from curiosity, others from interest.

When the speaker stepped upon the platform, Maggie felt a thrill of disappointment, not unmingled with disgust. She had from childhood, a reverential feeling for anything pertaining to religion. A minister of the Gospel she considered as one chosen of God, to be treated with awe.

Her dear old pastor, to whom she had listened Sabbath after Sabbath, was loved and respected by all his little band of faithful followers. And well he deserved it. The needy were never turned from his door, although to aid them his own family were often deprived of comforts. Only a look at his dear, kind face brought peace and rest to many an erring one, and courage to many a fainting heart that was striving to enter the portals of the heavenly city.

But this man was a portly, sleek, well-kept individual, with whom one could never associate the idea of self-sacrifice; on the contrary, he impressed her as being just the reverse,—greedy and selfish to a fault. In appearance, he was of medium height, broad shoulders, sandy beard, hair a few shades darker, florid complexion, and light-blue eyes. His full, thick lips covered a set of large, white teeth, which he was fond of showing.

He told of the beauties of Zion, the city of the Saints, where they were building temples to God, where there was no quarreling nor fighting, no backbiting nor jealousy, but perpetual unity, peace, and harmony. All were brothers and sisters, willing and ready to help each other. He was an earnest speaker, and while under the spell of his voice, doubtless many of his hearers agreed with him that the Latter-day Saints were God's chosen people, and thought that Salt Lake City must be a heaven upon earth.

Maggie's dreams that night were troubled, and she awoke the next morning feeling tired and ill. As Harry bade her good-by, he said: "Have a nice tea ready to-night, Maggie, for I intend to bring Elder Campbell home with me," and he hurried away as if he felt afraid he was doing something to offend or grieve her.

For a moment Maggie was tempted to call him back, and beg him not to invite this man to the house; but she saw it would be folly to do so without a better reason than she could give. Yet, all day a feeling as of some impending evil oppressed her, which she tried in vain to shake off. As evening approached she was her own sweet self once more, and greeted her unwelcome guest as pleasantly as if no evil fancies concerning him had ever flitted through her brain. He was entertaining in conversation, relating many pleasant stories and witty anecdotes. When the talk turned upon Utah, Maggie noticed that her husband seemed much interested, and from a remark dropped carelessly, she found to her surprise that the elder and Harry had met several times before in the village, and appeared almost like old friends.

Soon after tea, Maggie excused herself, in order to put Lilly,—her one little darling ewe lamb,—to sleep, and when she returned Elder Campbell said, "Your little girl looks very delicate, Mrs. Blake."

Maggie replied that she was not very strong.

"You should bring her to Utah, then, by all means. The air is so bracing, and the climate so delightful, that she would be sure to grow up healthy and robust."

"Do you think so?" Harry asked eagerly; while even Maggie thought, "Anything to benefit my darling."

Seeing his advantage, the elder resumed warmly:—

"I am sure of it. Why, madam, people come there from all parts of the world who are crippled and diseased, and in a short time they are restored to health and happiness. The climate is wonderful, wonderful!"

Harry asked if the journey overland was not very fatiguing.

"That depends a great deal upon the outfit you have, Mr. Blake," the elder slowly replied. "You can make the journey very comfortably if you have the means to do so."

After a short pause, he added:—

"Come now, say you will join the Latter-day Saints, and emigrate to Zion."

"We could go to your Zion without becoming Saints, I presume," Maggie laughingly remarked.

The elder seemed rather disconcerted for a moment, but he answered with a peculiar smile: "Certainly you *could*, but very few *do*. However, we should hope to convert you soon. We should be too glad to have you with us to quarrel over the terms." Soon after, he bade them good-night, and took his leave.

The days passed by, and Maggie, hearing nothing more of the elder, concluded he had left the neighborhood. She sincerely hoped so, for his influence seemed to have wrought a transformation in her husband, or at least she thought so; for his change of conduct dated from the evening Elder Campbell had taken tea with them. He was often gloomy and absent-minded. His evenings were occupied with business, he said; so his wife had little of his company. She was unsuspecting, and did not think of connecting his absence with the missionary from Utah; so when the shock came, it fell with greater force.

One evening, a few weeks after the elder's visit, Harry returned home earlier than usual, and as if to make amends for the past, he exerted himself to please to the utmost. Maggie's tender little heart accepted the olive branch extended, fluttering with joy at the gentle caresses and loving words. Perhaps they made the blow fall all the harder, when Harry, suddenly changing the subject said: "Maggie, I have joined the Saints, and intend to emigrate to Zion!"

"Harry! surely you do not mean that. Would you give up this dear little home where we have spent so many happy hours? And my dear old mother, and only sister, how can I part with them? Oh, my dear husband, I have never crossed you in any desire before, but in this I cannot yield so easily," Maggie pleaded when she recovered from the shock.

"Now, Maggie, your entreaties are of no use; we

must go, but you are welcome to take your mother with you. I cannot change my mind, for my word is given and cannot be taken back," was the almost gruff answer.

Maggie thought she would make one more appeal, so she said: "What has put this idea into your head? We have every comfort around us, a beautiful home and kind friends, your business is prospering; think of the sacrifice you will be compelled to make!"

"We can soon get another home, perhaps better than this, and make other friends as dear."

"But you know they will not be the same, Harry; do yield to me in this, and give up your idea of emigrating to that far-off country. Something tells me it is not for the best," and she clung to his arm in her earnestness.

He pushed her rudely aside, answering angrily: "No, I tell you, I am going; and if you do not choose to accompany me, you need not do so." And to stop further questioning, he walked quickly away.

"If you do not choose to accompany me, you need not do so!" It may seem almost incredible, but these are the identical words which the Mormon elders counsel both husbands and wives to say to their partners who do not willingly consent to ruthlessly sever all old ties and associations in order to emigrate to the promised land. And the numbers of wives and husbands that have been deserted, and the households that have been desecrated or totally broken up in obedience to this counsel, will never be known until the secrets of earth are revealed on the day of judgment.

Tears of wounded pride and affection filled the eyes of the loving wife. In all her married life, she had never been so rudely repulsed. What had so changed her husband's nature? Was this but a foreshadowing of coming events? If she thought so, would she not be doing right to take him at his word, and remain at home? No, a wife's place is at her husband's side in all changes of life, and vicissitudes of fortune.

The next morning, Harry, thoroughly ashamed of himself, asked her forgiveness, saying, "Maggie, I was a brute to talk as I did last night, come kiss and make up." She raised her face for the proffered kiss, but her heart was too sore for words.

Holding her still in his embrace, Harry continued, "You must not think that I could for one moment harbor the thought of being parted from you, Maggie. What could I do in that far-off country without my faithful wife? I am not always what I should be, I know, dear; but still, my heart is all right, and holds no idols but you and our child. Look up now, smile, and say you forgive me."

Hard indeed is the heart that is proof against warm kisses and loving words, and a woman's sensitive heart is swayed by love alone. Raising her eyes, she smiled through her tears, though her lips still quivered. The subject of emigration was not mentioned again for a few days, and Maggie began to hope that it would not be renewed. Alas! those hopes were soon shattered; for before starting to his business one morning, after kissing his wife and child good-by, Harry said: "Be in haste with your preparations, Maggie, for we shall leave here in a few weeks. I had an excellent offer for the house yesterday, which I did not think best to refuse, and the furniture can be sold at auction." And without waiting for a reply he was gone, which was always his way when he had grieved or wounded his wife's feelings.

Poor Maggie, who can depict the agony of that moment! Although partially prepared, she had not fully realized the sacrifice until then. Her brain whirled, and dropping into a chair, she wept bitterly. Lilly mingled her tears in sympathy. "O mamma, must we leave Grandma and Aunt Agnes, and my pony and rabbits and all our pretty things?"

"Yes, my dear, I am afraid we must."

"Then I won't go."

"Hush, Lilly, we must do whatever papa thinks best. Now, you go and tell Sam to have the pony at the door as soon as possible, and we will go and see grandma."

The more she thought of it, the more her grief increased. How could she leave this happy home, around which clustered so many tender memories. In a few short weeks strangers would own these cherished walls, while she would be miles away on the road to a new country, leaving every endeared object behind. No, not all she loved, her husband and child would be with her, and with them it was her duty to at least strive to be content.

The home of her childhood was but a few miles distant. Its sole occupants now were an aged mother and an invalid sister, to whom she was devotedly attached. She had not the courage to tell them sooner that this sad parting might be, but there could not now be longer delay. She was soon driving through shady lanes and over pleasant roads, passing field after field of waving grain, fast ripening for the harvester's sickle, and orchards, whose branches bent beneath their golden burden.

"See, mamma, there is grandma's house," cried Lilly, and through the tall trees with their heavy foliage, could be seen an old-fashioned country house, setting back from the road, with broad porches on every side, over which a variety of creeping vines lovingly twined their delicate tendrils.

Rover, the faithful old watch-dog, bounded joyfully down the path to meet them. "Even he will miss me," she thought. At the sound of the carriage wheels, an old lady appeared at the door, the dearest old lady, too, that ever was seen; not very tall, but plump and rosy, with soft brown eyes and silver hair, put smoothly back under the whitest of caps. At sight of her, another pang was added to Maggie's sorrow. How that loving heart will grieve! She kissed her more affectionately than ever, and asked: "How is Agnes to-day, mother?"

"She is feeling quite well for her, Maggie, and was just wishing you would drive over. But, my daughter, I don't think you are looking very well yourself." Maggie, however, assured her she was quite well, and hastened on to her sister.

The pleasantest room in the house had been fitted up for the invalid's use. Everything in it was dainty and pure. A couch was drawn to the window, and there, scarcely less white than the pillows on which she reclined, lay Maggie's only sister—Agnes. After the first anxious inquiries for her health, Agnes said, "I have been longing to hear you sing. I often think, when those fearful pains come on, if you were only here to sing to me, it would drive them away. I shall send for you next time."

"I hope you will, dear," Maggie faintly replied. Oh, how could she tell her!

"Now that you are here," Agnes continued, "you must sing until you are tired. Oh dear! the happiest days I spend now are in thinking of the old times, when our father and brother were alive; and of the songs we sang, and the merry games we played, in the long winter evenings. How we made these old rooms ring. I am thankful that we were so happy together, and never fretted each other as some families do, so that we can now look back with pleasure, instead of regret at those days."

"Yes, Agnes, we were happy, but you were always so good. I cannot see why such an affliction should be visited upon you."

"He knoweth all things best," sighed the invalid. "I do not mourn now as I used, but still it is hard to lie here so helpless, day after day. Yet, Maggie, I often think it will not be very long now. I feel that the end will come soon, and, dear sister, I am content. When I am gone, Maggie, you will comfort mother; for although I have been such a care and trouble to her, I know she will mourn me deeply, more than I deserve."

Maggie was weeping bitterly; never, it seemed, was heart so tempest-tossed. Where was her duty? with these helpless women, or with her strong husband, who was taking her away from all she loved, at the instigation of a stranger and a worthless adventurer, as she mentally called the Mormon emissary? But she could not tell them yet what must be; so, seating herself at the piano, she played soft, dreamy melodies, until her voice was firm enough to sing. Then one song followed another, until the old house rang again with the sweet music. Her mother's tears fell fast as she asked her to sing her father's favorite, that sweet old ballad, "The Land o' the Leal." Though her voice trembled, Maggie sang bravely to the end. Then drawing a stool to her mother's side, she rested her head on her knee, letting the tears flow freely.

Here little Lilly, who was also nestling close to her grandma's side, said softly, "Grandma, mamma is crying because we are going away to leave you and Aunt Agnes, and will never see you any more. Papa said so this morning; but mamma and I don't want to go, do we, mamma?"

"No, my darling," Maggie exclaimed, almost savagely, "and we won't go either." Then trying to calm herself she continued, "It is all too true, mother, we are going away from you, and yet it is for you to decide for me. Tell me, my mother, to whom do I owe the greatest duty, to you, or to my husband?"

"Quiet yourself, my child," said her mother gently, "you cannot know what you are saying; going away, where would you go to?"

"To Utah, to join the Mormons," Maggie replied.

"Oh, no, not that!" came the agonized cry from two loving hearts.

"Yes, mother, Harry has joined the Mormons, our home is sold, and in a few weeks we leave; but if you only say so, I will remain here at home with you. Oh, tell me, I entreat you, what to do, for I do not know!" she sobbed.

"You must go with your husband, my child, that is the only thing you can do. Your duty is plain in the matter; he has the first claim on you. Agnes and I have not long to stay until we are called to the Master's home. I wish that Harry would wait until we are gone."

"I have plead with him, mother, and he will not yield; yet how can I leave you?"

"Do not grieve, Maggie," said Agnes softly, "it will be a great trial to give you up, but the time for parting must come sooner or later. This only hastens it, but your place is at your husband's side, and no matter what follows, you will have the consciousness of knowing you have done your duty."

"I wish, Agnes, that I possessed a little of your resignation and submission, it would make trials much easier to bear; but putting aside all thoughts of our parting, something tells me not to go, and I cannot banish the thought, it seems an admonition that I dare not disregard."

"You are nervous and excited, my child, and no wonder. God will prepare the way for you, and I sincerely pray that your trials may be few. But should you be called upon to carry a heavier cross than you have borne before, try to be patient, remembering always, 'Whom the Lord loveth he chasteneth.'"

A host of warm friends escorted Maggie and her husband to the train to bid them God-speed on their journey. A number of persons from their own and adjoining villages were going also, but none with whom they were intimately acquainted.

Many were the comments of friends and neighbors on the step the Blakes were taking, but Harry was indifferent to all remarks, some of which were intended to reach his ear. Maggie had bade her loved ones farewell in the privacy of their own home, and we will not rend the veil from the sacredness of that parting hour.

Presently the signal was given, the train moved slowly off amid the waving of handkerchiefs and cheers of good-will, slowly at first, then faster and faster, until trees, fences, houses, and hills seemed flying past them, and they were fairly on the road to Zion.

Maggie's thoughts were at home with her loved ones. She could not weep, but there was a look of suffering in the soft brown eyes, unusual to them.

At Florence they met other emigrants with whom they were to travel across the plains. During their stay in this place, while making preparations for the journey, Maggie formed a few pleasant acquaintances among the emigrants, which, together with the excitement connected with the novel mode of travel, went far toward reconciling her to the change.

The first day's journey ended, they camped for the night very weary indeed, but the bright camp-fire and good, warm supper soon refreshed them. After supper they all gathered in a circle, and prayers were offered by the elders. Then came singing, in which all, young and old, joined heartily. As Maggie listened to the songs so earnestly sung by little children, strong men and matrons, and gray-headed patriarchs and aged women, whose life-journey was well-nigh ended, her heart was touched, and she felt that perhaps the Lord was indeed with those who were making such sacrifices to do his will.

But as the journey lengthened, and the days grew into weeks, and the weeks into months, and each night and morning she heard those apparently fervent prayers and songs of thanksgiving that they were "permitted to gather to Zion out of Babylon," echoed by women and men sick and almost dying from exhaustion and hunger, she grew to hate them, —they seemed only a mockery. The company had been late in starting, and as they had also met with some unavoidable delays, and the management was not of the best, their provisions ran low, and they were placed on half rations before the journey was two-thirds ended, and ere long one scant meal a day was all that was apportioned out to them.

The Blakes, who were traveling independently, were amply provisioned, and generously shared with others, until they, too, found starvation almost staring them in the face. Then, as the weather grew cold and stormy, the weaker ones died, and were hastily buried by the wayside. When the cheering news was at length given that on the morrow they would see Zion, those poor creatures rejoiced greatly, thinking that now their trials were ended.

A more beautiful sight than met the eyes of the weary travelers, when they reached the summit of the mountain, could scarcely be imagined. Before them lay the lovely valley of the Great Salt Lake, seeming to their weary eyes a very paradise of rest and contentment, while in the distance the briny waters of the lake glistened brightly in the sunlight. Many heartfelt prayers of gratitude went up to the Father above for bringing them safely to this peaceful harbor. Slowly they descended the mountain, and entered the city of the Saints, where they were warmly welcomed, shelter for all being freely proffered.

The Blakes were taken to the home of Bishop Parker. Leading them into a room where a pleasant-faced lady was sitting, their host said: "Mary, these are our guests, brother and sister Blake, and little Lilly; we must try to make them comfortable." His wife expressed her pleasure at meeting them, so cordially that Maggie felt irresistibly drawn toward her. Her face wore a sweet yet unutterably sad expression, showing to even a casual observer that she must have passed through some terrible trial. A little later, as she and Maggie were sitting alone, pleasantly chatting, a young woman entered the room, with a child in her arms. She asked Mrs. Parker some questions pertaining to household affairs, and Maggie presumed she was a domestic, and her astonishment can scarcely be imagined when her hostess introduced her as "sister Ellen Parker, my husband's fourth wife."

Maggie looked from one to the other in perfect bewilderment, and her eyes followed the comely young woman as she left the room.

"*His fourth wife*, did you say?" she stammered. "What do you mean? Do the Mormons marry more than one wife?"

It was now Mrs. Parker's turn to look surprised. "Is it possible, Mrs. Blake," she said, "that you have not heard that polygamy is practiced among our people?"

"I never have, though perhaps that is not to be wondered at, as I have not joined the church. But my husband has, and he has said nothing to me of such a practice, or—" Maggie checked herself ere the words were uttered. She would not hurt the feelings of her hostess by expressing her sentiments.

Mrs. Parker, smiling slightly, finished the sentence for her, "or you would not have come to this country?"

"I do not think I should," Maggie replied, adding

half apologetically, "but there was no need of my saying so; pray forgive me, I did not mean to offend you."

"No offense was taken," said her hostess. "Every pure nature recoils from such a system when it is first spoken of, but"—with a sigh—"like everything else, we become used to it in time." The fourth wife again passed through the room, eyeing Maggie curiously as if she would read her thoughts; and as the door closed upon her, Mrs. Parker resumed, and with genuine pity and concern in her voice, "I am very sorry, Mrs. Blake, that you were left in ignorance of polygamy. It might have saved you much misery, had you known it sooner."

"O Mrs. Parker," cried Maggie tearfully, "if my husband were to take another wife it would kill me. I know I could not endure it."

"Ah, my dear," Mrs. Parker answered, smiling sadly, "we all think that, but we manage to live through it after all. Let us hope your husband will not, at least until you understand and are reconciled to the doctrine; but should he do so, try to bear it patiently, and you will be rewarded in the next world, if not in this."

Maggie smiled through her tears as she replied, "Did you know me better, you would see the futility of such advice. There is not a particle of submission in my nature. I fear his home would be anything but pleasant, if he once made the attempt."

The old lady sighed: "So we all think, my dear, but continual dropping will wear away even the hardest stone. Now, my husband has four wives, and we get along very well, seldom having any difficulty. They do all the work, while I am housekeeper and general manager," adding with a forced laugh, "so you see, polygamy is not very bad for the first wife, after all."

The sad countenance and mournful eyes of Mrs. Parker belied her words, and Maggie felt in her inmost heart that she was not speaking truthfully; but she had not yet learned that the life of a Mormon woman is one continual dissimulation to the world, and warfare with herself. But not wishing to appear discourteous, Maggie said, "Well, looking on it in that light, perhaps it is not so bad, and anyway, I won't borrow trouble, for it may come of itself, soon enough."

They were soon called out to supper, and when all were seated at the long table, the four wives surrounded by children of all ages, each mother providing for her own, Maggie inwardly shuddered at the thought of such a life. There could be no privacy, or real home feeling in such a circle, though it might be called *home*. How could she endure to share her husband's affections with other women, as this poor wife was doing, and yet she fancied the husband's voice sounded softer and more tender, and that his manner was more gentle and respectful when speaking to her, his early love. As soon as they were alone that night, Maggie broached the subject nearest her heart by asking, "Harry, did you know of this doctrine of polygamy, before leaving home?"

"Well, yes, I heard a rumor of it, but nothing definite until we were on the plains."

"Why, then, did you not tell me of it?"

"Oh, I thought you would find it out soon enough," he answered indifferently.

"Yes, to my sorrow."

"Why, Maggie, you do not suppose I would bring another woman to the house while you were around? A house large enough to hold us could not be found. The girl's beauty would soon be spoiled, for if I took another wife, she would be a beauty of course; you know how I admire pretty girls," laughed Harry teasingly.

"Don't jest, Harry," Maggie said, her voice trembling; "to me it is no jesting matter, to think of sharing my husband's home and heart with another. I could not do it, I must have all or nothing."

"Maggie, you missed your vocation," cried Harry, still jesting. "The tone and gesture with which you said 'I must have all or nothing,' was worthy of a tragedy queen!"

"O Harry," exclaimed Maggie impatiently, "can you never be serious?" Then going to his side, she clasped her hands on his arm, looking earnestly up to his face. "Will you make me a promise?" she asked.

"A hundred, if you like, my dear," said Harry, now thoroughly sobered by his wife's manner.

"But I mean a solemn one, one that you will hold as sacred as your life; promise me never to take another wife while I live."

"Bless your heart, dear one, if that is all that troubles you, rest in peace, you are all that I can manage. But joking aside, you know, Maggie, that you and Lilly are dearer to me than anything else in the world, and I would sacrifice my own life rather than give you any unnecessary pain. Go to sleep now, my dear, and let us hope that our future will be brighter even than the past, in our new home in Zion."

Ah me! Harry Blake was not the only man in the history of Mormonism who solemnly pledged the wife of his youth that he would never trample her affections under foot, or pollute her fireside by the presence of another woman with whom he was living in sin under the guise of religion. The victims of those broken vows can be numbered by hundreds, yes, thousands, who are living to-day, and who envy their more fortunate sisters sleeping in nameless graves on the bleak hillsides of Utah.

The very next day after their arrival in Zion, Harry went out with Bishop Parker to look for a home, and upon his return informed their hostess that he had been fortunate in securing a house and lot, adding: "They told me it was church property. The house has been occupied, although it has never been finished, indeed it is a mere shell. The lot is a very good one, however, and in time I shall be able to make a fine place of it."

"I know the house," Mrs. Parker replied, "the poor man who built it is dead. When he reached the valley with his wife and three little ones, their money was almost gone, it had taken most of the savings of years to buy their outfit. The wife was a delicate little body, but cheerful and ambitious, the children, sweet and pretty. The husband seemed to worship them. But from the day they reached here misfortune seized them.

"The man rented a small house, but there was no barn or yard to keep his stock in, and the neighbors advised him to turn them loose. One morning they could not be found. As there was no brand to identify them, he could not prove they were his had he seen them."

"And did he never recover them?" asked Maggie.

"No, the country was full of Indians then, and every one said they must have stolen them. He purchased a lot on time from the church, and not having much money, he tried to build his own house. When the walls were up and the roof on, they moved in. That winter was very severe, and his wife took a cold, which, settling on her lungs, threw her on a bed of sickness. She lingered until spring came, then, when everything was green and beautiful, she died; the baby soon followed her, and the heart-broken husband and father gave up in despair.

"The church of Latter-day Saints demands a tenth of a man's earnings for tithing. This man had nothing to pay, whatever he turned his hand to failed. The lot had not been entirely paid for, and soon had to be surrendered again to the church. His home gone, he lost all hope, and one morning, soon after his wife's death, he was found dead in his bed. The two little orphan girls who were so sadly bereft of both parents are tenderly cared for by a family who have adopted them."

"What a shame, to take his home from him!" exclaimed Maggie indignantly.

"Yes, I thought so, too. Brother Parker tried to intercede for him, but was told that the interests of the church must be looked after, which of course is true, in a measure. But," she said, changing the subject, "you can make a nice home of it, and you must not mind if you hear it said that it is an unlucky place, as I am sure that both you and your husband are too sensible to pay any attention to foolish gossip."

When Maggie was fairly settled in her new home, which Harry had fitted up with taste and comfort, she might have been content, had it not been for the grim specter, polygamy, continually staring her in the face. But thrust it aside as she would, the fear of it would ever creep back into her heart.

To please her husband, she accompanied him to a few dances, the popular amusement among the Saints, but what pleasure she might have had was turned to bitterness, in sympathy for her sex. To see a man enter the hall, followed by several women who called him husband; to note the angry, jealous looks bestowed by the rest upon the favorite, or upon some girl young enough to be his grandchild, with whom their lord and master was flirting, filled her with indescribable disgust.

Why do they submit to such treatment, she thought; if it were her, she would kill herself before she would suffer such indignities! But ere long, she learned the estimation in which a woman is held among the Latter-day Saints.

Neither did the meetings at the Tabernacle and ward meeting-houses hold attractions for her. The sermons consisted principally of maledictions hurled at the Gentiles, and eulogies of celestial marriage, which were often too disgusting to listen to.

Some of the apostles were profane and obscene, as well as illiterate; and Maggie felt it an outrage to be compelled to sit and hear such libels on religious teachings. Gradually her husband ceased to invite her to accompany him, and she was not loth to remain away.

She was greatly attached to her friend, Mrs. Parker, at whose house she was so pleasantly entertained upon their arrival, and her intimacy with the bishop's wife was a shield to her in many ways; for Maggie was fast learning some of the mysteries of Zion, and was not as careful in expressing her opinions as wiser people would have been. Mrs. Parker always had a good word to speak in defense of Maggie, who would, indeed, have been almost friendless without her.

As she sat sewing one afternoon, some one rapped at the door, and walked immediately in without waiting to be bidden to enter. The visitor proved to be an old Mormon lady who had called several times. That her visits were never returned did not disconcert her in the least. "How do you do, sister Blake?" she asked in her blandest voice. "I had not seen you to ward meeting lately, and I thought I would come and inquire after your spiritual situation."

Maggie replied politely, asking her to be seated, when the old lady threw back her bonnet and shawl, and took out her knitting. Seeing she was likely to remain some time, Maggie resumed her work with a sigh of resignation.

"You have been here some time, sister Blake," the old woman remarked, "and I have been wondering when you were going to be baptized."

"I am sure I don't know," Maggie replied, "I have no intention of doing so at present, and for that matter, I do not know that I ever shall."

"What! sister Blake," she cried in amazement, "never be baptized? Now, I know you can't mean that. Why did you ever come to Utah, if you did not intend to join the Saints?"

"I came to please my husband, as many other women have done, I suppose. He is a Mormon, but I am not, and never intend to be," was the decided answer.

"But, sister Blake, you will never get to heaven if you do not join the church. Don't you know that only the Latter-day Saints can enter the celestial kingdom?"

Maggie smiled quietly as she said, "I will take my chances. I should indeed be sorry to think that all the dear friends I have lost are not in heaven."

The old lady interrupted her, saying eagerly, "But if you should join the church, you could redeem them by being baptized for them, for they are in purgatory, I am sure."

"Baptized for them!" said Maggie in surprise. "Please explain."

"Well, I never, sister Blake, but you are ignorant of the doctrines of the church. Did you not know that we Latter-day Saints were allowed to be baptized for the dead? And as we are the only ones permitted to enter the kingdom of heaven, we should try to redeem others who never embraced our faith, or rather who died before it was revealed to our prophet, Joseph Smith. I have been baptized twenty times," and the old lady drew herself up proudly as she added, "and as soon as I find out the names of some other relatives, I shall be baptized again."

Maggie threw back her head, and laughed more heartily than she had done since their arrival in the valley. "Truly," she said, "this is a wonderful Gospel! You deserve a rich reward for sacrificing your comfort for so many people. It could not be very pleasant to be ducked under the water so many times, especially in cold weather."

"No, it was not very pleasant, but as it was my duty, I did not mind it."

"Do you really believe, Mrs. Foote, that you have redeemed the souls of your friends from purgatory, as you call it?" Maggie asked seriously.

"I do, indeed, sister," she answered; "our prophet says so, and it must be true."

"I must say, then, that your religion is a very selfish one. I could never have faith in any doctrine that claimed to be the only one by which people could be saved. I believe there are earnest Christians in every denomination who will be saved at the last day. Their judgment may have been at fault in some things, but so long as they tried to do right, God will overlook all involuntary errors, and commend them for the good they have done."

But this good Saint was not to be convinced. She had been too thoroughly grounded in the errors of Mormonism, and was, in consequence, too bigoted to see things in any light but the one she was told.

"I must get some of the elders or bishops to talk to you, sister; it will never do to let you continue in that way; your fate will certainly be to be turned over to the buffetings of Satan. I suppose now, you don't believe in celestial marriage either?" she said, cunningly watching the expression of Maggie's face as she spoke.

Maggie could scarcely conceal her contempt, as she replied, "Certainly not, how *could* any true woman believe in it?"

"Why, it was a divine revelation from God. It must be true, and we are taught to obey God's law, are we not?"

"We certainly ought to follow God's law," Maggie said, "but I cannot believe he would give a law of that kind to his people. His teachings have ever been loving and merciful. Such a law or practice as polygamy is a source of never-ending misery and wretchedness that no loving father would willingly inflict on his children."

"That is the way the women all talk, sister, until they are regenerated by the Holy Spirit. I used to say the very same myself. But I have lived to learn better, thanks to the counsel of our holy elders, and I'll see you believing in polygamy before you leave Utah, and giving another wife to your husband with your own hand, as I have done."

Maggie considered this conversation simply the chatter of an old fanatic, but she found afterward that even worse and more absurd things were taught and believed by the majority of Mormons. Soon after, sister Foote rolled up her knitting, said good-by, and wended her way to another house for a friendly chat, where Maggie's words were repeated, and her dreadful heresy very severely commented upon. And as we all know, a story never loses by repetition. In this case, it gathered strength until it assumed wonderful proportions and finally reached the prophet's ear.

On the day following the visit of sister Foote, Maggie's servant, an intelligent young English girl, who seemed mature and sober beyond her years, said to her, "Do you know, Mrs. Blake, that Bishop Proctor's wife died early this morning, and that the baby is dead too?"

"Why, no, I had not heard it," replied Maggie in surprise. "I thought they were both doing well. How did it happen?"

"Happen!" cried the girl indignantly, and then

PROF. J. M. COYNER,
PRINCIPAL SALT LAKE CITY COLLEGIATE INSTITUTE.

almost under her breath, she whispered the word, "Murdered!"

Maggie grew pale as death as she said, "Why, Mary, what do you mean; how can you talk so; are you out of your mind?"

"No, ma'am, I am not, though I often think it strange that I have been able to keep my senses, considering all the wickedness I have seen done, and all that I have suffered myself through this accursed religion. Excuse me, ma'am, for making so free as to talk in this way; but although I have been with you only a few days, yet I know that you can be trusted; and now that Mrs. Proctor is gone I have lost my only friend, and it grieves me almost to death to think how cruelly she has been treated," and here the poor girl burst into a flood of tears.

Maggie endeavored to soothe her, and as soon as she was quieted, the girl resumed, "You keep so much to yourself, ma'am, that you do not see or hear one-half of what is going on around you, almost by your own doors. You know Bishop Proctor has tried to keep out of polygamy because his wife hated it so, and she was such a loving, delicate little woman that he could not bear to grieve her. But the priesthood have been hounding him for months past, and he has been threatened with being sent on a mission, or even being cut off from the church, if he would not live his religion.

"It was rumored but a short time ago that he had really married Louisa Young, and when Mrs. Proctor questioned him, he denied it; but when she pressed him closer, he told her it was none of her business,—such an answer as he had never given her before in all their married life.

"I had expected to go and stay with her, but to our surprise, as soon as she became unable to attend to the house, Louisa was brought there by the bishop.

"When poor Mrs. Proctor saw that she was really making herself at home, and acting as if she were mistress of the house, she again implored her husband to tell her if he was married to her. His reply was that it was the duty of a Mormon woman to do as she was told, and ask no questions,—a duty that she had always failed in, but must learn now. She then begged that Louisa might be sent away, and some other person procured in her place, but this request was also denied.

"This confirmed her suspicions, but it was not until yesterday that the entire truth was told her. She went right into spasms, and"—here the girl lowered her voice again to a whisper—"they say that this morning a blue mark was found upon the baby's throat. Anyway, when Louisa went to take it up it was dead, and the poor mother died soon after. I don't believe she ever got her senses again after she found out that Louisa was really her husband's second wife."

"Oh, how horrible!" exclaimed Maggie shuddering. "Surely, as you say, the poor woman has been cruelly murdered!"

"Yes, and she was such a good woman, too. She

was such a good friend to me when I came here an orphan, alone and unprotected. Oh, ma'am, if there is a righteous God, how can he let such things go unpunished as are continually happening here! Why, there was that poor wife of James Knight"—

"Don't, Mary, I cannot bear to hear about these things, they are too dreadful," said Maggie, still pale as death. "You spoke of coming to the valley alone and unprotected; how did that happen?"

"Ah, it is a long story, ma'am, and it almost drives me wild to tell it. It makes me so angry when I think how my poor sister and myself have been robbed and oppressed by the authorities of this church. But if you will excuse me now, ma'am, I shall be proud to tell you my story whenever you will be pleased to hear it."

Mary's story, as Maggie afterward heard it, was the following, as told precisely in her own words:—

"I was born in England. I was one of a large family of children, all well brought up and tolerably well educated. When my father was converted to Mormonism, he was the owner of quite a comfortable property. The missionary under whose preaching he was converted (and who is now one of the twelve apostles) instructed him that he should sell everything and prepare at once to emigrate to the valleys of the mountains.

"In obedience to the command, my father disposed of all his property, and was then told that he must place the proceeds in the hands of the missionary, who would secure a passage across the Atlantic for himself and family, and provide all things necessary for the journey. My father obeyed in this also. I was present when he delivered over the money to the missionary. I saw him place on the table two bowls filled with English sovereigns and silver. The money was emptied on the table and counted, and the missionary took it away. Shortly after, he disappeared from the town, and we soon learned that he had sailed for America, carrying the money with him, and making no provision whatever for us.

"Still my father did not give up his faith in Mormonism, nor his determination to emigrate to Zion. After a great deal of effort, he scraped together a little more money, enough as he thought to pay our way. Such goods as we could take with us were shipped, and we started on our journey.

"When we reached the Missouri River our money was exhausted. We had no teams, and no means of getting any; and though the winter had already set in, we with many others started to cross the plains with hand-carts. I have no words to describe the horrors of that journey,—the suffering and death from hunger and cold. *My father and mother and five brothers and sisters starved to death before my eyes.*

"I saw a young man of our company, in the agonies of starvation, gnaw the flesh off his own hands. After many had perished, we were at last met by teams sent out from Salt Lake, which brought necessaries that, for the time being, saved us from death by starvation.

"But our sufferings were not yet at an end. The weather continued fearfully cold and stormy. The provisions brought out by the teams were insufficient, and all of us were near perishing with hunger before our journey's end. *But while the women and children were starving, the captains appointed by the church to lead the companies of emigrants had plenty to eat.*

"At length we reached Salt Lake. I was a young girl, known to almost no one; and my sister who had survived the journey was much younger than myself. We were a sad pair of orphans, penniless, friendless, and helpless. I knew of nothing we could call our own, except the boxes of goods which my father had shipped from England. I made inquiries for them, but could learn nothing. Afterward I saw in the tithing office the boxes marked with my father's name upon them. I asked that at least a part of their contents might be given to us, but no attention was paid to my request.

"My sister found a place immediately, with a kind woman from our native town, who has been like a mother to her; and I was fortunate enough, also, to find a kind friend in Mrs. Proctor. Both she and the bishop tried to recover some of my father's things for us; and although they were not successful, I shall never forget their kindness to me, the poor, desolate orphan that I was. And it makes me feel so wicked to go to the Tabernacle, and see the man who robbed us sitting on the platform among the twelve Apostles. I would go a long way to see that man hung, for I count him the murderer of my father and mother, and my five brothers and sisters."

This tragic story of poor Mary, which Maggie ascertained was true in every particular, together with the sad death of Mrs. Proctor, affected her so deeply as to render her almost ill for several days. And to add to her distress, her husband, to whom she had communicated her grief, told her calmly that she *must learn to take as a matter of course everything of the kind she might hear of;* for though such incidents were very sorrowful, yet it would do her no good to fret over what she could not help or prevent.

CHAPTER XVIII.

A Heart History Continued.

A Happy Home Picture.—"Brother Ellis."—The Message.—A Stormy Scene.—Attempt at Reconciliation.—Mrs. Parker's Visit.—Her Advice.—Christmas.—Sealed to Jesus Christ —Joining the Church.—"Brother Ellis" Again.—Interview with the President.—The Terrible News.—" One of Papa's Women."—Attempt to Escape. —Death.

LITTLE dreaming of the storm that was brewing over her head, the days dragged slowly along with Maggie, whose thoughts were constantly occupied with the sad change which had taken place in her husband since their arrival in Zion.

He seemed to be gaining rapidly in the estimation of the Mormon dignitaries, and was constantly called upon to attend meetings and gatherings of the priesthood. She felt they were slowly, but surely, drifting apart.

The little caresses so dear to woman's heart were now seldom bestowed, the many acts of gallantry and attention, as much a woman's due in married as in single life, were now seldom performed. Even when at times he appeared like his former self, she still felt there was some evil influence working upon him, to which he was gradually yielding.

Looking from her window one morning, she saw that King Winter had dropped his snowy mantle over the valley,

"While all were asleep and dreaming."

The pure white flakes were still lazily drifting down from heaven, and her spirits rose and her heart fluttered with joy, when Harry, on awakening, talked of sleigh-rides and a big Christmas dinner, and went whistling and singing about the house as in the olden days.

"The short winter day drew to a close. The little family gathered round the cheerful fire, Maggie busily sewing, Harry reading aloud, while Lilly sat on a low stool resting her head on her father's knee and gazing steadily in the glowing coals before her.

It was a simple home picture, and one that dwelt in their hearts for many years after.

"Hark," said Harry, "surely I heard footsteps. Yes, some one is knocking at the door. It must be an urgent errand that brings people out on such a night as this." Hastening to the door, he opened it, to admit three men. To his surprise, they were men of high standing in the Mormon church.

"Why, brother Ellis," he said, "is it you? Good evening, brother Wright, and you, too, brother Handley. You are very brave to venture out in this storm."

The men seated themselves, although two of their number seemed rather embarrassed; the other, however, who was first to enter, was perfectly at ease.

Maggie had never seen him before, except on the stand in the Tabernacle, and she shuddered inwardly as her eyes rested with aversion on his face and form. He was short and broad, his feet and hands uncommonly large, his face—but how shall I describe it? The forehead was very low, the nose broad and flat, the lower jaw projected, giving the appearance of an ape, more than a human being. It was hard to tell the color of his eyes, for they were never still a moment, but continually shifting from one object to another. Crown this image with a shock of stubby reddish-brown hair, and you have a perfect picture of brother Ellis, a high-priest of the church of Latter-day Saints, and a fit person to send on such an errand as had brought these men here.

"I fear we intrude," brother Ellis commenced, taking in the pretty home picture at a glance. "You look quite comfortable here, brother Blake, —your wife and daughter, I suppose."

"Yes," said Harry, "I thought you had met my wife," and turning to Maggie, he introduced her to these good brothers. Maggie merely bowed in acknowledgment, but the men stepped forward, offering their hands and calling her sister Blake.

After shaking hands with them all, Maggie involuntarily sought her handkerchief, and furtively wiped her hand. Had she looked at brother Ellis as she did so, she must have seen the angry gleam in his restless eyes, for nothing could escape them. Harry noticed both, and frowned angrily at his wife, who colored at the rebuke, and hastily replaced the offending handkerchief in her pocket.

After a slight pause, in which no one seemed inclined to speak, brother Ellis said, "We came on a little matter of business;" and from his tone, one might have inferred that it was quite to his taste, this little matter of business.

"Indeed," said Harry, in a tone of surprise, "it must be very important, that it needed attention on such a night as this."

"Will you permit us to ask sister Blake a few questions?" he continued, in a tone that plainly said, "We will do it, whether you permit it or not."

Harry looked up in astonishment, but answered "certainly," for he had been in Zion long enough to know that it would be dangerous for him to offend these miserable spies, from whom no Mormon household was safe.

Brother Ellis turned his face, if not his eyes, in the direction of Maggie, and asked, "Did you not tell sister Foote some time ago that you would never be baptized in the church of Latter-day Saints?"

Maggie looked at him, astounded, and her first impulse was to ask him politely if it was any of his concerns. But as she glanced at the almost infernal expression of his face, a sense of fear took possession of her, and she could scarcely steady her voice to reply, "I did."

"Did you not laugh at our doctrine of baptism for the dead?"

Again came the answer in tremulous tones, "I expressed my disbelief in such a strange and peculiar doctrine."

"Did you not scorn the idea of celestial marriage being a divine revelation?"

To this Maggie made no reply, she was becoming indignant at being cross-questioned so, in her own house, too. What was her husband thinking of, to allow it? She cast an appealing look at him, but his face was turned away from her, and wore a scowl of displeasure.

Brother Ellis continued, "You know the old saying, 'A bird that won't sing must be made to sing,' holds good in more cases than one."

"Sir!" exclaimed Maggie indignantly, "I do not understand you."

"Don't you?" he said with a malicious smile. "Then we must make our meaning a little plainer. Your husband is a good Mormon, and it is your duty to be one also. We know that it is his desire, and the good Book you profess to believe says, 'Wives obey your husbands,' don't it?"

"Yes, but—" Maggie began, but this high-priest mildly interrupted her.

"We won't listen to *your* interpretation of the words. In *our church* it means that a wife should have no will of her own, but should be in subjection to her husband, who is her lord and master; and he, in turn, is to be in subjection to those who are in authority over him."

"But you would not have me join your church when I do not believe in its doctrines, and abhor its teachings?"

"The wife should never follow her own judgment

in preference to that of her husband, for God has placed him at the head. Be obedient, and God will cause all things to work for good."

"Mr. Ellis," she could not call him brother, "do you consider woman an inferior being, not capable of judging for herself?"

"Certainly I do. It is woman's place to minister to man, and he in return will do her thinking for her, and save her in the eternal kingdom. A woman should not be a clog on a man. And that is just what you are, sister Blake; you are keeping your husband from living his religion." Then turning to Harry, he added, "Brother Blake, unless your wife consents to be baptized into the church, you must put her away and take another wife."

"What!" cried both husband and wife in one breath. Brother Ellis hastened to say, "Yes, and we were sent to deliver this message, brother Blake. It will not be necessary to say anything more; for you know very well that the rule of the church is, 'Obey counsel and ask no questions.'"

Harry sank back in his chair without a word, but his face was pale and stern. He knew very well that brother Ellis spoke true, that they had not come of their own accord, but were emissaries of a higher power,—a power that could and would crush relentlessly any who dared withstand its iron will. Although he had not yet sacrificed all his manhood to it, still he dreaded it enough to fear its threats and the penalties it imposed.

But she had no such fears, so she rose and confronted the speaker, her form drawn to its fullest height, her eyes flashing with scorn and contempt.

"Such a command is worthy of your church," she said, her voice ringing out sharp and clear, "and persons more fit to convey the message could scarcely have been chosen. Your office, gentlemen, is truly a most enviable one. You are worthy teachers of such a doctrine. When I feel myself on a level with the rest of your dupes and slaves, I will become a Mormon; until then, I claim the right to think as I please, even at the expense of your threat. There is the door, *gentlemen;* you will oblige me by walking out of it," and pointing to the door, she fixed her eyes steadily on the men, who left the house without venturing another word.

Maggie's anger was now thoroughly aroused, and seeing that her husband did not speak, she looked fixedly at him for a moment. He moved uneasily under her gaze, but would not raise his eyes. Presently she said slowly, as if speaking to herself:—

"I was to love, *honor*, and obey; you were to cherish and *protect*, until death did us part. You played the part of a *man* well to-night. I congratulate you. It was so manly to sit still and let your wife be insulted by the infamous tools of a more infamous priesthood, without resenting a single word. You did protect me well. *Truly, you are a good Saint.*"

Never before had such words fallen from her lips; but she was only human, therefore liable to err, and surely she had just cause for anger.

Harry, too, was now thoroughly aroused, and like many another man, he took refuge in harsh words, putting all the blame on the weaker shoulders.

"A nice fool you made of yourself to-night, talking as you did. It will be in every one's mouth by to-morrow, and I shall be a laughing-stock for the whole town. Had you kept still, instead of gossiping with that old woman, nothing would have been said to us; and now, who knows what the consequences will be? But of one thing you may be assured, and that is, I will not be a laughing-stock any longer. I have been told often enough that I am under a woman's thumb, and that it is because I am afraid of my lady wife that I do not go into polygamy. But they shall see who is master."

"You may take a *plural wife*, as they call it, *a mistress*, as I term it, as soon as you desire; but I will not remain to witness your disgrace."

"You will not leave this house, or if you do, it will be alone. Lilly shall not go with you, and you will do well to remember that you are in a country where a woman can do absolutely nothing without the consent of her husband."

"Yes, I know that woman is considered no better than a fool, and treated as a slave; but for all that, I will not be forced to join this infamous church."

"You know the alternative then."

"Very well, I understand you," and Maggie walked proudly from the room.

When alone, her anger and pride gave way, and

throwing herself on a couch, great sobs of anguish shook her frame. Oh, why had she left the dear ones at home? Why had she not obeyed that inward monitor? Then these bitter trials had never come.

Lilly had been a silent though awe-stricken listener to all that had passed, and stealing quietly to her mother's side, she slipped her hand in hers, and tried to comfort her with soothing words and tender caresses. Her child's sympathy quieted her aching heart, and the tears that had refused to flow now came in torrents, but their force soon left her weak and exhausted.

Mary, who knew that the visit of these men boded no good to her mistress, came in to offer her sympathy; but Maggie could not speak to her, and the girl soon left the room, feeling that her presence was only an intrusion.

Rising, Maggie wiped away the traces of her tears,—would to God the events of the past hour could be as easily effaced, she thought. In silence she assisted Lilly to prepare for bed, and when the child knelt to offer her evening prayer, again the flood-gates were opened, and Maggie herself prayed long and earnestly for help and guidance. It was long past Lilly's bed-time, so the eyelids soon drooped over the bright, blue eyes, and she slept calmly and sweetly.

Not so her mother, whose heart was torn and convulsed with conflicting emotions. Pride and love each fought for the mastery; pride, wounded by neglect and unjust accusations, refused to be comforted. Love called up the past, the bright, happy past. Between it and the present was a barrier, mighty it was true, but not entirely immovable. A few words of contrition and repentance might remove it, a few tears and loving caresses might break it down. It was not the loving husband of her youth who had spoken harsh words, and permitted those creatures to insult her; but it was the influence of an evil spirit within him, which had been called into life by daily contact with those wicked, unfeeling, and degraded hirelings of the Mormon hierarchy.

Thus her woman's heart plead until pride was entirely subdued. And as she had been the first to speak harshly to him, she would also be the first to acknowledge her fault and seek a reconciliation. Ah, a woman's heart! It is something to cherish. Would that man could always think so, then—

> "There were fewer sobs in the poet's rhyme,
> There were fewer wrecks on the shores of time."

Stepping noiselessly across the floor, Maggie opened the door of the adjoining room. All was silent within; a faint glow from the dying embers lighted the room but dimly. Going to her husband's side, she knelt down and took his hand. "Harry," she said softly, "forgive me, I am sorry I spoke as I did."

He did not answer, but coldly withdrew his hand. Although chilled by the repulse, she continued, "Take back the cruel words you said to me, Harry,

OFFICERS AND DIRECTORS OF ZION'S CO-OPERATIVE MERCANTILE INSTITUTION, 1881.

let us forget they were spoken. We have been so happy in the past, let our future be as cloudless. Do not perjure yourself any further by following the teachings of this false religion."

Still no answer.

She would yet plead a little longer. "Oh! my love, my husband, will you not listen to me, if not for my sake, then for our child's? Would you disgrace yourself in her eyes, she, so young and innocent?—"

"There, there, Maggie, you have preached long enough," said a voice—could it have been her husband's?

She staggered to her feet as if a blow had been struck her. Was it to such a being she was pleading for love and protection? Had she mistaken his character all these years? Had she been worshiping an idol, to find it clay at last?

Alas! no, but she had yet to learn how the slavish and corrupt system destroys all that is manly and chivalrous in man, and makes him a mere puppet in the hands of his masters, to be moved by the strings of fanaticism and lust.

Her heart was wounded afresh, she went silently back to her sleeping child,—now her only treasure; and toward morning she fell asleep. When she awoke, her husband had left the house, and did not return until late that night.

For days and days, Maggie was utterly miserable. The unavoidable intercourse of daily life, such as must exist between persons sleeping under one roof, and eating at one board, was all the communication she had with her husband, and the estrangement told sadly in her hollow eyes and pallid cheeks. But in real life, whether sorrowful or joyful, the days pass somehow, and Maggie strove to console her dreary hours with the companionship of her child.

It was, however, with feelings of sincere pleasure that she welcomed her friend, Mrs. Parker, about a week following the visit of those *fiends*, as she mentally called the Mormon elders, who had forced themselves into her presence. To this dear friend she felt she could pour out her troubles, and find relief in the sympathy of her loving heart. As Maggie kissed the dear, kind face, she burst into tears. The kind old lady took her in her arms, soothing her with loving words as she would a little child, but did not strive to check the flow of tears. Too well she knew the relief they bring to an aching heart, for,—

"The eyes that cannot weep, are the saddest eyes of all."

Presently, when the storm of grief had spent itself, she said: "I knew you were in trouble, dear child, but could not leave home sooner to offer you my sympathy."

Maggie repeated all that happened on that never-to-be-forgotten night, adding, "Can you blame me, Mrs. Parker? Had I not cause to speak as I did?"

The old lady shook her head, saying, "You were rash, my child, although I cannot blame you, yet it may bring more trouble on your head. It is as brother Ellis says, the Mormon church considers man the master, and woman should have no will of her own. She is an inferior being in its estimation. Sometimes I think it were better for us if such were the case; we would then suffer less."

"I cannot think," remarked Maggie, "how women of intelligence can submit to such indignities as they are subjected to in the Mormon church."

Her listener smiled sadly as she replied, "My dear, it is easy to see you have yet to learn the sad truth that the *helpless must submit*. And with some, the slavery comes so gradually, the links of the chain are forged so silently, that they are scarcely aware of their condition until they find the chain so securely fastened that it cannot be broken."

"Cannot, do you say?" said Maggie, in surprise. "Then it is true, that you women in this religion are nothing but the meanest and most abject slaves."

Again the smile that was sadder than tears shone on the wrinkled face of this good woman. She did not reply directly to Maggie's cutting remark, but went on to say, "It is not an easy matter for a woman to break all the ties of married life; she has her little children to think of: if she left her husband, who would provide for them? The world is not always kind to a woman who struggles alone for existence; but if she bears a man's name, no matter how heavy the yoke she carries with it, she is, seemingly at least, not unprotected or friendless. And here in Utah it is *absolutely impossible* for a woman to sever those ties with safety to herself or children.

"But pardon me, my dear, if I say that you have no trials at all, in comparison with those of other women in this Territory. I rarely speak of my own, even to the most faithful friend I have on earth, my venerable mother, who accompanied me to this wilderness in order to be near me in my sorrows. But think, before leaving the house, I had been ministering to the wants of one of my husband's wives, who has just borne him another child." The convulsive clasp of the hands which had been lying gently folded in her lap, and the quivering lip, revealed the anguish which she would not put in words, almost for her life.

Maggie's generous and sympathetic heart soon forgot her own grief in the greater one of her friend. "How could you do it!" she exclaimed. "If I were in your place, I believe I should have killed them both, sooner than minister to their wants. What right have such children in this world, any way? But you are not a woman at all, you are an angel," she added, reverently, taking one of the withered hands in hers, and tenderly kissing it.

"It is hard, oh, so hard, to subdue the flesh," continued the old lady; "for in spite of the constant teachings and admonitions of the church, that it is the sacred duty of all first wives to love our sisters in marriage as our own souls, yet the thought cannot be banished that they come between us and what is far dearer than our own souls. We are told that we must think only of the celestial glory which will be the reward of faithful adherence to the doctrine of celestial marriage; but in spite of all pretense of spirituality, we cannot forget that there are children in whose veins there can be the commingling life current of but one father and one mother,—children of our husbands, but not *ours*. Strive as we may, struggle with all the strength of our natures, we cannot divest ourselves of the belief that a true marriage can be only between one man and one woman, and all other alliances are contrary to both God and nature."

"But if women believe in this way, why do they submit to the degradation of polygamy?" asked Maggie. "Surely, if they would be firm, the system would soon die out."

"In every religion there are fanatics, and more, I think, among the Latter-day Saints than any other. They are taught that polygamy is their only way of salvation, and I know there are many who firmly believe it, though against their better judgment, and though all their womanly instincts revolt against the system. Then there are so many ignorant ones whom it is easy to make believe. So the evil grows and thrives, taking deeper root daily, its fibers spreading wider and wider, until it has taken so firm a hold that it cannot be rooted out. And we who have the most experience, always find it the *wisest plan to submit quietly*, and make the best of what we cannot alter.

"Look at me, for instance. My husband went into polygamy because he honestly considered it his duty. I had faith in his sincerity, and though I thought it would be my death blow, yet I loved him too well to desert him, *if I could safely have done so.* He has never failed in his duty to me; he has always stipulated that the other women should treat me with deference and respect, and I have always tried to treat them as well as I possibly could. I suppose there has been less unpleasantness in our family than in any other polygamous household that I know; and I leave it to your own common sense if it was not wiser for me to retain the affection and esteem of my husband than make his home a place of torment, and entirely alienate him from me."

Of course Maggie was not convinced, so she answered, "As I said before, dear friend, you are more of an angel than a woman. I would not answer for myself what I should do under such circumstances. But surely, if these principles and doctrines were preached by the missionaries among their converts before coming to Utah, there would not be so many dupes."

"They know that perfectly well, and are therefore on their guard. Many good men and women come to these valleys to enjoy their religion, thinking it a peaceful, favored spot, where evil and crime are unknown," rejoined Mrs. Parker.

"Well, why do they not return when they learn the true state of affairs?" asked Maggie.

"For many reasons. You know the difficulties of the journey over the plains, as well as the expense. The majority of the people have but very little when they arrive, and those who are people of means almost invariably give what they have to the church authorities for *safe-keeping* before they start for Zion, *and it is not usual for the church to be in a condition to refund it all at once—*"

"Ah, yes," interrupted Maggie, "I see it all very plainly, but if I were a man and free to come and go as I pleased, I would leave the country in some way, and denounce these creatures to the world as a set of swindlers as well as tyrants."

"No doubt that you would make the attempt, my dear, but you might be forestalled in your intention. You might not reach your destination."

"Why not, pray," Maggie began; then she remembered something she had heard hinted before. A look of horror stole into her eyes, blanching her cheek as well, and she added in a whisper, " Surely you do not mean they would be foully dealt with?"

"I cannot say, my dear, but I do know that some who have made the attempt, have never been heard of again."

"Then Heaven help *me;* how can I escape from their toils?" exclaimed Maggie.

"Do not attempt it; submit with what patience you can; believe me, it is best."

"But I would be living a *lie*. It would be only an outward acquiescence, against which my heart would constantly rebel."

"Nevertheless, I say you will be wiser to obey counsel in this case. After all, it is the first step that is the hardest; in grief, as in sin, the heart becomes callous, and ceases to feel the pain of each new dart that pierces it."

"Would you advise me in all good faith, to profess a belief in the teachings of a church for which I feel nothing but contempt?" Maggie asked earnestly.

For a moment there was silence between them. Maggie, watching her friend's face, saw it work with emotion. When she spoke, her voice trembled, and her eyes glistened with unshed tears.

"God forgive me," she said, "if I advise you wrongfully, but I think you would be happier were you to join the church. You know it is not likely that your husband will leave it. I believe that he cannot, or will not, and a man likes his wife to be of the same mind as himself, and especially he does not like her to set herself in opposition to all his wishes."

"I know all that," Maggie sighed, "but—"

"I realize all you feel, my dear child, and if you were not in Utah, I would not give you this advice; but since you are here, and no prospects of leaving, I say, join the church; take no notice of what does not concern you, and ask no questions. Then you will not be persecuted."

For awhile Maggie sat in deep thought, then she said slowly, "I will think of it seriously, but my better nature revolts at the sacrifice. It is disgracing my womanhood, besides acting the part of a hypocrite, and I fear I shall be sinning in God's sight. Yet *he* will know that I am trying to act for the best."

Christmas came—a day observed by all Christians as one of rejoicing, when the merry bells ring forth the glad tidings that a Saviour is born. And following the example of the "three wise men of the East," who brought gifts from afar to lay at the feet of Jesus, a tiny babe lying in a manger, we, keeping the ancient custom, give to our loved ones gifts and tokens of remembrance, and for his dear sake, not forgetting even the poorest of his creatures.

Here in Utah, the morning dawned bright and beautiful, and yet on his birthday, no bells rang out the glad tidings to the Saints in this valley, no anthems or carols were sung to his praise. Little children were not taught that Christ was once a child like themselves. They were not told that he loved them, took them in his arms, and blessed them, saying to those who would keep them away, "Suffer little children to come unto me, and forbid them not; for of such is the kingdom of heaven."

The Mormons do not hold services on Christmas-day in their Tabernacle, to tell their people that a Saviour was given them on this blessed morning, many years ago. But they tell them Christ was a polygamist, that Mary and Martha were his plural wives, and the marriage at Cana of Galilee was his own. Think of that, ye Christian women of this enlightened country! was there ever such sacrilege? Our Saviour, the embodiment of all that was pure and holy, following this lustful doctrine! They tell them also that here in Salt Lake Valley, a temporal kingdom shall be set up, and that Christ will personally rule and reign therein.

And though it seems almost too monstrous to be credited, there have been women so utterly unbalanced and led away by the pernicious and immoral teachings of this church, that they have been *sealed to Jesus Christ*, some Mormon brother standing as proxy, so that they might be numbered among his plural wives in the resurrection.

Maggie thought of her last Christmas among her dear friends in her far-off Eastern home. The time that had passed since then seemed ages to her,— every month a long dreary year with neither spring nor summer, only dark and stormy autumn and winter days.

Lilly aroused her by calling in her ear, "Merry Christmas, mamma." Kissing her affectionately, she returned the caress with a smile, thinking it would not be a very merry one to the poor child.

While these sad thoughts were flitting through Maggie's mind, her husband was taking himself to task for his treatment of her. "Peace on earth, good will to men," sang in his ears.

"I cannot stand this life any longer," he said to himself. "What made me talk as I did to Maggie, I wonder? In all our married life, such words never passed our lips before. I used to consider myself a gentleman; it must be the influence of the country. The men out here don't treat their wives as they should, and I have been foolish enough not to resent it when they have laughed at me for the way I speak of my wife, as though she were my equal. But I will be man enough to acknowledge I was in the wrong, for she is the dearest little woman in the world, and as people always said, much too good for a fellow like me."

His hand was on the door knob ere he had thought what to say, or how he should plead for pardon. Opening the door softly, he entered the room where Maggie sat; her attitude was one of the deepest dejection, and she was quietly weeping. No thought then had Harry of the words to be spoken; at sight of those tears, words of penitence rushed to his lips.

"Forgive me, Maggie. Dry your eyes, dear wife, and we will forget the hasty words spoken; bury them with the past, and let us try to think of them no more." These and many more words were hurriedly uttered, and Maggie, smiling through her tears, nestled lovingly in the arms outstretched to enfold her.

After a short silence, Maggie said, "Harry, I have concluded to join the church, that is, if you desire me to."

"You have!" was the surprised answer.

"Yes, I thought it might be pleasanter for you, perhaps," she added hurriedly, as if afraid her motives would be too closely questioned. He did not seem as well pleased as Maggie expected he would be, so she asked rather timidly if he did not wish her to be baptized into the church.

Harry answered in a more serious manner than was his wont, "Yes, it would certainly please me, because I think a man and his wife should be of one faith; but, my wife, if you should ever regret it, do not blame me. Remember that in spite of what I have said, which I will own frankly was not meant, I did not urge you to this step, and if you join the church, it must be of your own free will."

"But, Harry, suppose that horrible threat should be carried out!"

"Oh, my dear, those were only idle words. What man or set of men in the world could force me to do anything against my will?"

"Alas! my husband, I fear they were not; for though we have only been here a very short time, yet I have learned a great deal, and besides, my good friend, Mrs. Parker, has been telling me some fearful things," and she related their conversation.

"Mrs. Parker was very foolish, Maggie, to alarm you so. I have no doubt but many things have happened that need explanation, but for all this, you need not feel afraid. However, if you are willing, perhaps it is just as well that you join the church."

"Unless, Harry, we might return to the old home," Maggie said eagerly.

"That is impossible at this time of year, we may think of it a little later. Besides, we are here, and I like this country —"

"Do you like the church, Harry?" interrupted his wife.

"Don't question me too closely," he laughed. "I shall never be carried away by any religion, but this one suits me as well as any, and to be frank, I have better business prospects than I ever had in my life before, for this is a growing country, and I believe I am the only one of my profession in the city."

"Then, Harry, you may say I am willing to be baptized, but—I do not wish them to think that I consent out of fear of their threat. My only motive is that our life may flow smoothly on in the old channel. If the future be as cloudless as the past, I shall be content, but—"

"Well, dear?"

"You will never forget the solemn promise you made me on the first night we entered the valley; you will not let them persuade or frighten you into polygamy, will you, Harry?" Maggie pleaded.

"Pshaw!" laughed Harry, "what a jealous little body you are. There is no fear of that, for I despise the practice as much as yourself."

After this the days were full of joy for Maggie. *Love* was *life* to her, and now she felt perfect trust and confidence in her husband. When the day for her baptism arrived, she went into the water, and received the blessings calmly and earnestly, with a conscientious desire to do her duty faithfully, thinking also, as many another deluded woman has done under the same circumstances, that her troubles had ceased. But, alas, she found, as many other women have done, that hers was only a brief respite.

"I tell you, brother Blake, you must take another wife. We have one already picked out for you, and she is pretty enough to please even your fastidious taste."

"But I have told you before, that I do not want another wife," replied Harry Blake, "and I mean what I say."

"Oh, that's nonsense; you don't want to be tied to one woman for life, I hope. Just go to see this girl a few times, and I'll warrant you will soon change your mind."

"No, brother Ellis, I think not. Let us talk of something else."

"But I tell you, you *must* take another wife, brother Blake, you are not living up to your privileges. You have but one child, and the church tells us to marry and raise up children to increase our kingdom."

"That is all very well for those who desire it, but I am content as I am, and do not desire to enter polygamy."

"I must say you are very ungrateful, brother Blake; the church has been very kind to you, and placed you in the way of prospering in temporal affairs, and you are very remiss in your spiritual duties. But it seems I must make my meaning clearer; the church commands that you take another wife, and as you do not seem inclined to take my word for it, although I am your presiding bishop, I hope you will call at the president's office, who will bear witness to the truth of my words."

The speakers, Harry Blake and brother Ellis, were walking quietly along the street, conversing in an undertone. As the last words were spoken, brother Ellis turned and left his companion to his own meditations.

Harry Blake quickened his steps as if in that way he could dispel the disagreeable impression the conversation had caused. Daily association with polygamy, for almost all his friends in the church were polygamists, had lessened his horror of it to a certain extent, but if he had ever thought of the monster's invading his own home circle, he had thrust it aside ere the thought was fully born. Now, he did not crush it out of his mind, but lingered on it until he felt ashamed of himself, and almost ashamed to meet the pure face of his loving wife. He wandered on and on, till the twilight shadows warned him of the day's decline. And when he turned toward home, it was with a guilty feeling in his heart.

A few days afterward he was summoned to a "special interview" with the president in his office, from which he emerged in rather an agitated frame of mind. However, that very same evening, he made a very careful toilet, and when Maggie asked him where he was going, the reply was, "Only to a meeting of the seventies."

Although no thought of treachery entered her brain, yet she felt an indefinable dread of some coming evil, that made her nervous and low-spirited throughout the evening. This feeling increased as the days went on, and her husband avoided her eye, seeming careless and indifferent to her wishes and feelings. The old shadow of doubt and distrust ever and anon loomed up before her, but she dare not put her fear into words, even to her own heart. She would not admit there was anything amiss, lest the fancy become a reality. She would crush back the cruel thought yet a little longer. The winter had passed away, and the pure air of spring was fragrant with the odor of blossoming trees. But Maggie's heart was too sad to enjoy this beautiful springtime.

One morning as her husband left the house, he said to himself, "I know it is cruel not to tell her, but I cannot, I am altogether too great a coward. I will get her friend, Mrs. Parker, to break the news to her, and to help her bear up under it; for Maggie is not like the rest of the women in this country."

When her friend came, Maggie relieved her overburdened heart, by telling her all her fears, adding imploringly, "Tell me, do you think he could break his solemn vow? do you think he could take another wife?"

Mrs. Parker took her in her arms, kissing her tenderly, and then said in tremulous tones, "My dear child, I wish I could comfort you, there is great sorrow in store for you."

Maggie started up in affright, but the words she would have uttered refused to pass the pale lips. Seeing her distress, the old lady thought it best to end her suspense. "How can I tell you?" she said, "but your husband is to go through the Endowment House this very day with one of brother Ellis' granddaughters.

When Maggie heard those fatal words, her heart seemed as if it were turning to stone, her brain was

Rev. D. J. McMILLAN,
Superintendent of Presbyterian Missions, Utah.

on fire, and in that moment her love died. She now saw her husband's treachery,—a nice reward for all her faith and devotion to him,—and she felt that she could strike him dead without the slightest compunction, should he enter her presence then. But she could not speak; it seemed as if an iron hand were on her throat, the fingers tightening their hold until she was suffocating; she heard a voice say, "My child, my child, don't look so!" and then darkness encompassed her. The face of her friend, the room in which they were sitting, faded from her sight, and in their place she saw two figures, one a young girl, scarce more than a child, a smile on the rosy mouth, love shining in the eyes raised to a face tenderly bending over her; the other, a man whose face and form were only too familiar, for they were those of her own husband. No, not her *husband*, the man who had so cruelly deceived her had forfeited all right to that sacred title; henceforth they should be nothing but strangers to each other. While she looked steadily at them they faded gradually until lost to view, and again she saw the tearful, sympathizing face of her dear old friend bending over her, and heard the kind voice saying, "Thank God, you have recovered," and her little daughter crying at her side: "Mamma, don't die, don't leave me, mamma!"

Maggie shuddered, and said in a strange, harsh voice, "I have seen them, and I will kill them both."

Mrs. Parker put her arms around the poor child, and said soothingly, "Seen whom, my dear?"

Maggie described the young girl she had seen in her vision or trance, in company with her husband, and continued, "Yes, they are married; but if they dare to enter these doors, I will kill them as sure as there is a God in heaven!"

The old lady, who had experienced all these feelings herself, but had outlived their bitterness, said to her gently and sorrowfully: "Calm yourself, my dear. I pity you from the bottom of my heart, but take my advice, and try to bear the burden as bravely as you can. What is done cannot be undone, and if you are rash and imprudent, you may cause more trouble for yourself and your child than you have any idea of in your present excited condition. Remember how helpless and powerless we Mormon women are, and how they always *stab us through the hearts of our children*. I know it is a heavy cross, but may the good Lord give you strength to bear it. Go now to your room and lie down, and I will stay here until they return, and assist you all I can."

When Maggie was alone with her child in her own room, she became again almost crazed, and clasped the little one so tightly in her arms that she cried out, "Don't, mamma, you are hurting me; let me go out to Aunty Parker!" The poor heart-broken mother tried to control herself, and soothed the child, endeavoring to make her understand as well as she could that she was in great trouble, so great that death would be only too welcome, were it not for the worse anguish of leaving her alone and friendless.

Lilly, who was intelligent and womanly beyond her years, seemed to comprehend it all, and said, as she kissed away the fast-falling tears, "Never mind, mamma, you have me, let us go away from here together, back to grandma, and then everything will be all right again."

Before Maggie could answer, they heard the front door open, and apparently a large and merry company entered and took possession of the house. During the remainder of the day and evening, footsteps were continually coming and going, and peals of laughter ever and anon reached the ears of the wretched woman whose heart was being so cruelly crucified, and whose terrible grief was the theme of more than one coarse jest down-stairs.

Once Mrs. Parker had come to the door of the room, bringing her some refreshments, but she did not dare trust herself to say more than a word or two to the wronged and outraged wife. Maggie took the food, knowing that her child would need it before morning, and then she closed and securely fastened the door, after warning Mrs. Parker not to allow her to be disturbed on any account.

How she lived through that night she never could tell. When morning dawned and Lilly awoke, she said, "Why, mamma, you look just like Aunt Agnes, when she was sick so long. What is the matter? are you going to be sick too?"

"No, my darling, I hope not," she answered, trying to smile, and walking to the mirror, she pushed back the disheveled locks from her face, and looked to see if *one* night could have wrought such a change that even Lilly should mark it so quickly.

She was almost frightened herself at the ghastly image she saw, and as she started back, Lilly commenced crying. "I know you are sick, mamma. You are going to die, and be put in the ground, and then what shall I do?"

While soothing the grief of her darling, Maggie endeavored to look into the future. All night she had lain as one bereft of reason, incapable of thought; but now she must decide as to her future course, and that without delay. To live in that house now would be an utter impossibility. She could work for her child, or if the worst must come, they could die together; but remain with *him* she would not.

She made several attempts to leave the room, but her courage failed; she would have to wait a little longer; she dared not meet them yet; she would have to wait until she was less reckless of consequences, until she could be sure she would do nothing rash, that would result in more trouble for her innocent child. When she did at last succeed in leaving the room, *he* had left the house.

When Maggie entered the cozy little dining-room, —now *her own* no longer,—the new wife, a sweet-looking, fair, young girl, scarce more than a child, was engaged in clearing away the breakfast things. There had not been any servant in the house for some days, as her faithful Mary had married rather suddenly, and her place was not yet filled.

When she heard Maggie enter, she turned and

asked politely if she could prepare anything for her; and seeing the poor, pale, faded face, inquired kindly if she were ill. Maggie could not command her voice to speak, but shook her head as she tottered to a chair.

Lilly asked, "Have you come to work for us, and what is your name?"

The girl laughed pleasantly as she replied, "My name is Rosa, and I am brother Blake's second wife."

"You are *not* my papa's wife," Lilly exclaimed vehemently.

"Yes, I am, my dear," Rosa answered quietly, "that is if brother Blake is your papa."

"No, you are not," reiterated Lilly angrily. "Mamma is his wife, and he can't have any other," and she stamped her tiny foot. Then, as if a thought had struck her, she added, with undisguised contempt in her baby voice, "I guess you must be one of my papa's *women;* Jessie Parker told me her papa had lots of women, so perhaps that is what you mean. Well, you will have to do the work, and mamma will boss you, as Jessie's mamma does them," and seating herself at the table she continued imperiously, "I would like to have some breakfast."

Maggie attempted to reprove her, but found she could not utter a syllable; her lips parted, but no sound came from them. Although this was the woman that had stolen what was dearest to her on earth,—the heart of her husband,—yet she was too thorough a lady, and too just a woman to permit Lilly to deliberately insult her.

But Rosa did not seem in the least offended, she was accustomed to hear Mormon children speak in far more contemptuous terms of plural wives, so she only smiled pleasantly, and waited upon Lilly as if she had been the servant of the house. While Lilly was eating her breakfast, Maggie rose from her chair, thinking that she would return to her room and remain there until *he* should come back; but she staggered, and would have fallen if Rosa had not sprung to her assistance.

Perhaps this second wife realized in part the depth of her anguish, and seeing how helpless she was, Rosa helped her to her room, and laid her on the bed. She was a good, kind-hearted girl, and was not altogether to blame for the misery her presence in the household had brought to Maggie. From her earliest babyhood she had been taught that her salvation depended on celestial marriage, that her soul would be forever lost unless she was sealed to some good brother in the church. So when she was told it was decided by the priesthood that she should marry brother Blake, she never dreamed of objecting for one moment, especially as she had heard him discussed frequently, and set down as a very desirable match. He was reputed to be well-off, able to maintain in comfort a much larger family than he possessed, which was a very great inducement; for even in her short life, poor Rosa had seen enough of the poverty side of polygamy to dread that, although she was too faithful a Saint to disobey any counsel given by the authority of the church.

But we must do her the justice to say that in

being sealed to Harry Blake, she did not exult over the prospect of bringing humiliation or sorrow to Maggie, as only too many young girls in her position have done. She simply thought polygamy must be all right because she had always been taught so, and of course it was to her advantage to secure as rich and as good a man as possible. If she ever thought of the sorrow that the first wife would endure, it was in a vague, desultory manner, or as something which was a matter of course, which could not be helped one way or the other.

And this is the way in which hundreds of young girls reason to themselves, if they think of this phase of the subject at all: "Of course the first wife will feel bad for awhile, but it will soon pass over, and it will be just the same if he marries any other girl." Their moral natures have become so deadened, and their finer susceptibilities so blunted, by daily contact with the monster, that they cannot realize there is any holiness or sanctity about the marriage tie, and that it is a deadly crime against God and nature to come between two whom that sacred ordinance has made one. Instead of marriage being the symbol of a spiritual bond between two souls, their education has taught them to consider it simply as a compact between one man and an indefinite number of women, made for the sole purpose of bringing children into the world to build up the man's kingdom on earth, so that he may be a monarch and ruler in the celestial world.

Rosa was naturally a pure, innocent, affectionate child, worthy of a better fate; but what soul could be subjected to such infamous teachings, and escape without a stain?

Strange to say, when Maggie first saw her, she did not feel that bitter resentment that she thought she should; her hatred and indignation were directed toward *him*, the man she had so devotedly loved, and so blindly trusted; for he had not married this girl, she was fully assured, from *religious* motives. No, it was her youth and beauty which had won his love, and made him false to the wife who had sacrificed her all for him.

For several days, Maggie's life hovered on the borders of the dark river. Rosa waited on her faithfully and kindly, and her friend Mrs. Parker watched by her bedside night and day. During her hours of delirium, her conscience-stricken husband—for he was not yet entirely callous—would steal into the room and minister to her wants; but at the first indication of returning consciousness, he would vanish like the guilty creature he was; he could not meet the eye of the woman he had so cruelly deceived and wronged.

During all those long days of suffering, after the delirium had fled, Maggie spoke rarely, and then to no one but her child. It seemed as if she would be dumb for the rest of her days; her voice refused to act, and it was only in whispers that she could speak to Lilly. Had she remained bereft of reason she would have suffered less, but who can depict the anguish of that crushed and bleeding heart! At last, strength came back gradually, but the woman who rose from that bed of sickness was a different creature from the former trustful and affectionate Maggie Blake.

One morning Rosa said that if Maggie was well enough to be left alone, she and Harry would like to go away for a day or two. Maggie received the announcement without further comment than the simple words that she was perfectly well. She had already decided upon her course. She would have the day to herself, and could make her preparations for flight without interruption; but she dared not give any sign of the feeling of relief and thankfulness with which she saw Rosa leave the house.

The first task before her was to gather her own and her child's clothing together, and she set about this as quickly as her weakness permitted. Busy, and absorbed in painful thought, she did not hear a footstep outside, and only raised her head when the door opened to admit her husband. The shock of his unexpected appearance at the moment when she was preparing to leave him forever, quite overcame her, and she sank helplessly into the nearest chair, with both hands pressed over her heart to still its throbbings.

Harry looked at her a moment in silence. A little pity, a little remorse, stirred within him as he mentally contrasted the haggard face and wasted form with a vision that rose from the past,—that of the fair young girl he had wooed and won in those years whose memory he would gladly banish if he could. Very gently he laid his hand on the bowed head, and pronounced her name. The act, the tone, roused her, and she faced him with the look of a hunted creature at bay.

"You dare to touch me and speak to me like that?" she cried. "You, who have made me what I am! You, who have not only broken my heart, and made my life a burden, but have killed all the good in me!"

"Maggie, surely you do not know what you are saying."

"Do I not? then hear me repeat it, and remember what I say, for they are the last words I will ever speak to you. Before this day ends, I will leave your house with my child,—leave this accursed country forever."

"You will?" the man's face hardened, and every impulse of pity or compassion was instantly crushed. "Then hear me. You may go where you please, but Lilly stays with me."

For a moment she looked at him in a dazed sort of way, as though not comprehending the meaning of his words; then, as the truth dawned upon her, and she realized her own utter helplessness, her pride forsook her, and falling on her knees, with clasped hands she plead that the sentence might be revoked,—that she might be permitted to take her child somewhere—anywhere, only out of sight of the home that was hers no longer.

"This is folly, and worse than folly," Harry answered, "and you will see it yourself in a little while. Your home is here. You and Lilly have every want supplied, and if you cannot agree with Rosa, why keep to your own apartments, and I will see that she keeps to hers."

Why protract the recital of an experience that has been lived over so many times in Utah? The unhappy wife and mother was helpless, and did as the helpless must,—submitted to her fate. Sunk in the apathy of despair, she lived on for months and years,—for it is only in books that people die when all that makes life worth living is gone. Misery did the work of years in bleaching her hair and furrowing her face; and when at last the boon so long prayed for was granted, and she

> "Bound the slow bleeding of her stricken heart
> With the chill comfort of the sepulcher,"

no one, looking into her open coffin, would have dreamed that she who lay there had lived out but half of her allotted time on earth. She sleeps to-day in the bleak, barren burial-place over-looking the beautiful city in which her husband lives with the three women who have been "sealed to him for time and eternity."

She has one mourner,—the child for whose sake she bore the burden of life. And when Lilly brings her weekly offerings of flowers, and lays them on the unmarked grave, a woman comes with her, and stands beside her with pale face and bowed head. It is Rosa, who, supplanted by later favorites, and experiencing in her own life something of the sorrows of her who lies here at rest, seeks to make atonement to the dead by kindness to the child she has left.

CHAPTER XIX.

Spread of Mormonism in the United States.

The People of the Nation Have the Power.—The Let-Alone Policy not Sufficient.—Steady Influx of Foreigners.—Concealment of Second Marriages.—Mothers Will not Make Known the Fathers of Their Children.—Mrs. Young's Letter.—Danger to the Nation.—"Danger to Every Household in America."—Mormon Church at Covington, Ind.—Mormonism in Michigan.—Canton, Ill.—Young Girl in Colorado.—An Appeal.—Young Lady in Indiana.—An Infatuated Daughter in Massachusetts.—Will Another War be Needed?

ONE of the most specious and dangerous arguments which has been advanced as a reason why Congress should not take measures to arrest the evils of Mormonism, and one that has influenced the opinion of thousands of well-meaning, intelligent, and law-abiding citizens, is the plea that if left alone, Mormonism will execute its own death sentence. Never was there a more fatal and less excusable mistake,—an error that if perpetuated will become a deadly crime.

There are other crimes also, which bind the wrists of justice. The great railroad corporations which practically rule Congress, many of the large wholesale business houses which sell goods to the Mormon merchants, and a great number of the commercial newspapers, are covert friends of the Mormons, and covert enemies of all who would have United States laws obeyed in Utah. But beyond Congress, a majority of whose members go to the legislative halls bound hand and foot to corporations, there are the *people*, and when they become aroused in earnest, corporations and a venal press are all too glad to hedge, and to become as furious in attack as before they were subtle to frame reasons why nothing should be done. It was so in the old slavery days; it has always been so. When the people of the United States understand that the leaders of the Mormon church, knowing the utter fraud of the entire institution, employ it as a gigantic political and commercial machine in order to impose upon, rob, and make slaves of the masses; that their weapons toward their people are superstition and ignorance, and toward the world hypocrisy and perjury; and that beyond all, they are doing what they can to overthrow all respect for, and all power of, the United States Government,—then avaricious merchants, soulless corporations, and a subsidized press, will stand aside, even as they did in 1861, and the *will of the people* must prevail. It is essential, then, that the people should not be misled by false theories, or specious arguments, nor by those who willfully circulate falsehoods for the purpose of retarding or preventing the administration of justice.

The let-alone theory is a very plausible one, and the let-alone policy a very satisfying one, for those who do not wish to bear the reproaches of conscience for neglect of duty. It is very easy to say, "Mormonism is a crime, and a disgrace to the nation. It ought to be, and shall be, abolished, but there are other methods than congressional interference."

Yes, we answer, there are other methods, and so thought those who were continually opposing the old Anti-Slavery agitation. But those "other methods" terminated in the blood and wreck of a civil war.

It is also very easy to say, "Open the doors of Utah to the outside world, and let civilization, wealth, fashion, luxury, and culture pour in. These will prove more effective than the most stringent legislation."

Even people who have been in the Territory, and think they have studied the subject, will say, "Send bandboxes instead of troops to Utah. Let the milliners and dressmakers have full sway, and they will soon make it impossible for a man to have more than one wife. Then let schools, churches, and civilization (that much abused and misappropriated word) do the rest."

These people will do well to remember that the gates of Utah have now been opened to the world for more than ten years, and that the great transcontinental railroad, which the advocates of the let-alone policy contended would destroy the barbaric institution, has actually given the system the means of indefinite growth, enlargement, and power. Look at the facilities for importing whole cargoes of foreign dupes and slaves, as compared with those of twenty years ago! *Then*, the long, toilsome journey over the plains by ox-teams, or perhaps on foot, with household and personal effects in a hand-cart, was a matter not to be lightly considered, or undertaken without a large measure of faith and courage. Now, the iron horse whirls them over that ground in a very few days, and in such numbers that the railroad companies deem them not unprofitable travelers, even at very low rates of transportation.

Who has not marked in the coast journals almost every week from early spring to late in the fall, the announcement that another ship-load of Mormon immigrants has arrived *en route* for Utah?

And when it is recollected that a large majority of these imigrants are gathered from the most ignorant and credulous classes of Europe, that they are steeped in superstitious fanaticism, and already shorn of manhood and womanhood by being pledged to obey their leaders in all things, temporal as well as spiritual, it may easily be seen how the system is kept up in Utah by these constant reinforcements.

A late writer in *Harper's Magazine* has remarked with great truth that, "But for the steady influx of foreigners—low, base-born foreigners, hereditary bondmen,—the two dreadful features of the Mormon church, polygamy and the exalting of the Church over the State, would die out in America in two generations."

But instead of dying out, one feature, polygamy, is alarmingly on the increase. The Mormon priesthood know only too well that they have an additional fetter on a man when he becomes a lawbreaker; consequently, men are continually being urged into polygamy, who, if let alone, would never think of committing that crime.

The times may not be quite as bad as the old "Reformation" period, but there is no disguising the fact that the Mormons weld their forces together by polygamy, and more of these plural alliances have taken place lately than can be estimated or even imagined.

People who have every opportunity for knowing, state as an undeniable fact, that hundreds of first wives are wretched beyond expression because they are afraid their husbands *have* taken other wives, though they have not sufficient evidence to prove it. The men of course deny it, but there are many attending circumstances which go to prove that they are acting under orders in declaring what is not true.

It seems to be the present policy to conceal second marriages from the first wife, especially if it be thought that she cannot be implicitly trusted, so that if she should be inclined to prosecute her husband, she has not the slightest evidence against him. The plural women are sworn to the greatest secrecy, and are even enjoined to deny the paternity of their infants, rather than compromise their saintly husbands.

Almost any day in the week, women may be seen in the streets of Salt Lake City, carrying infants whose fathers they would not reveal under torture. If it came to an issue, and these women

Mrs. ANN ELIZA YOUNG.

were brought into court, they would declare under oath that they were never married to any man, and did not know who were the fathers of their children.

The demoralizing influences of the system are now being felt in hundreds of homes which only a few months ago were as happy as pure. Hundreds upon hundreds of children have been and will be ushered into the world, the innocent victims of priestly tyranny and licentiousness. And yet, while this system is daily spreading and being strengthened in Utah and the adjacent Territories, the people of the country do not seem to be much concerned. They even complacently assert that Congress has no right to interfere in the matter. The system must be left to die out before the influences of Gentile fashions!

It is not so much of foreign reinforcements to Mormonism that this chapter designs to treat, as of the spread of the evil in our own country, and the consequent danger to American homes. The following statements of recent personal experience are from the able and trenchant pen of

MRS. ANN ELIZA YOUNG.

For the benefit of those who think Mormonism is a matter about which the American people need not concern themselves, or who believe that it is confined to Utah, and is even there in process of self-extinction, I write of some late experiences of mine, and other facts which decidedly negative these ideas.

To those who know what Mormonism is,—what

its designs are, and what it will soon be able to accomplish,—the indifference to the subject shown by so many intelligent people is simply astounding! They may have read in history of religious fanaticism, and the bloody wars it has caused, but they do not realize that Mormonism contains all the elements for producing such a conflict. They know that the issue of a contest for the presidency may depend upon a single vote, but they do not seem to remember that with Utah admitted as a State, the Mormon church may hold that decisive vote, and may demand and *obtain*, as the price of that vote, privileges which would add ten-fold to its power for mischief! I am glad that the Governor of Utah has taken so brave a stand, and that the Governor of Idaho has sounded the note of alarm. *We* know that their fears are not groundless. In addition to the Territories,—Utah, Idaho, and Arizona,—in which the Mormons now hold the balance of political power, it will not be long, according to present appearances, before Colorado, Nevada, New Mexico, and perhaps Oregon, will be in a like condition.

These facts cannot be repeated too often, nor with too great emphasis. Those who do not care for "the balance of political power," may be aroused by calling attention to the fact that the fairest and richest valleys, and the best town sites, are being taken up by Mormon colonies. It often happens that the Mormons control the schools, but not at all in the interests of good education. And the fact that a family will have Mormon neighbors, with the debasing practices of polygamy under their eyes, contaminating and corrupting their children, will certainly be no inducement for them to settle in such a locality.

But it is not only in the "far West" that Polygamic Mormonism is at work, and at work earnestly and successfully. It is safe to say that no place is secure from its attack, no home sacred from its encroachments.

It should not be forgotten that Mormonism originated in Central New York, among people whose religious culture was of the highest kind. It is a fact that should be more widely known than it is, that the Mormon missionaries are reaping rich harvests in the Southern States. In Georgia alone, many hundreds of converts have been made, and dispatched to Utah and Colorado. From one place in Kentucky, twenty proselytes were forwarded to Utah last spring, and Mormon emissaries are doing a deadly work even in cultured New England and the enlightened Middle States. It is only a short time since a number of converts were made in the neighborhood of Oberlin, Ohio, almost within the shadow of that well-known and widely influential Christian College. The emigration and spread of Mormonism in the Territories and some of the Western States is terrible to think of. And yet in the face of all this, our newspapers have little to say against the crime, and some of them raise the cry of "persecution" if the Government shows the slightest signs of dealing with it.

The people do not know the institution. They think and often say, "It will never hurt us or ours." But there is danger to every household in America, as the following incidents will show:—

I went to Covington, Ind., recently to fulfill a lecture engagement. I found there three Mormon missionaries, actively engaged in preaching Mormonism and polygamy. But so quietly and cunningly had these men conducted their work, that many of the best people in the place had no realization of the mischief that had been done, although the work had been going on for nearly three years.

My lecture seemed to have aroused the first general attention to the subject. There was an organized church of fifteen or twenty Polygamic Mormons, and the number was constantly increasing. Their meetings were held in a Methodist church,* a short distance from the town.

The elders and several of their converts attended my lecture, and it was plain that the audience, although evidently much interested in the subject, were so decidedly influenced by Mormonism that they hesitated to show positive approval of words which directly attacked and condemned the proselyting there going on. They acted as though they had come to regard the system as having some respectability, or to feel that policy demanded silence when it was attacked.

---

* The trustees of that church are either extremely ignorant or almost criminally indifferent. It is certainly not true "liberality" to permit those Mormon elders to scatter "firebrands, arrows, and death," as they are doing in that community.—EDITOR.

I must not be understood to say that Mormonism is predominant in the place. The best people are now thoroughly awakened to the evil which has so long been developing itself among them. They not only showed me great kindness, but sympathized with my work. They asked me to give a second lecture, which I did. But it was alarming to find Utah Mormonism existing, tolerated, making proselytes, in such a place. It may appear to some a little thing, but I hope that the great majority of my readers will see what it reveals. The Mormon leaders desire only to be "let alone." Their missionaries work quietly and cunningly until a few converts are made. Social and business relations,—"policy,"—cause many to be silent, and some to excuse. Before the people are aware of it, the evil becomes established. Sometimes the missionaries are helped by a mistaken "liberality." The newspapers at Covington had not only said nothing against Mormonism, but I was informed that their columns had been open for the use of the Mormon elders.

If this was the first instance of Polygamic Mormonism in the United States, it would not seem so serious, but it is only one among many thousand cases.

In Northern Michigan, converts are constantly being made. I have been told, upon seemingly reliable authority, that polygamy is actually practiced there, one man having six wives, and another two. I cannot vouch myself for the truth of the statement, but I have heard it repeated several times, and believe that it is true. One of my informants claimed to have boarded in a Mormon family where the man had two wives. But such is the slavery of Mormonism that if this man were arraigned for bigamy, the probabilities are that both women would swear in court that he was only married to *one* of them, that the other was an inmate of the household in some other capacity. To each other they will not only excuse their atrocious falsehood, but consider it a meritorious action. Truth with them means simply that to a brother Mormon they must be true. The rule does not apply at all where outsiders are concerned. It is by this means that the courts are baffled in Utah, and justice defeated.

At the close of a lecture delivered at Canton, Ill., a lad of about sixteen came behind the scenes, and introduced himself to me. He was so bright, intelligent and well-informed that he seemed much more like a grown man than a boy. He expressed his sorrow at hearing me speak so harshly of Mormonism, and said he hoped I would see the error of my way before it was too late.

I asked in surprise, "Are you a Mormon?"

He replied that he was, and that his parents had recently been converted by Mormon missionaries, who had been that evening in my audience. He said he knew they were good men. He was so enthusiastic and vehement that at first I was speechless from astonishment. I asked him how he knew they were good men.

He replied, "By the way they talk."

SPREAD OF MORMONISM.   295

I told him that hypocrites and fanatics *might talk well*, that he must not judge people by what they said alone. I also told him how I was born and reared in Mormonism, and had had full opportunity to see its baneful results; that my knowledge had come through terrible suffering, while he had but the words of those men from which to form conclusions. He said it would be impossible for me to destroy his faith, and that he and all his family were soon going to Utah.

I inquired about the matter, and found that his statements were true. I was informed that the family had been universally respected before their conversion to Mormonism, and that the people of Canton felt great regret at their course. This lad was as bright, intelligent, and handsome a boy as any mother ever need wish for, and it made my heart ache to think of his future under Mormon influences.

I found an intelligent and well-educated lady, a teacher in a public school in Iowa, who avowed her firm belief in the Mormon doctrines, and it is not improbable that she, too, will soon find her way to the promised land. May Heaven comfort her when the day of her awakening comes!

But the case which touched me most of all was that of a young girl from Colorado. She was sent to Utah by her parents for the benefit of her health, in the summer of 1879. The Christian Gentile family to whom she had letters of introduction were temporarily absent, and she was unfortunate enough to be directed to the house of a Mormon elder, who keeps a number of boarders. There she met another prominent Mormon polygamist, the editor of the Mormon church organ. She spent but two weeks in Salt Lake City, and what black arts they employed to pervert and fascinate her young mind I cannot conceive; but she returned to her home not only a baptized convert, but determined to go back to Utah and there spend her life. Her parents were horrified to learn the change that had come over their daughter. From being an innocent and pure-minded girl, she had come to believe in the horrible doctrines of Mormon polygamy. She carried on a secret correspondence with the *high-minded* and *honorable* editor. This the parents accidentally discovered. They also ascertained that he had asked her to be sealed to him as a plural wife, while she was in Utah, and was now urging her by letter to return and make her home at his house. The intense grief and strong opposition of her parents caused her to postpone for some months her departure for Utah, but her determination remained unchanged. This girl's father was a lawyer, she herself a teacher who had been tenderly nurtured, and whose mental strength seemed more than ordinary. She was fairly successful as a writer, modest and womanly in her demeanor. I went to the place to lecture last summer, and the mother, whose health was utterly broken by her grief, sent the young lady's aunt and her father to ask me to call and try to save their daughter. I went, and for several hours, with most intense feeling, I talked with her, but she seemed intrenched against every possible influence. After telling her my own history, and of the pain and sorrow I had seen polygamy bring to women, I asked her how she could leave her broken-hearted parents who loved her so dearly? She said she should pray for them, and she believed that they, too, would soon embrace the Mormon faith. Later, when in a room alone with her I said:—

"Gertrude, what reason do you think I have for talking to you as I am doing? Do I not seem sincere and truthful? and do you not feel that what I have said comes from my heart?"

She replied, "Yes, you do seem sincere; but you know how I have been taught by the Mormons to regard you They told me you were an ambitious, dissatisfied woman, only seeking notoriety."

"Well," I asked, "do you still believe that? Do I look or act like such a woman? Will you not have faith in my sincerity, at least?"

She placed her arms around my neck, and replied: "I will, Mrs. Young; I am sure you are a true woman, and have spoken only for my good; but if an angel from heaven should come and tell me that Mormonism was not true, I could not believe him until I had gone there and tried it for myself."

I said, "Yours is a hopeless case; nothing but the sorrow that it has in store for you will open your eyes."

These instances show that it is not alone from the

ignorant and degraded that Mormon converts are made, but that cultured, intelligent people can also be deluded. It would seem that belief in any false doctrine does not necessarily depend upon ignorance, but rather that peculiar organizations are easily fascinated by the idea of direct communication with Heaven. Their readiness to accept everything marvelous makes them willing to receive as a divine revelation and a modern miracle the story of the golden plates, and to believe in the prophetic power of Joseph Smith, Brigham Young, and John Taylor. However this may be, Mormon missionaries are at work, and Mormon converts are being made all over the country, North, South, East, and West.

And now, in the face of these indisputable facts, comes the question, How do the American people dare to permit Mormonism to flourish and increase? How can they ignore or trifle with it any longer? The population of Utah does not show how fast Mormonism is increasing, because there are so many settlements of Mormons in the surrounding States and Territories. Over 3,000 came from Europe in 1880, and the Southern States contributed hundreds which were sent to Colorado and other parts of the country.

From a sad personal experience, I solemnly aver that Mormonism and polygamy bring no good to man, woman, or child; but on the contrary, darkness, destruction, and despair.

I appeal now to our new President and his Cabinet, to our Senators and Congressmen, to our ministers of the Gospel of every denomination, to our newspapers, which are so mighty a power, and most strongly of all, to the people of this country, whose will can accomplish anything,—I beseech you all to allow no opportunity for action to pass by unimproved. Permit no law by which Mormon polygamy may be abolished to go unenacted. Leave no prayer unspoken, no word unsaid, that may help to destroy this foul and shameful crime against religion, society, and free government.

Mrs. Ann Eliza Young.

These experiences of Mrs. Young are supplemented and confirmed almost every week in the year by events which are happening all over the country. The Mormon church papers are continually publishing correspondence from their missionaries, giving glowing accounts of their success in proselyting; and although some of these letters may be written for effect among the people of Utah, yet results prove that they contain a great deal of truth.

During the month of September, 1881, a prominent United States Federal Official in Salt Lake City received a letter from a young lady in Indiana, who thought he must be a Mormon from the position he held. The writer, who from appearances was possessed of some education and culture, and who said she was a school-teacher by profession, after apologizing for addressing a stranger, avowed that she had been completely captivated by what she had learned in regard to Mormonism, and had a strong desire to investigate the system still further.

She was convinced that a greater knowledge of Mormon doctrines would conduce both to her physical and spiritual advantage, and desired to know where to obtain the proper books and papers. She also wanted to know how she should proceed in order to reach Salt Lake City, as she ardently wished to gather with the Saints. The gentleman referred the letter to some non-Mormon ladies, who undertook the task of trying to enlighten her and break her infatuation, but with what success their labors will be crowned remains yet to be seen.

Another recent case is that of a young girl from a highly respectable and cultured family in Massachusetts. She became infatuated with the teachings of a Mormon missionary, and with himself; and when he wooed her for his wife, she never thought to ask him whether another woman had a previous right to that name. Her family tried to reason with her, and when that proved of no avail, more stringent means were adopted. She managed, however, to elude their vigilance, and escaped to Utah with the Mormon elder, who, in order to satisfy her, "married" her on the way. She had no sooner reached Salt Lake than she found that she was only the *third* woman whom the wretch had deluded in the same way. She met some kind friends who assisted her with means to return to Massachusetts, but she never wrote after she left the city, and they know not whether she reached her home again. She felt herself a ruined and betrayed woman, and the probability is, that instead of returning, like the prodigal, to the home which her folly had left desolate, somewhere out in the great world wanders another woman, eternally lost!

And now the important question presents itself, What is to be the end? Is this absolute theocracy which holds itself above the Government of the United States, which teaches its adherents that "all governments founded by men are illegal, which claims that its founder was a prophet inspired by God, and that when he died his mantle fell upon his successors with all its divine powers,"—is this institution to be permitted to wax stronger every year, and without let or hindrance, flaunt its treasonable presence in the face of the American nation? Worse than all, shall it be permitted to continually forge the chains of an ignominious slavery on the wrists of women, to offer a perpetual permission for men's lusts in the name of religion, and to blast and destroy the honor and sacredness of home?

The people of America will do well to remember "that once before there was an institution in this country around which there was a shield of sympathy: its divine rights were declared from a thousand pulpits; Congress was too sordid and too cowardly to deal with it; wholesale merchants and great corporations lent their influence to perpetuate it, and a venal press rang with anathemas against any who dared to denounce it. But there came a day at last when men had to choose which should live and rule, that institution, or this nation. The history of what followed is fresh in all minds; and little as the masses believe it now, there will come a time, if this monster in Utah is left to grow, when there will be another call for volunteers and for money; and as before, tens of thousands of brave young men will go away, never to return; as before, there will be an enormous debt incurred; as before, the country will be hillocked with graves, and the whole land will be moistened by the rain of women's tears!"

CHAPTER XX.

What Are You Going to Do About It?

BY THE LATE REV. LEONARD BACON, D. D., LL. D.*

Something Now.—Thirty Years' Compromise.—National Sovereignty.—People Unfit for Self-Government.—No State Rights.—The First of Human Rights.—Jim Fisk.

THERE are indications that the Mormon question is coming to the front. It has been trifled with too long, as if it were of no urgent importance. One House of Representatives after another has permitted a notorious criminal, reeking with the filth of his so-called "plural marriages," to sit as the delegate from Utah. The presence of that man in that place, drawing his pay and mileage as a member of Congress, has been an insult to the people of the United States and a defiance of their moral sense. But

---

*This unfinished article is the last work of Dr. Bacon's pen. It is published just as he left it. A letter from his son, Rev. L. W. Bacon, to *The Christian Union*, N. Y., in which the paper was first printed, says:—

"He wrote to the end of the line, wrote beneath the last line the word '[over],' and laid his pen beside the paper, having first entered in his pocket-diary, 'Utah article nearly finished.'

"Then he spent the evening in bright, cheerful conversation with his family, taking great delight in talking with his youngest

there are indications that the people will endure the insult not much longer. Something must be done, not merely with the delegate from the Territory of Utah, but with the Territory itself, and with the malignant enemies of the United States and of Christian civilization who have been permitted to govern it. Every Representative in Congress, and every Senator, will do well to consider carefully, not how to evade the question in the hope that something will turn up, but how to grapple, at once and effectively, with the hideous barbarism which is already the reproach of our country throughout the civilized world.

We have had more than enough of the wisdom, which, being in high places of responsibility for the nation, was amiably confident that Mormonism (or at least its beastly co-ordination of the sexes) would die out of itself. The men are already old who can remember that marvelous stroke of policy when Millard Fillmore, acting as President of the United States, appointed (with the advice and consent of the Senate) Brigham Young as Governor of Utah. Mr. Fillmore knew perfectly well at that time, and every Senator who advised and consented to the ap-

---

son, just returned from the Rocky Mountains, and went to bed at the usual hour. He woke at six o'clock on Saturday morning to a few minutes of consciousness, and not apparently of extreme distress, and then fell asleep.

"We all hope that these earnest pages may be the more seriously heeded for being his last words to his fellow-citizens.

"Ever truly yours, L. W. BACON."

pointment knew, and every citizen of ordinary intelligence knew, that Brigham Young was nothing better than a consummate scoundrel. But Mr. Fillmore, and others like him, in that day when compromise with wrong was thought to be statesmanship, had a pleasing opinion that if the lying and lecherous prophet of the Mormons would consent to become an office-holder under the Government of the United States, all would go smoothly, civilization would somehow displace polygamy, and instead of the prophet's cruel despotism there would be liberty. More than thirty years have passed, and Mormonism is to-day stronger, more defiant, and more dangerous to the nation, than ever.

What can we do? A feeling is abroad that the time has come for a more vigorous policy in regard to this great moral and political danger. It was hoped that the trans-continental railroad would do great things by bringing travel and trade to that great metropolis of despotism by the sea of Sodom. It has done great things. It has added millions to the wealth of the Mormon chiefs; it has facilitated the going forth of emissaries from Salt Lake City to the ends of the earth, and the coming in of wretched dupes by thousands to swell the Mormon population and the Mormon vote, not only in Utah but in the neighboring Territories. There was hope that acts of Congress against polygamy, and prosecutions before United States Judges for marrying more wives than one, would break up the harems of the hierarchy, and open the way for Christian civilization to displace the bastard Mohammedanism invented by Joseph Smith. But Mormonism laughs at such expedients, like leviathan at the shaking of a spear.

Let us understand the situation. The Territories, whether before or after being inhabited, are the property of the States, and under their united sovereignty. When Brigham Young, with his accomplices and the horde of their dupes, marched into the Territory now known as Utah, neither he nor they acquired any rights there save such as were given them by the laws of the United States. The Constitution gives to Congress "power to dispose of and make all needful rules and regulations concerning the territory or other property belonging to the United States," for the very purpose of enabling the States, as represented in Congress, to determine in what method civil society should be organized, and what sort of new States should be founded on the soil which is their common property. In a State of this Union there is a divided sovereignty. Each State, by consenting to the Constitution, has ceded a portion of its sovereignty, carefully guarding the remainder. But in a Territory the sovereignty is undivided; the inhabitants, till they shall have been admitted into the Union as a State, are simply under the sovereignty of the United States. In that sovereignty they have no participation. They must shape their social order and morality, their notions of right and wrong, their entire civilization, in such a fashion as shall be acceptable, not to the King of Ashantee, nor to the Sultan at Constantinople, but to the sovereign people of the United States.

The government, then, of Utah is under the control of Congress so long as Utah is a Territory. No rule or regulation can have any legitimate force there, otherwise than as it derives force from an act of Congress. Whatever regulations have been made for the temporary government of the Territory, may be rescinded by Congress whenever experiment has proved that they are inefficient, and that they give no adequate promise of raising up a civilized State, fit for admission to the Union.

For thirty years we have been making the experiment of a Territorial government in Utah, and it is manifestly unsuccessful. It has not answered the purpose for which Territorial governments are established. We, the people of the United States, have never yet acknowledged that the number of inhabitants is the only thing to be considered in receiving a new State into our Union. The question is not merely, How many are they? but also, Of what sort are they? Are they a civilized people? If they are in some sense civilized, then in what sense? Are they as a people capable of self-government? If they become a State, will that State be a fit partner in the sovereignty of the United States? Will it be a disgrace and a danger to the Union? The population of Utah is at this moment numerous enough for a State; but notoriously that population, taken as a whole, is unfit to be invested with the dignity and power of a State in this Union; and there is no reasonable hope of its becoming fit under the present Territorial organization.

Already a plan has been proposed for a different method of Territorial government in Utah. Without discussing the details of the plan, I may say it looks in the right direction, inasmuch as it proposes that Utah shall be governed not by the Mormon hierarchy but by the United States; and that instead of a Territorial legislature and Territorial courts, (whether called Probate courts, or by any other name), there shall be in that Territory such a representation of the national sovereignty as will cause the laws of the United States to be respected and obeyed. The emergency may come in which it will be necessary to proclaim martial law in the strongholds of Mormon power. In one way or another, the sovereign people of the United States, acting through their Government at Washington, can guard their own Territory of Utah against an organized and barbaric despotism, and can make effectual arrangements there for the establishment of a civilized and self-governing State, fit to become a partner in their united sovereignty. Will they not do it? Not to do it would be a base surrender of the trust which they hold for their posterity and for the world.

Doubtless there will be talk about the rights of the inhabitants of Utah. Let their rights be respected and guarded; but let it be remembered that those inhabitants are not a State. They are not even a body politic save by force of an act of Congress, which Congress can repeal at any time when such repeal shall be deemed expedient. They are citizens of the United States, as many of them as are not like the [late?] delegate Cannon, foreigners not naturalized. They are citizens in the same sense in which minors and inhabitants of the District of Columbia (to say nothing about women) are citizens; but their citizenship gives them no political power. As individual citizens they are entitled to protection by the National Government within the limits of its jurisdiction, and any of them who pass out of a Territory into a State are entitled to the protection of the State. As individuals they are entitled to the same protection with other American citizens in foreign countries. Every individual of them has a right to personal liberty, to the possession and lawful use of the products of his lawful industry, to whatever property, whether real or personal, he has acquired in any lawful way. But let it be remembered that there is nothing of State rights in the case—no sovereignty or *quasi* sovereignty with which the United States is to negotiate or make some compromise. The whole matter is that in a certain Territory belonging to the United States there are (or were in 1880) 143,906 human beings to be governed by such rules and regulations as shall be deemed just and expedient by the wisdom of the United States in Congress.

As for the rights of settlers in Utah, it is worth remembering that the first of human rights—first in order of time, and first in importance—is not the right to govern and vote, but the right to be governed and to be well governed,—the right, in other words, to be protected, to be restrained, to be incited to well-doing, by the beneficent influences of well-ordered civil society. Civil society implies government; and well-ordered society is good government. The right to be well-governed includes and carries with it every other civil right. Of that first and comprehensive right, the inhabitants of Utah, under existing arrangements, are deprived. It is the duty of Congress to make other arrangements, such as will put them under the beneficent influences of good government, protecting them against violence and fraud, restraining them from wickedness, and inciting them to become good citizens.

The failure, hitherto, of all attempts to suppress or punish the barbarism which Mormons call "plural marriage," is more remarkable than wonderful.

For the sake of showing that the fact, however remarkable, is not wonderful, let us suppose a case elsewhere than in Utah. "The memory of the wicked shall rot;" and there is no contradiction of the Scripture when I suggest that the memory of a certain wicked man who was commonly called Jim Fisk remains in New York to this day. I am not aware that he was ever married, but all who remember the occasion and means of his death remember that he had a concubine who lived in great splendor at his expense, and whom it was his pride to exhibit at Central Park and elsewhere. That was a bold defiance of decent people; but will anybody please to tell me that it was an offense against the laws of New York? Suppose, now, that not being satisfied with one harlot, he had been rich enough and shameless enough to keep thirty, having them all to himself. Suppose him to have bought a block of houses fronting on Fifth Avenue, and to have established one of his harlots in each house, assuring it to her as her home and the home of her children. That would have been just about what Brigham Young did in Salt Lake City. In such a case, what would the State of New York do? Mr. Fisk, if anybody should remonstrate, might say, as one Mr. Tweed said on a somewhat similar occasion, "What are you going to do about it?"

CHAPTER XXI.

The Twin Relig.

BY HON. P. T. VAN ZILE, U. S. DIST. ATT'Y FOR UTAH.*

Philadelphia Convention, 1857.—No Easy Question.—Mormons Completely Organized.—Tithes.—Polygamy not Publicly Announced at First.—Wonderful Power of Forgetting.—You Cannot Protect Me.—Proportion of Polygamists.—"Brooming a Bishop."—Polygamists Holding the Offices.—Spiritual Exaltation.—Mormon Jurors.—Congress Guilty.—Evil Results of Polygamy.—Laws Suggested.

A NATION seldom moves deliberately to correct an evil upon its first appearance. But when that evil becomes strong and defiant, when "right is crushed to earth" and it seems for a time that evil will prevail in spite of the laws of God or man, when thousands of bleeding hearts, with their last gasp for life, appeal to a strong nation, when streams of innocent blood have been spilt upon the ground, and cry to Heaven for vengeance, then governments are aroused, and often adopt stern measures to correct the evil.

---

* Read before the Michigan State Association of Congregational churches, at its meeting in Detroit, May 21, 1880.

Hon. P. T. VAN ZILE,
U. S. District Attorney for Utah.

On the 17th day of June, 1856, at the city of Philadelphia, that grand old city where the nation had its birth, a convention of men assembled,—men who had been moved by appeals for liberty and a better civilization.

The air was full of rumors concerning the oppression of four millions of human beings almost within the shadows of the National Capitol, while mingled with the wail which came up from the sunny South, asking for freedom from the bonds of American slavery, came a petition over the snow-capped Rocky Mountains, from the wilds of the frontier, from a land two thousand miles away, asking for freedom from an oppression which ruins soul and body, and makes life worse than a blank.

From this convention of noble men came the first public expression upon the subject with which we have to deal. So to-day let these men speak again, and would that they might arouse and stimulate to action,—earnest, determined action,—the people of these United States and its Congress. Hear them!

Resolved, That the Constitution confers upon Congress sovereign power over the Territories of the United States for their government, and that in the exercise of this power it is both the right and the duty of Congress to prohibit in the Territories those twin relics of barbarism,—Polygamy and Slavery.

Since that declaration, the nation has arisen in its majestic strength, and carved the one ulcer, slavery, from the body politic, but the other "twin relic," as foul and abominable an ulcer as was slavery, still fills our nostrils with its stench, still disgraces that which we declare is the greatest and best of governments, still spreads and thrives; and raising its "hydra head," bids defiance to people, to government, and to law. The extent and magnitude of this evil is not understood by the majority of the citizens of the United States. It is generally looked upon as one of the tenets of a church or organization of fanatics who occupy an out-of-the-way country, and by many a wiseacre it is confidently asserted that the evil can at any time be easily and readily set aside when the United States desires to do so. This is by no means true. By reason of inattention and careless indifference, this monstrosity has grown and thrived until it has become bold and defiant, and now, when the Government begins to wake up to the fact, and look toward eradicating it, they find it an ugly question to solve.

Stop and consider, you who would have the Government make laws that will be effectual in suppressing polygamy. What laws will you have enacted? Is your answer, A law forbidding the practice under heavy penalties? That law has been enacted, and for nearly eighteen years has been upon our statute books. We can no longer close our eyes and cry out, This is an easy question to solve. We must awake and realize the fact that to-day this question has assumed large proportions, and that its solution will puzzle, and is puzzling, the brains of some of our wisest statesmen.

Let us notice some of the difficulties in the way of enforcing the law of Congress, prohibiting polygamy in the Territories. If you look at your maps, you will discover, lying in what is called the great basin, the Territory of Utah, composed of mountains and valleys, and containing 84,276 square miles,—a country about one and two-thirds times as large as the State of Michigan; and by a little crowding, it could embrace in its polygamous folds the States of Michigan and Indiana, while Massachusetts or Vermont could lie down in one of its valleys without being the least inconvenienced for room.

If you notice the physical geography of this country, you will observe that it has ranges of mountains running north and south, the Wasatch and the Oquirrh, and that its agricultural lands are scattered here and there throughout the Territory, wherever a valley susceptible of cultivation can be found. The consequence is, the hundred and fifty thousand people who believe, or pretend to believe, that this monstrous doctrine is a revelation from God, are collected in small settlements here and there in these several valleys, while the people opposed,—the Gentiles, as we are called,—consisting of perhaps ten thousand or less, are centered in the mining camps and in Salt Lake City, and thus those who advocate the doctrine are left by themselves in most cases, with no one to report their violations of law.

This vast Territory is divided into three judicial districts, and for each of these districts the United States appoints a District Judge. In these District

Courts this crime must be prosecuted. This means bringing witnesses and jurors one hundred and fifty miles out of a country where there are no railroads. Add to this the fact that most of the people in the Territory are opposed to this law, and will do everything and anything they can do to defeat its execution. Over this large area of country this "Church of Jesus Christ of Latter-day Saints," as they call themselves, with polygamy as one of its cornerstones, has complete sway, and is continually reaching out into adjoining Territories, and attempting to fasten its poisonous fangs upon them and bring them under its control.

Never was a body of men so completely organized as is this Mormon people. It is so arranged that the president of the church can know the sentiment of every man in the Territory, Mormon or Gentile.

The building up and strengthening of Mormonism is the chief object of every Mormon; and consequently, he opposes and cripples every effort made by the Government or its officers to punish polygamy. So every move that is made by a Government official, and almost every word spoken, is known by the leading Mormons, and arrangements are made accordingly. All the telegraph lines in the Territory, except the through lines from east to west, are controlled and owned by the Mormons, and run into the office of President Taylor. He can know every dispatch that is sent, and by whom. If a United States officer telegraphs for the arrest of a man, or for a witness, John Taylor knows it; and if he has no objections, the officer will get his prisoner or witness; if Taylor objects, he will not. The Mormon church is the largest business concern in the Territory. It owns millions of dollars' worth of property. It carries on stock raising, and has large herds of cattle and sheep scattered all over the Territory. These herds are called the church herds, and are branded with a cross. They have large co-operative mercantile institutions in nearly all of the settlements, with a mammoth institution to supply them, situated in Salt Lake City. You can always know these stores by the sign over the door, which reads: "Holiness to the Lord. Zion's Co-operative Mercantile Institution," and in the midst is a representation of the all-seeing Eye. All their goods are marked with the letters Z. C. M. I.; even to the horse-block in front.

The church collects from its members a large amount each year for tithing. Taylor reported one year one hundred and forty-five thousand dollars, and how much more was collected I do not know. Brigham Young, although often requested, never made but one report about the tithing, and that was in the tabernacle and consisted in this: "It is none of your ——— business how much tithing has been collected."

The marriage ceremony is performed in secret, and the most terrible oaths are taken never to reveal what transpires. To these oaths are attached the most horrible penalties, some of which are that the participants will have their tongues torn out by the roots, their throats cut from ear to ear, their bodies sawn asunder, and their knee-joints broken, and the like, should they ever reveal what they see or hear while in the Endowment House. Think of putting a witness on the stand to testify, who feels himself bound by these oaths! And these penalties are not meaningless, as many a poor victim would testify if his voice could be heard. Many men and women have lost their lives for no other offense than revealing what has transpired in this sink-hole of iniquity,—the Mormon Endowment House. I mention these facts that you may understand some of the difficulties we have to meet when we undertake to enforce the law of Congress forbidding polygamy in the Territories.

Polygamy is antagonistic to decency, and would not be tolerated by a civilized community. The Mormons understand this as well as you, and they would never undertake to practice it openly and in defiance of law in the State of Michigan, or any other of the States. But Utah seemed peculiarly favorable to its growth, and until recently it has grown and flourished without molestation. The pretended revelation from God upon which this doctrine of polygamy is founded, is claimed by the Mormons to have been received in 1843, by their prophet Joseph Smith; and although a fair construction of the language of that revelation would seem to make it not only the privilege but the duty of every true Latter-day Saint to practice polygamy, nothing of the kind was done until they passed the boundaries of civilization and settled in the valleys of this Territory, except in a few cases, and that very secretly. And even after their settlement in Utah, some of their leaders,—among them John Taylor,—denied that it was a tenet of their church.

When, however, they became well established, and over a thousand miles intervened between them and the Missouri River, with the great Rocky Mountain range, which in those days was almost impassable between them and the outside world on the east, and the Sierra Nevadas on the west; when they found the land they had chosen surrounded by snow-capped mountains,—a perfect prison-house, from which no man, woman, or child could escape,—then it was that in the Mormon Tabernacle in Salt Lake City, nine years after their pretended prophet claimed that God spoke to him and revealed his will concerning this people and polygamy, this infamous doctrine was publicly announced by Brigham Young. But there were those even at that early day who would not and did not receive this doctrine, and who believed it came rather from the devil than from God. And to-day, in the city of Salt Lake, there lives a respected old lady who has stemmed the tide of Mormon opposition for over thirty years; and although she saw the husband of her youth leave her and take to his embrace other women whom he called wives, and although she became to his affections an outcast, still that grand woman has been sustained in all these tribulations, and has, in the midst of all, succeeded in raising up her family, which was large, and, thank God, there is not one of them that does not despise Mormonism. That woman is no less a personage than the first and only legal wife of Orson Pratt, one of the chief apostles of the Mormon church.

But the Mormon leaders of those early days made excuses to their followers for not publicly announcing this revelation. Among others, the following were given: That influenced by certain notions of duty, even good men may try to steal a march upon their fellows, for the purpose of doing them a service; that it was determined in those days that the world has no business to know everything the Lord has revealed, and that evasiveness on the subject of marriage was an obligation for the protection of the church,—an *aid* to the Lord in the establishment of that institution until it became strong enough to take care of itself; that great truths fully offered to the world would be casting pearls before swine; and a dozen other reasons.

One thing is certain; from that day to this, falsifying among the leaders has been cultivated as a fine art. They study the *art* of forgetting what they have seen and heard, and so it often happens that a Mormon, perhaps one of the everlasting priesthood, as they call them, goes upon the witness stand, and testifies that he cannot remember having performed a marriage ceremony that took place within a week past. He will not swear that he did not, but he has no recollection on the subject. They all have wonderful powers of forgetting—I have never

MORMON TABERNACLE.   MORMON TEMPLE (IN COURSE OF ERECTION).

TEMPLE BLOCK.

EAST TEMPLE STREET, SALT LAKE CITY.

found one who had a retentive memory when a polygamy case was on trial.

With this doctrine of polygamy, a fundamental principle of Mormonism in Utah, there grew up and became well established, a Theocratic Government with the president of the Mormon church at its head; and it exists to-day. No despot ever had more absolute control over his subjects than Brigham Young, nor more than John Taylor has to-day over the members of the Mormon church.

Their victim once in polygamy, they have him chained and manacled,—there is no retreat, no escape. He at once shuns the Gentiles, for fear of being exposed, and like a cringing cur, obeys the "Mormon priesthood" for fear they will withdraw their protection, or as they term it, "turn him over to the buffetings of Satan."

The first lesson learned by a Mormon is to obey counsel, right or wrong, and ask no questions. Whatever he is told to do must be done: if it is a good deed, he should be thankful; if it is bad, or even criminal, he must not hesitate, but do as the "Servants of the Lord (?) have directed, and let the consequences take care of themselves."

The result of this is that to-day many and many a man is bound to the Mormon church and its institutions by no other bond than a consciousness that the "priesthood" know of too many instances where he obeyed counsel, and in obeying committed some dreadful deed. He has heard, may be, for these many years the blood of his victim crying from the ground, and has seen before him the last look mingled with the agony of death; and with this comes the consciousness that all is known by this Mormon priesthood, and he dares not break loose.

Some have come out and confessed, upon being promised immunity, but they are comparatively few. Less than a year ago, I witnessed the struggle of one who had "obeyed counsel" to the fullest extent. I promised to protect him if he would confess to me, and give him the word of the Attorney General of the United States if necessary. He listened to me, waited, seemed to consider the proposition favorably; but finally with a sigh he said, "No, it will not do, *you cannot protect me;*" and with this he left my office.

Polygamy is in every sense of the word an ulcer on the body politic. It does not belong in America, and should not be tolerated in America; and if there is no other way, we should apply the knife and carve it out.

These people delight in calling themselves "a peculiar people," and they are indeed peculiar. They hav'n't a single sentiment of Republicanism in their souls.

They are mostly foreigners, and as I have heard them often express it, they came to this country because it is a free country. Freedom, to them, means license. Under such circumstances, do you wonder that there are obstacles in the way of enforcing the law?

But not all of those practice polygamy who belong to the Mormon church, and claim to believe in the so-called revelation from God, received by the prophet, Joseph Smith. Just what proportion do, it is impossible for me or any other outsider to say. It may be, and undoubtedly is, known by those in authority; but no outsider is permitted to examine or even cast his ungodly eyes on one of their records, and especially the record of marriages. Nor is any Latter-day Saint permitted to disclose the fact, if he knows, and so it is variously estimated from one-tenth to one-seventh. There is, in the Mormon Endowment House, a record of marriages. The time of the court has been occupied for hours and days, trying to find the man who could, or rather would, produce that book. I have found witnesses who would swear they had seen it; but none of them would testify to its whereabouts, or who was the custodian. The art of forgetting was always invoked, and was generally adequate to the task. Now does n't it seem strange that the president of the church himself could not tell where that record was? I have had him on the witness stand on two different occasions, and on each occasion he swore—this man of God (?)—that he could not tell where that record was, and that he had no idea where it could be found. Oh what blasphemy, for such men to claim that they are the prophets and servants of the most high God!

But you at once ask, If polygamy is believed to be a law of God, especially to this people, why do they not all practice it? There is one very good reason: there are not women enough. Several of the leaders have appropriated from six to a dozen, and have thus prevented others from living up to their privileges, as they call it.

This is not the only reason. It is not every man who feels able to take upon himself the burden of so large a family.

This is by no means considered a good reason by all; for a great many, if not the majority of the polygamists, take plural wives for the support it gives them,—the women supporting the husband and children both, and all growing up more like animals than human beings.

Another reason is, there are now a good many wives among the Mormons in Utah, who have independence enough to stand up for right and decency, and give their husbands to understand that if they undertake to go into polygamy, the United States officers will be informed, and they will be prosecuted.

Some women go so far as to settle matters themselves; as, for example, the following, clipped from our morning paper, will testify:—

"The other day a little flurry was created on one of our principal streets by the sight of a dignified and portly individual, no less a personage, in fact, than one of the bishops of J. C. of L. D. S., rushing along the sidewalk in breathless haste, closely followed by an indignant woman armed with a broom. Twice or thrice in the course of the pursuit, the fly-

BROOMING THE BISHOP. SEE PAGE 324.

ing bishop received a well-directed blow from this weapon, which had the effect of causing him to break into a mad gallop, keeping it up until he disappeared around the nearest corner. An inquiry as to the meaning of this unusual spectacle developed the following facts:—

"A good Saint, whom we will call brother Jones because that isn't his name, has resided in Salt Lake City many years, and accumulated considerable property; but he has lived beneath his religious privileges, and contented himself with one wife. On the day referred to, the bishop, feeling called upon to admonish him with regard to his neglect of the glorious privileges of Latter-day dispensation, called at his house and reproved him in the presence of his wife, telling him that his chances of exaltation would be slim indeed if he did not set about looking up another spouse at once.

"Sister Jones only waited to hear him finish the first sentence of the latter portion of his admonition, when, seizing the broom, she exclaimed:—

"'Get out of this, you villain; I'll teach you to come into an honest woman's house and advise her husband to take another wife. Take that, and that'—laying the broom-handle vigorously about his head and shoulders. The wretched bishop grabbed his hat and made for the door; but before he could reach it, the blows fell thick and fast on his defenseless head. Once outside, he thought himself safe, but he soon discovered his mistake. Nemesis was behind him in the shape of that broom, and his flight through the gate and down the street was accelerated every few steps in the manner we have described. When he reached home and counted up his bruises, he registered a vow. Henceforth, when he counsels an erring brother, he will choose his opportunity more wisely, and the admonitions that he gives on the subject of celestial marriage will be uttered far from the hearing of indignant wives armed with brooms."

There are two classes of Mormons. One class is liberal in its views, and appears to be trying hard to get a knowledge of the manners and customs of the outside world. And although those who compose it are still Mormons, members of the church, they are not willing to adopt or believe in this doctrine of polygamy. This class is composed principally of young men and young women, often the sons and daughters of leading Mormons, generally the children of the first or legal wife, who are, as a rule, bitterly opposed to polygamy. From this class every year comes a multitude of what the Mormons call, and properly, too, apostates.

The other class, which is largely in the majority, consists of those who shut their eyes to everything except the curses of the Mormon priesthood. They are mostly foreigners, brought here by the Mormon missionaries from almost every country on the globe. The greater part of them are ignorant and superstitious, and really believe all that the priesthood claim for their religion. With this class, polygamy is growing in favor, and I am inclined to think that more people are entering polygamy today than ever before. In some settlements, where the inhabitants are all Mormons and away by themselves, polygamy is very generally practiced.

It will undoubtedly seem strange to you who live in a country where law is respected, and if violated, punishment follows, that in the face and eyes of the law of Congress these people continue to enter this relation; but so it is.

The reasons for this are not wanting. The people hear the leaders, especially John Taylor, boast of the fact that no government on earth can prevent the practice of polygamy in Utah. George Q. Cannon, home on leave a year ago from Congress, said the same in substance, and polygamy is openly preached in their meetings. Public sentiment favors it. The man who opposes it is opposing the whole community, while he who favors it is a hero, and the leaders see to it that he is rewarded.

No man in Utah can expect any political preferment who is opposed to polygamy. This rule is carried out down to the lowest office in the Territory.

The legislature which was in session this last winter, was composed almost entirely of polygamists. And the United States Congress appropriated out of Uncle Sam's money from $20,000 to $25,000 to pay these law-breakers their *per diem*. Men who not only live in open violation of the laws but preach and advise others to do so, will reach out their hands and take from the Government they despise, this $20,000, while in their hearts they are continually planning the violation of its laws, and defying its power to punish them.

The Mormon leaders decide who shall hold the offices. Brigham Young did not conceal this fact. When the law passed Congress forbidding polygamy, Brigham Young openly boasted that he would crowd polygamy down the throats of the United States Congress, and he did it. Captain Hooper, then in Congress, was a monogamist. He was kept at home, and Geo. Q. Cannon, who has four wives, who was twice indicted, and who is notoriously a polygamist and defiant so far as the law of Congress is concerned, and who openly preaches the foul and abominable doctrine, was the pill prepared by Brigham Young.

The Gentiles protested, sent a man to contest his seat; but the Congress of the United States opened its precious mouth and swallowed Geo. Q. Cannon, polygamy and all, and to-day he sits among the law-makers for this Government as the Honorable member from Utah; so Brigham Young was able to say, and John Taylor can say, "This is the way the truly faithful are rewarded." Another incentive for entering polygamy and advocating it is, it shows fidelity to the church. But the reason paramount to all others with the truly sincere, and there are some sincere ones, is that by it they expect to obtain spiritual exaltation. It is taught by the Mormon priests that a monogamist will occupy a very humble position in the other world, if he gains celestial glory at all; that those who have practiced polygamy will, in the next world, be kings and queens, and that they will obtain excellence and exaltation in proportion to their faithful performance of the tenets of the church, especially polygamy. And so, if a Mormon has a friend who died unmarried, in order to save that friend in the next world, he gets some one to be sealed to his friend for eternity. It simply means marriage for eternity.

But I am not willing to concede that any of these reasons are what actuate very many men. I think that in a great many cases, lust is the only incentive, and that the church and this bogus religion is only a cloak they use to cover their real reasons.

There is, however, among a large class of Mormons a growing feeling of dissatisfaction, particularly among the younger people. They are beginning to understand the hollowness of the doctrine of the church, and I am inclined to think the examinations to which we have recently subjected Mormons who have been summoned as jurors has had something to do in bringing this about.

Let me give you a sample of one of these examinations. At the last term of court in the Southern District, I was examining persons summoned to sit as a grand jury. One man was called who lived in the extreme southern portion of the Territory. He was sworn to answer such questions as should be put to him. After asking the usual preliminary questions, I asked, "Do you believe that the revelation claimed to have been received by Joseph Smith, with reference to polygamy, came from God?"—Ans.

"Yes, sir." "Do you believe that polygamy is a law of God to this people?"—Ans. "Yes, sir, I know it is." "How do you know it?"—Ans. "I have been told it was." "By whom?" To my utter surprise the answer was, "By the Holy Ghost." "When?"—Ans. "When I was nine years old."

I am convinced that there is a large class of men in Utah to-day, living in polygamy, who if they could honorably release themselves, would certainly do so, and will welcome the day, if it ever comes, that frees them from this bondage.

These men have raised and have about them large families, in many cases dependent on them for support, and they feel in duty bound to keep the families together, and so continue in this relation.

The apostasy from the Mormon church is very great, and would in time break up the institution, were it not for immigration which largely exceeds the apostasy.

Some of the causes which tend to perpetuate polygamy I have already mentioned; namely, for the sake of obtaining the favor of the leaders—political preferment,—to show fidelity to the church and its doctrines, and to obtain spiritual exaltation.

To the reasons already advanced, I will add: The inability of the Government under the present state of the laws to effectually convict and punish polygamists.

And I charge upon the Congress of the United States, in a great measure, the perpetuation of this foul crime. Never in the history of the contest has a bill tending to the extinguishment of this damnable institution been offered in Congress except it had all the vitality amended out of it, and a compromise measure passed which was an elephant to handle. More often a bill has been entirely defeated in the committee to which it was referred, by some man like Proctor Knott, who shows every symptom of being retained in the interest of the Mormon church, and never reported back to the House—never even introduced.

Think of it! The crime of polygamy in Utah actually outlaws in three years' time!

A man takes a plural wife, keeps it secret, perhaps sends her home to her own parents for three years, then takes her to his harem and openly lives with her as his wife, and he can snap his fingers at the officers of the law. The statute of limitation protects him. There is no law punishing adultery or lewd and lascivious cohabitation, and so the man who can hide his crime for three years, (and there is no difficulty where he has the whole community to help him as he has here,) goes scot free, and can practice polygamy openly.

We hear the cry coming up to us, Why don't you punish the leaders? The answer is, Their crimes by the laws of the United States have outlawed, and they see to it that every offense does outlaw before it becomes known.

Representative Willits, of Michigan, introduced in Congress, this session, a bill repealing this law of limitation so far as it affects this crime, and other bills, which, if they could be passed and become laws, would shake this institution from center to circumference. On being introduced in the House, they were referred to the Judiciary committee of which Proctor Knott is chairman, who referred the bills to a sub-committee of two, of which he himself was one, and that has been the end of the Willits bill.

The Mormons have always had a man or two in Congress through whom they have been able to shape legislation.

If there is one thing more than another in connection with this matter to be hoped and prayed for, it is that men who understand and feel the importance of looking after this problem in Utah will be elected to Congress this fall. It is high time for the people all over this country to make themselves heard upon this subject, and in such a way that they may be understood.

I have not the time to discuss in this paper, as fully as I would like, the evils that result from polygamy. I can only mention some of them.

The first great evil, and one more noticeable in Utah than any other, is licentiousness and prostitution. All the men, women, and children hear this abominable relation discussed every day of their lives; the attention of young men and young women is called continually to the social evil, and licentiousness and prostitution is the natural result.

The second is a general disregard of morals, resulting from the manner in which the children are raised. A man with from twenty to sixty children, and from half a dozen to a dozen women who think no more of themselves than to become concubines, can hardly expect, if he cares to consider it, that this numerous family will grow up possessing a high standard of morality.

The third evil is untruthfulness, and when necessary, false swearing. It is instilled into the minds of all that they must keep as a secret the relation in which their fathers and mothers and brothers and sisters are living; and if brought into court, it is no crime to swear 'that they have no knowledge on the subject, or that these parties are not living in polygamy. Indeed, they are told, and impressed with the idea, that if they undertake to divulge the facts of a plural marriage, their memory will be taken away, and so they generally swear that they cannot remember.

At the last session of the Third District Court in Salt Lake City, I heard more perjury to shield polygamists, in one day, than I ever heard during all the time I lived in the State of Michigan.

The fourth is its destruction of all the finer sentiments of men and women, and they become coarse and gross. Especially is this true in the case of woman. It reduces her from a woman, devoted, trusting, loving, and to be loved, to a mere animal or machine. She no longer lives; she simply exists, to be used by, and to serve the foul purposes of, a licentious, beastly man.

Love and hope that once glowed and burned

within her, have gone out and become dead, ashy embers.

She looks into the eyes of the child at her breast without hope, and almost shudders for its future. The eyes once full of hope and bright with anticipation, have become lifeless and sunken; and if you were to write the cause of all this, it would be but one word—*polygamy*.

With this great evil upon us, we naturally ask, What is the best course for the Government to pursue to abolish it?

Upon this I can only suggest a thought or two, and must leave you to carry out the argument; for this, if fully discussed, would consume the whole time allotted to this paper.

First, I would repeal the law of limitation so far as it protects this offense, and let it be understood that if a man goes into polygamy, and thus violates the law of Congress, the crime committed would *never* outlaw,—that he would be liable to prosecution at any time during his life. This is my favorite measure. I believe it would be more potent in breaking up polygamy than any law Congress could pass. The little dodge I have mentioned, of keeping quiet till the offense outlawed, would not be so effectual.

Second, I would pass a law prescribing what should constitute marriage, and among its provisions I would require a public record of the marriage, which should be in all cases proof of the marriage; and I would not recognize the legality of the Endowment House marriage.

Third, I would disfranchise every person who is living in polygamy, or who would swear he believed it right or a religious duty to practice it.

Fourth, I would pass a law forbidding, and providing punishment for, adultery and lewd and lascivious cohabitation.

Fifth, I would make cohabitation and the admission of the parties evidence of marriage.

Sixth, I would make polygamy odious in every way, and would commence by expelling from the United States Congress the notorious polygamist, George Q. Cannon, who to-day has four wives living. I would do this if for no other reason than because I think it a disgrace to the Government to allow such a man to sit in its Congress.

Seventh, I would abolish the Territorial legislature, of which nine-tenths of the members are polygamists.

These are a few mild remedies I would apply to this ulcer, and I would increase them as I discovered the needs of the patient. And if mild applications proved ineffectual, I would carve the infamous thing from the body politic.

A work is being done here by men and women who are true missionaries. Gentiles, Christian ministers, and teachers are establishing schools all over the Territory. I wish I could give you the history of these schools, and the good they are doing; but you can imagine, knowing as you do that education is the forerunner of civilization, and the lighting up of dark places. Every church that has a foothold in Salt Lake City, has established a school; and among the prosperous schools is Salt Lake Academy, under the management of the Congregational church, with Prof. Edward Benner as principal.

The mining resources of the Territory are bringing business men into the country, and will in time be powerful in abolishing the peculiar institution.

You Christian ministers of the State of Michigan have a work to do in this matter, and if you fail to do it, you must be held responsible for that neglect.

I call upon you to arouse the people in your several congregations upon this subject. So shape public sentiment, and so interest the community, that your influence will be felt in the Congress of the United States, to the end that we may have such legislation as will lead to the utter overthrow in this country of this infamous practice.

I would not have it understood that all is utter darkness, or that we feel discouraged in the work, for it is not so. There are times when discouragements seem to cast a shadow over us; but the light is beginning to dawn, and I believe there will come a day—how soon is for the people of this great nation to say—when this "Twin Relic of Barbarism" will, like American Slavery, be in the history of this country a thing of the past. May God hasten the day.

CHAPTER XXII.

Some Suggestive Letters.

BY HON. P. T. VAN ZILE, U. S. DIST. ATT'Y FOR UTAH.*

Difficulties in the Way of Convicting Mormons.—How to Crush It.—Law of Limitation.—Disfranchise the Polygamists.—Punish Adultery.—"Don't Persecute Us."—Mormon Buncombe.—Treason.—No Kid-Glove Proceedings.—The Young Men

LETTER NUMBER ONE.

SALT LAKE CITY, UTAH, Jan. 11, 1881.

YOUR letter of December 28, 1880, asking in substance why the law of Congress forbidding polygamy in the Territories is not enforced in Utah, is at hand, and I take occasion at this, my earliest opportunity, to answer you.

In your letter you seem to assume that no efforts are made to execute the law. This is by no means correct. Every effort that can be made, is made by the officers; and some cases have been prosecuted and convictions obtained. It is true, however, that a majority of the offenders go unwhipped of justice, and this must continue to be the case until Congress takes this matter in hand, and enacts

---

* These letters were addressed to the editor of the *Inter-Ocean*, and were published in that paper in 1881 and 1882.

some further laws. This question has been handled with gloves when handled at all. The poultice policy has been too long in favor, and to Congress belongs the blame for not ridding the country of this foul stain, polygamy. They have, to be sure, enacted a law forbidding polygamy and declaring it a crime; but for these many years they have permitted our hands to be tied by failing to enact measures that are necessary for the enforcement of the law, so that to-day the law is not respected.

The law we are called upon to enforce reads as follows:—

Sec. 5352. "Every person having a husband or wife living who marries another, whether married or single * * * is guilty of bigamy and shall be punished." * * *

It will be observed that the offense consists in "marrying another." In other words, it is the marriage that constitutes the offense, and therefore, it is the marriage that must be proven. In order to convict a man of bigamy, it is incumbent upon the prosecution to prove beyond a reasonable doubt—

First, That the defendant at the time it is alleged he committed the offense had a lawful wife living.

Second, That having a lawful wife living, he married another—not that he lives and cohabits with another, but that he married another.

Third, That this bigamous marriage was solemnized within the last three years past. For, strange as it may seem, Congress has allowed this crime of bigamy to be subject to the general limitation law.

Now, with these propositions in our mind, let us look at some of the difficulties in the way of successfully prosecuting one of these Mormon saints (?).

The first thing a federal officer has impressed upon his mind when he undertakes to enforce this law, is that he is in Utah, and not in the State of Illinois, or in any other of the States in this Union, and it is by no means fair to judge us by what would be expected of the prosecuting officers in the States. There the entire community demands and expects that if a man commits bigamy he will be punished. Every man, woman, and child cry out against the crime. In Utah we have the reverse, or nearly so. The last census gave Utah 143,900 inhabitants, or thereabouts. Out of this number at least 100,000 are real or pretended believers in, and advocates of, this foul crime of polygamy. They preach it and hear it preached in their church openly from week to week. Their fathers and mothers, sisters and brothers, perhaps, practice it. Many of them are the children of polygamous marriages. This public sentiment, which has possession of the whole Territory, urges every individual to obstruct, in every way possible, the enforcement of this law of Congress. They excuse their acts to their own consciences by about this kind of reasoning:—

"God, through his prophet, Joseph Smith, has revealed it unto this people that they should practice polygamy. God's law sanctions, if it does not command, that this people practice polygamy. Opposed to it is the law of man. Which, when they conflict, should be violated, God's law, or man's law?—Why, man's law, of course."

Every Mormon marriage is solemnized in the Endowment House. No person is permitted to enter this house except the tried and faithful Mormon, and all who do enter are sworn never to reveal anything that transpires. Because of this secret marriage ceremony, the greatest difficulty is experienced in executing the law. You, who wonder that this law is not enforced, stop for a moment and consider the situation here in Utah, in the light of these facts. The sentiment of the whole Territory is opposed to the enforcement of the law, and the offense is committed only in the presence of those who swear never to reveal it, who are, in fact, *particeps criminis* to the offense. With this state of facts can you expect successful prosecutions of polygamy cases?

Daniel H. Wells, the first counselor to President John Taylor, was summoned by the prosecution in the case of John Miles; but rather than reveal what took place in the Endowment House, he suffered imprisonment for contempt. Before the court made the order, however, he testified that he was under a sworn obligation not to reveal what transpired.

A third obstruction to the enforcement of this law is, these offenses are generally known only to Mormons, who believe that polygamy is a law of God unto the people, and that the law of Congress is simply enacted to persecute the Mormons. Upon these persons the prosecution must largely rely for proof of the offense charged. It is difficult for you to understand that it is almost impossible to get the facts before a court and jury from such witnesses? Why, perhaps the very witness you rely on is himself a polygamist, at that moment as guilty as the man on trial; besides, he does not wish to see a conviction, and is opposed to the prosecution in every way. He has taken an oath, to which is attached a horrible penalty, never to reveal the very matter concerning which he is asked to testify.

Do you think for a moment that such a witness is available?

What is the result generally? These witnesses have convenient memories, or rather a convenient way of forgetting. They can't remember. I have known witnesses to remember every other circumstance connected with the case except the all-important fact, the marriage,—that they had no recollection of (?). And horrible as it may seem, it is nevertheless true that these witnesses, when pressed to the wall, and the general answer "I don't recollect" will not do, will perjure themselves, rather than reveal the facts.

Mothers and fathers will testify they know nothing about the marriage of their daughters who are living with polygamists and rearing children; plural wives will swear that they are only mistresses; and, in fact, almost any statement will be made to evade the law, and they will satisfy their consciences, by the all-consoling belief that they did it for "Christ's sake."

The first or lawful wife is not allowed to testify

as a witness, and so it often happens that the first or legal marriage is more difficult to prove than the second or polygamous marriage. Often the first marriage was solemnized in a foreign country; for it will be remembered that a large proportion of the Mormons are foreigners. The certificates of marriage will not do; the defendant must be confronted with the witnesses.

The fact that the offense must have been committed within the last three years, shields nine-tenths of all the polygamy in Utah to-day. It is generally understood that this crime outlaws in three years; and with this limitation law in view, a Mormon takes a young girl into the Endowment House, and she is sealed to him as a polygamous or plural wife. She then goes home to her father's house, and lives for three years apart from her polygamous husband. The fact is kept quiet by those who know about it until the offense is outlawed; then the polygamous husband calls for his concubine, and lives with her in open defiance of the Government or its officers.

The honorable member from Utah, one of the nation's law-makers, George Q. Cannon, who has four wives, slipped his neck out because of this limitation law; and to-day, instead of being in the penitentiary, he is allowed to disgrace the Government of these United States—a Government for which he has no respect, and whose laws he violates and openly counsels others to violate—by sitting in the House of Representatives as delegate for this Territory. Is it to be wondered at that loyal, law-abiding citizens become disheartened?

It should further be understood, in connection with the difficulties I have mentioned, that there are no laws forbidding adultery, lewd and lascivious cohabitation, incest, or seduction in this Territory, otherwise we might arrest these offenders for adultery, the plural marriage being void. The only law we have to correct the evil is this law of Congress above quoted.

In view of the situation I have urged the passage of certain bills by Congress, which, it seems to me, would go a great way toward helping out the difficulty. Concerning these bills I will write you at some future time.

LETTER NUMBER TWO.

Salt Lake City, Utah, Feb. 10, 1881.

It is a very easy matter to deal in generalities. It is no hard thing for us to say, "Congress should pass such laws as will effectually put an end to this vile practice—polygamy—in the Territory;" but when we come to specify what measures should be enacted, then it is that we are often bewildered.

There are in this country two distinct parties that have taken issue with each other upon this Mormon question. One party contends that this problem must be solved by moral suasion, that there is no necessity for Congress to pay much attention to the subject, but that the missionary, school-teacher, and preacher, will solve the question and regenerate

Utah. The other party believes and advocates that the school-teachers and ministers are necessary, but that Congress must also step into the breach and pass rigid laws,—laws that carry with them such provisions as will enable the officers to enforce them. To this latter class I belong.

I know the cry raised by our friends upon the other side is, "You are asking for class legislation; you are making a specialty of these Mormon fanatics." Call it what you please; I know that the United States must act in this matter, or soon this ulcer will have spread and assumed such proportions that the Government can only rid itself by severing it from the body politic.

You who cry, "Let it alone, and apply moral suasion," do you remember that the other "twin relic," American slavery, which, thank God, is no more, set up the same cry? And, oh, to the shame of this great nation it must be witten! for years and years we did let it alone, until the bitter wail of five million souls went up to God, and this nation was drenched in blood. To-day, not millions, but thousands, of burdened souls, who have experienced the beastly practice, polygamy,—souls whose light has nearly gone out in this world, and whose faith in mankind is weak, if not extinct,—are praying for the day when they may be disenthralled from a slavery which has been a living death to them.

If every Congressman could hear the experience of some of the legal wives in Utah related by themselves, and hear the earnest prayers often spoken

Pres. JOHN TAYLOR.
The Successor of Brigham Young.

aloud, but oftener prayed in secret, there would be no need of any lobby at the Capitol to urge that laws be passed that would eventually stamp out this relic of barbarism.

The time has passed, if it ever was, when this sickly sentimentality, "Moral suasion and let-it-alone doctrine," would satisfy the ends of justice. The time has come, and now is, when this Government must act, must see that its laws are vindicated, and that its dignity is upheld. But how is this to be done? What laws are needed?

We all agree that the leaders, those who are not only violating and living in open violation of the law themselves, but are urging others to violate and disregard the law, should be punished. How is this to be done? John Taylor, the president of the saintly (?) gang, will stand up and proclaim to the public that he is in polygamy, and is glad of it. And there are plenty of others who do the same thing. They have all violated the law of Congress prohibiting polygamy, but they are protected by the law of limitation. More than three years have expired since they "married another," that is, committed the crime of bigamy. This law of limitation is a perfect protection to them, and will successfully ward off any and all attacks that the Government with its present weapons can make upon them. In other words, the United States says to them, "Now, you *must not live in polygamy,* for if you do, I shall punish you unless you keep it quiet for three years; but if you keep it quiet for three years after your plural marriage, why then you can live in polygamy all the rest of your lives, and you may even go to Congress, and help to make the laws."

First, and above all others, I would have the law of limitation, so far as it affects this crime of bigamy, repealed. Let it be understood by every one, that at no time during his natural life can a man live in polygamy in this country without being liable to prosecution.

It seems to me no worse to live in polygamy the first three years after contracting plural marriage than any subsequent three years. A bill of this kind was introduced by Mr. Willits, of Michigan, during the early part of the present session, and is now in the hands of the Judiciary Committee of the House. Why that committee does not report, is a mystery to the friends of the bill. That such a measure is proper, there can be no question. Why, then, should that committee withhold their report, and thus prevent Congress from acting, and the bill from becoming a law? Let it be once understood by these Mormon law-breakers that time will not cure the offense, but that the strong arm of law is raised, and may at any time fall on their defenseless heads if they dare to violate the law, and there will be a hesitating and reflecting before they take the step. If such a law had been enacted at the time the law forbidding polygamy in the Territories was enacted, three-fourths of the leaders could be punished to-day. If I could have but one law, I would have this to aid the law of '62.

Secondly, I would by law disfranchise every man or woman who lives in polygamy, or aids, abets, or counsels polygamous marriages. Let it be understood that before they can have a voice in governing this country, they must be loyal, and respect the laws. The ruling party here not only violate the solemn mandates of the United States Government, but they openly and publicly defy the Government and its officers to enforce the laws. They laugh in our faces at our efforts, and openly and publicly counsel their people to disregard this law prohibiting polygamy. Polygamy *must be made odious*, and no longer allowed to be a prerequisite to civil Territorial office, as it has been, and is now, to a large extent in this Territory. At least, ninety-five per cent of the last Legislature were polygamists. A monogamist is not, as a rule, allowed to hold an important office. Thus polygamy is at a premium.

A bill should be passed by Congress, and become a law, providing that no man or woman can cast a a vote or hold an office until it clearly appears that they are not living in polygamy; that they have not, and do not, cause, aid, or abet others to contract or consummate plural or bigamous marriages. This bill should contain a test oath, which in substance should be that the person proposing to vote or hold office is not at the time living in polygamy, or with more than one woman whom he calls wife; that he has not, since the passage of the law, counseled, aided, or abetted others, either directly or indirectly, to violate the law prohibiting bigamy or polygamy in the Territories.

That the object of the law might not in any way be defeated, it should further provide that any persons desiring to do so may question the vote of a person required to take the oath, and even introduce witnesses to contradict him; and if it appeared, either by the test oath or by outside testimony, that the person was disqualified by reason of his polygamous relations, or his counsel or acts in relation to others, he should be disfranchised.

Let us no longer press the venomous reptile to our bosoms, and thus, while caressing him, allow him to thrust his poisonous fangs into our bodies; but rather let the Government rise up and throttle him. Let loyalty, not disloyalty, be at a premium. Let the law-abiding American citizen rule the country by his vote, and be the officer who shall make and enforce the laws.

I am convinced that the young men of Utah, sons of the leaders in the Mormon church, would hail the passage of such a law. Such a law would not only make polygamy odious, but it would open the way for the young men of Utah to hold offices of trust and importance. And those young men who do not believe in polygamy, but rather believe in obeying the law, would greatly assist in leading this Territory out of its midnight crime and bigotry into the light of free government. Such a law would Americanize Utah, and this, above all things, is what it needs.

To-day, John Taylor, president of the Mormon church, and his counselors dictate who shall hold

ZION'S CO-OPERATIVE MERCANTILE INSTITUTION.

DESERET NATIONAL BANK BUILDING.

the offices, from delegate down to the lowest place.
This is a theocratic government through and through.
Let Congress pass the law I am asking for, and the
Samson would be, to a great extent, shorn of his
locks. The people who are law-abiding would at once
recognize the fact that the government of this Territory was referred to them, and like true Americans, they would step to the front, and a Republican form of government would be vouchsafed to
Utah. Liberty and freedom to speak, vote, and act
would lighten up benighted Utah. Theocracy, bigotry, and fanaticism would perish, and become as
dead in the black midnight of ignorance. May
God speed the day! Such a bill as this was also
presented by Mr. Willits, early in the present session, and is now in the hands of the Judiciary Committee of the House.

Thirdly, I would have a law enacted forbidding,
and providing a punishment for, adultery and lewd
and lascivious cohabitation in the Territories, and so
define these offenses that there could be no doubt but
that they applied to those living with plural wives;
and I would give the first or legal wife a right to
testify. Such a law would bring consternation to
this polygamous institution. But that there might
not be any spirit of persecution exhibited toward
these deluded women who have been living in polygamy, I would give them a portion of the property, and a reasonable support out of the estate.

This law would reach out and take into its fond
embrace all these leaders, who, week after week,

preach this outrageous doctrine, and advise others to adopt and practice it.

Fourthly, I would say that, next in importance, there is needed a marriage law, something like the Ohio law, which requires a license to issue before a couple can be legally married. This license should be issued from the United States District Court by the clerk, and a record kept; and this, together with the certificate which should be required to be issued by the person performing the ceremony, ought to be made proof of the marriage in all cases in court, including bigamy cases. This law should also forbid, and provide punishment for, secret Endowment House marriages. A law of this kind could be so drafted that we should no longer be at the mercy of those who, in the Endowment House ceremony, have sworn never to reveal what took place.

The present election law is a fraud upon every outsider or non-Mormon, placing everything in the hands of the Mormon church. Also the jury laws need revising. But I will not take time to explain them. We cannot expect all our ills to be cured at once.

There has been too great fear that some law-breaking Mormon might be persecuted. This has been the cry of the Mormons. At home they stalk abroad defying the Government and its laws; but when the Government attempts to put its hands upon them, they go cringing about like whipped curs, and cry, "Don't persecute us, don't persecute us! We are only worshiping God according to the dictates of our own conscience."

I want to see this Government rise up in all its dignity and power, and no longer listen to the whimpering curs who cry persecution. Let it be understood in this Territory that the Government will no longer tolerate this dirty business, that it will enact such laws as those polygamous Government-haters cannot evade and escape, and in a dozen years this country will be regenerated, and polygamy will be odious.

We have soothed and petted this institution too long. Whenever it has cried out persecution, too many have, like Sargent of California, sympathized to the extent of granting that it was their religion, when there is no religion about it, but the reverse—crime.* Don't let us have any more warm, soothing applications, but let us have purgatives in allopathic doses. Let it be understood that this institution will no longer be tolerated. No one need fear the result. They have threatened, and may do so again, but don't fear; there will not be even a ripple on the wave.

When these chaps who are loudest in their threats, once understand that Uncle Sam means business, they will not only subside, but in ten years swear that they never advocated the doctrine.

---

*See Decision of the Supreme Court, in Appendix, page 401.

LETTER NUMBER THREE.

SALT LAKE CITY, UTAH, Jan. 9, 1882.

In a recent publication we were treated to a report of an interview by a *World* reporter with one of our leading Mormons now in New York, himself a polygamist and bishop of the institution called the Church of Jesus Christ of Latter-day Saints.

Our bishop tells the reporter, among other things, "I do not anticipate that Congress will act rashly or unadvisedly, and our own people express no fear of any such action. It would be hard to say what would be the result should the Government act indiscreetly. Our people are peace-loving and law-abiding, but they are not to be trodden upon with impunity."

To us who have lived in the Territory and had to do with this "monstrosity," who have desired so long to see the Government assert itself and stamp out this accursed relic of barbarism, this kind of talk is not new. But this is genuine Mormon buncombe of the mildest kind.

The fact is, there are, out in Utah, a few thousand men and women who are supported by a so-called church, having the base and diabolical doctrine of polygamy as one, if not the principal, of its corner-stones. This so-called church, with its dastardly, law-defying leaders and law-breakers, largely foreigners, occupies a portion of the United States, and enjoys the protection of the laws and the general prosperity brought its members by reason of being within the boundaries of this nation. These men and women say to this Government: "We admit that we violate and destroy your laws. We have done so openly and defiantly since 1862. We have gathered together, out on the mountains and in valleys of one of your Territories, a few thousand people whom we advise to violate your laws, and teach defiance to this country. We never have obeyed, and do not now intend to obey, the law. On the contrary, we openly and defiantly assert, and it is one of the tenets of our so-called church, that we will disobey your laws, and advise others to do so." And now, this bishop, one of the leaders, addressing this Government and its Congress, says, in substance, Be very careful how you act. His exact words are, "It would be hard to say what would be the re-result should the Government act indiscreetly. Our people are peace-loving and law-abiding, but they are not to be trodden upon with impunity."

And this same man claims to be a naturalized citizen of the United States. And to become such, he swore in one of the courts of the United States that he was well disposed toward the Government, that he was attached to the principles of the Constitution, and that he would obey it.

What do you think of this, gentlemen who are called upon to make the laws, and who have the welfare and honor of your country at heart?

In those turbulent days of 1859, '60, and '61, when we heard some of the citizens of this nation say that slavery was a divine institution, and this

Government had better be careful how it interfered; that a certain faction in the nation would resist any such interference, or using the language of this bishop, "It would be hard to say what would be the result should the Government act indiscreetly," such talk in defiance of law, in defiance of loyalty, and in every way opposed to good citizenship, was then called treason. It meant treason then, and no other construction can be put upon it to-day.

And has it come to this, that these Mormons, one hundred thousand strong, are to dictate to the Congress what laws are to be passed?

There is no danger that Congress will pass any laws that will be too extreme. The subject to be dealt with is one that demands heroic treatment. Extraordinary cases demand extraordinary remedies. That something must be done, and done at once, we all agree. And I think I may say that it is generally conceded that mild measures will hardly meet the case. That this is a matter that must receive immediate and decided attention is evident. What shall we do? What will be adequate? These are the questions, and the only questions, to be considered.

I have already expressed myself in a former letter upon the question of needed legislation. I do not intend to again go over the ground, but only desire to call attention to one of the measures I then advocated. A religious fanaticism is very difficult to regulate. It can hardly be done by punishing a few individual fanatics. Every man who has been convicted of polygamy has been looked upon as a martyr, and thus is rather raised in the estimation of the rest of the people. Prosecutions should be pushed, and the law so amended as to make convictions more easily attainable, I might say, possible; but prosecutions and incarcerations in the penitentiary will never break up polygamy in Utah. There was a day when it would, but that day has passed, and to-day something more radical, something determined, must be resorted to. Every man and every woman who lives in polygamy, or who advocates it, and aids and abets the commission of the offense, should be disfranchised. And don't let's have any kid-glove proceedings to arrive at these facts. Let the bill be so drafted that when it becomes a law it will be effective. Let the law be that when a man or woman is challenged at the polls for being a polygamist, he himself must be sworn and examined by his neighbors; that his alleged plural wives and his lawful wife may be called and examined under oath, either privately or publicly, as demanded by the challenger.

No one need be afraid of the consequences. There are a hundred thousand men, women, and children in Utah who would hail the day when such a law would become operative. The Utah Legislature would not have, as it generally does, ninety-five per cent of its members polygamists, and be run by John Taylor and the Mormon leaders in the interest of the Mormon church. Instead of this, the young men of Utah, who are heartily sick of the institution, would come to the front, and we should see a law-abiding people where now we see a law-defying people. Why, think of it! to-day in Utah there is a premium awarded to those who will defy and violate the laws. The polygamist is rewarded by the best and most honorable positions. This law would change this, and the men who obey the law would be rewarded, and so it should be; for I tell you, the man in Utah who resists the demands of these Mormon leaders, and dares to "come out from among them" and be a law-abiding American citizen, is deserving of a reward, whereas to-day he receives just the contrary. He abandons every hope, and shuts out every chance of ever obtaining official position, and subjects himself to the vilest kind of abuse. The passage of this law would revolutionize the politics of Utah, and this alone would be a power in this land which would help materially to solve the vexed question.

But more than this, it would be a continual punishment inflicted upon the men and women who violate the law. There would be no escape, but like the black night of despair it would hover about them, and polygamy would be a mark upon whomsoever dared to violate the law, like the terrible mark that was set upon Cain. And soon they who wear the mark would be driven out, not by force of arms, but by the continual consciousness of being aliens and enemies to the country and its laws.

The passage of such a law would be acting discreetly, and the consequences would be as I have predicted, the bishop to the contrary, notwithstanding.

CHAPTER XXIII.

Views of a Statesman.

BY HON. SCHUYLER COLFAX.*

Mormon Defiance.—Juries.—Female Suffrage.—Right of Dower.—Abolish the Legislature.—Heed the Gentiles.—The Golden Time.

NO one can shut his eyes *now* to the insolent defiance our Mormon Turks have flung into the face of the nation. The worn-out subterfuge of years past, that the United States Supreme Court had not affirmed the constitutionality of the Congressional prohibition of polygamy, is cast aside, since their unanimous decision, as of no further avail. And now the Mormons boldly force the issue. Their many-wived President, John Taylor, has on the eve of the reassembling of Congress, added a wealthy widow to his harem. Their many-wived Congressional Delegate, whose polygamous family has been supported for many years out of the people's taxes by his

---

*This chapter was published in the *Chicago Advance* Dec. 22, 1881, under the title "THE MORMON DEFIANCE TO THE NATION. SUGGESTIONS AS TO HOW IT SHOULD BE MET. The present heading is selected by the Publisher.

salary from the National Treasury, no longer uses words of evasion, nor suggests any policy of compromise or postponement. But to the House of Representatives, over his own signature, he boldly avows his contempt of the national law, both as to his polygamous family and as to his preaching against it to his followers.

Thus Mormonism insultingly asks the nation, "What will you do about it?"

If we are not the most pusillanimous of peoples, if we are worthy the blood so freely shed, first to establish and finally to maintain our Government, our law-makers will answer this bold Mormon challenge by replying that "by the Eternal," who turned our weakness into strength, and gave to us the nation whose protecting flag floats over these ingrates, the laws of the land *shall* be obeyed in Utah as in Dakota, by Mormons as by Protestants and Catholics, Jews, and Gentiles. The Chief Magistrate of whom the cruel bullet of the assassin so recently robbed us,—"inspired," as the murderer claims, like the Mormons, by "a divine revelation"!—pointed the path of duty to the American people in his Inaugural, in which he declared it "a reproach to the Government that, in our most populous Territory, the authority of Congress is set at naught," and demanded that Congress should prohibit within its jurisdiction, all criminal practices, especially that class which destroys family relations, and endangers social order. His successor, who has so won the confidence of the nation, spoke trumpet-tongued in his recent message to the nation, of the duty "to suppress this iniquity, the existing statute for the punishment of this odious crime so revolting to the moral and religious sense of Christendom, having been persistently and contemptuously violated ever since its enactment." The press has responded to both of these Presidential proclamations of national duty with no uncertain sound. The people are aroused on the subject as never before in the past twenty years. The Senators and Representatives of the Republic are at their official posts. The hour for action has come!

What shall be done?

Whoever has studied the Mormon problem on the ground in Utah, and through *their* sermons, speeches, and proclamations, must realize that no halting, mincing, temporizing, tender-footed policy will be of the slightest effect. Better nothing at all than that. A physician might as well treat a malignant, growing cancer with rose-water.

If this polygamous defiance of law, which, through the mistaken and too-forbearing policy of the nation, has been growing and strengthening for over a quarter of a century till it absolutely controls the home legislation of "our most populous Territory," and claims the balance of power in others adjoining, is to be stopped at all, it must be by bold and fearless legislation in the spirit of President Arthur's forcible declaration of "the duty of arraying against the barbarous system ALL THE POWER which, under the Constitution and laws, can be wielded for its *destruction.*" Golden words, indeed! The nation must strike at this defiant monster-evil with all its might, vigorously and emphatically, to show the offenders that it has resolved on its extirpation; and so effectively, also, that what it destroys in a Territory shall never be able to be revived in any future State, to become bastioned against attack thereafter by State power and State rights.

To achieve this result, the following suggestions are offered, although the writer is conscious that they may be much improved and strengthened by our law-makers:—

1. Juries should be impaneled by the U. S. Marshal of Utah exactly as in other Territories and States, from law-abiding citizens only. How few of the readers of this article know that by a most unwise law, enacted under our unwise "conciliating" policy, the Mormon officials select, in Utah, half the names from whom the U. S. jurors are to be drawn! As well expect to put down gambling by allowing gamblers to select half the juries who are to try them for their offenses!

2. Without any reference to the general question of Female Suffrage in communities where what President Arthur justly calls this "barbarous system" does not prevail, the Mormons of Utah should not be allowed to vote their submissive harems by the wholesale in favor of polygamy, at either Congressional or Territorial elections. Nor should these surplus wives be allowed to claim land as "the head of a family," to help enrich their husbands,—a right

denied to legal wives anywhere,—both cases holding out a premium, in power and in possessions, to polygamy as against law-abiding citizens.

3. The right of dower, which has been abolished by the Utah Legislature (so as to render a polygamous wife slavishly dependent on the husband's favor for any share of his property after his death, for herself or her children), should be re-enacted by national legislation, and carefully guarded for the legal wife, who, in polygamy, is not the favorite as a general rule. This would greatly discourage women from marrying a polygamist.

4. The District of Columbia had for years a Territorial Legislature. Congress, however, by the assent of both parties, believed such a body could be dispensed with there, and it is now governed by three Commissioners, under the supervision of the direct legislation of Congress. Every member of the Utah Legislature whose *per diem* and expenses are paid for out of the National Treasury, holds the national law in utter contempt; and nearly, if not quite, all of them are practical polygamists. Why not try *there* exactly the same experiment that is being tested now in the District of Columbia; namely, abolish the Legislature, saving all its expense to the Treasury, and have instead, a Board of governing Commissioners, under the supervision of the National Congress. The Constitutional power is the same in both regions. The need for its exercise is far greater West than East. Only in this way can the union of Church and State in the Legislature be effectively abolished.

5. Enact that as Utah is confessedly exceptional in its outspoken determination to defy the national law, no citizens thereof shall enjoy the benefit of the Land, Patent, or Naturalization laws, unless they declare under oath that they have not violated any law of the land, and specifically the law that is so contemptuously trampled under foot in that Territory; and this should also be subject to disproval by competent evidence. The exceptional crime and the willful criminals should be banned by exceptional law.

6. Heed the Gentile appeal from Utah that the open living in polygamy should be the crime punished rather than the ceremony, which is guarded by secret and oath-bound ceremonies of the Endowment House, which the leaders refuse to testify about in court.

7. I do not underrate the value of the suggestion that in the Territories a woman married to a bigamist should be a legal witness against him on his trial. There is the same justice in this as in allowing a woman, imposed on by a mock marriage, to testify. But this would be more effective *after*, rather than *before*, the legislation suggested above.

But by itself this seventh proposition would be of little avail. Beguiled, induced, almost forced by the public opinion there, and by the increased happiness in heaven promised by their creed, the women debased by this relation, must needs justify and eulogize it thereafter, or else proclaim themselves and their children dishonored.

Now is the golden hour of Opportunity and of Power too. Congress, by fearless, direct legislation, can cleanse the Territory, while it is a Territory, from this barbaric institution which degrades woman, defies your national law, scouts at your national judiciary, mocks at your national authority, stains your national escutcheon, and reviles all who lift their voices against it. No matter what may be one's politics—Republican, Democrat, or Greenbacker—Northern or Southern by residence, Eastern or Western—this is a question outside of party and, indeed, higher than party. Strike at it with bold, vigorous legislation; with prohibition that *will* prohibit; and when the leaders realize that the nation is in earnest, and has stirred itself in righteous wrath, the beginning of the end will be here, and the institution will tumble into ruin and disgrace.

But if the insulting defiance of Mormondom to the nation does not arouse Congress to the duty of vindicating its insulted laws, do not ask the Gentiles there—a faithful few among the faithless found—to keep up the unequal contest. They have, against all the ruling influences of public opinion and of numbers, kept the flag flying there on which is inscribed that true motto of a Republic, "Obedience to the Law." They have petitioned the American people for effective help in the struggle. They have voted and argued, written and spoken, year after year, Congress after Congress; but all in vain. Mormonism at last takes the aggressive. For decency's sake, if nothing more, the Gentiles plead that while dungeons open for bigamists elsewhere, Congress shall not honor with one of its chairs the publicly avowed representative bigamist of Utah. If this ulcer is not to be extirpated, what is to become of the heart of our Republic in the next quarter of a century? Rapidly growing in numbers by natural causes as well as by immigration from abroad, the Mormons will control the other Territories around them by their great resources of colonization; and Interior America will be given up to the worst phase of Asiatic barbarism. May patriotism, and firmness, and fearlessness, before it becomes too late, avert this direful consummation.

CHAPTER XXIV.

The Redeeming Agencies.

BY C. G. G. PAINE, A. M.

Threatening Aspect.—Past Political History.—Legislation Powerless to Reform.—Congregational Churches.—Salt Lake Academy. New West Education Commission.—Roman Catholics.—Episcopal Church.—The Hebrews.—The Presbyterians.—Salt Lake Collegiate Institute.—The Methodists.—The Baptists.—The Press.

NO thoughtful and intelligent reader has carefully perused the preceding pages without being forced to the conclusion that there is a great and growing evil in our country, which not only threatens the peace of every home in the land, but has already become a source of great anxiety to those who desire national happiness and prosperity.

The supporters of this great evil hold the exclusive control in some, and bid fair soon to have it in several, of those large Territories in the New West, which should soon become States. And unless they are speedily checked in their hitherto victorious career, they will ere long control the nation.

Those who have studied the Mormon question only superficially, but yet think they know all about it, may say these are the words of a croaker and a false prophet, and assert that it is utterly impossible for so small a body of men to attain such power.

But surely those who assert this must have forgotten the past political history of the Mormon church. They do not remember how the Mormons, while located at Nauvoo, and when only a few hundred in number, controlled the government of the great State of Illinois, deciding who should hold the offices in their county, who should represent their district in Congress, and who should be the governor of the State.

They must be ignorant of the fact that for more than thirty years the Mormon priesthood have set at defiance the national authority, and have killed or driven out of the Territory many of the United States governors, judges, and other officers who were sent there by the strong (?) arm of the nation.

They have not read how the Legislature of Idaho, when the Governor sent a message urging some action against polygamy, contemptuously laid it upon the table.

These facts concerning the past and present of Mormonism show how skillful it is to use its strength, and to what it aims. As evenly as parties are balanced, it needs to have the control of but two or three States to control the nation; hence the national danger.

The facts in the chapter on "The Spread of Mormonism in the United States" show how quietly and insidiously it steals into our homes, and robs us of our loved ones before we even suspect danger.

When these facts have made their due impression upon the mind of the reader, the question naturally springs to the lips of every one, "What can we do?" The very asking of the question shows that all instinctively feel that something ought to be done; and that feeling has a good and right foundation. Something ought to be done, and that speedily.

The preceding papers by Judge Van Zile show that much radical legislation is needed,—legislation which will place the power in the hands of men who will see that just laws are made and executed.

But legislation is not the only thing that is needed. Says Rev. Chas. R. Bliss, Secretary of the New West Education Commission, in a recent letter to the *Advance*:—

"The question at issue is not one of justice, but one of discretion; not whether it is right to uproot Mormonism by law, but whether it can be done by law. What is Mormonism? It is not polygamy, but something deeper, more subtle, more menacing. Polygamy is only a branch of Mormonism, not its root. Were it destroyed, the system, with its organized disloyalty, its hostile purpose, and its social corruption, would be but slightly impaired. Mormonism is a firmly-knit social and religious organization, bound together by memories of common suffering and ties of common interest, interlinked by a thousand cunning devices, administered by numerous eagle-eyed, secret officers, and so managed as to place in a few hands large revenues and the reins of a subtle and pervasive power. It is an organization so compact and vigorous that it can and does retain and increase its power, found peoples, and govern new towns, send its outposts far into surrounding Territories, and through them control the ballot and shape political action hundreds of miles from Salt Lake City.

"It is folly to expect that such an organization will yield to the ordinary forces of civilization, and die of itself. For at least fifteen years it has been brought face to face with the ordinary forces of civilization, and yet to-day it is stronger in numbers, confidence, and inherent energy than it ever was before. Polygamy, save in a few centers where Gentile influence is marked, is increasing. Said a prominent apostle in a country town to the writer last October, 'There have been more polygamous marriages in this community in the last eighteen months than for ten years before; even very young men and women are being urged into it.' Temples are being pushed to completion, sermons are as confident, ceremonies are as carefully observed, conferences as numerously attended, as ever. Certainly, if the ordinary forces of civilization are strong enough to destroy it, some impression ought to be visible. There are reasons for the failure, and these are in the organization itself. It has vitality. It inures to the pecuniary advantages of many. It is a powerful political engine. It appeals to certain lower instincts, which makes it welcome to the mass of its adherents. It finds in the ignorance of its dupes full opportunity to enforce its monstrous claims to divine inspiration. It appeals to an honest, though mistaken, religious feeling. It inflames devotion by pointing to martyrdoms and hurling epithets of scorn at the National Government, which it denounces as cruel and vindictive. To call such an organization a 'mere local nuisance' is easy; but to say that, being such, it will yield to the ordinary forces of civilization, and die out, is to betray a lamentable ignorance of what it is."

No great question of morals can be settled simply by law. One of the Representatives to Congress has recently stated that the great difficulty in enforcing laws against polygamy is that the sentiment of the people is against the laws.

That is no excuse for not making laws in such a form as to remove the difficulties as far as possible in the way of their execution, and this is what the Gentiles have been urging for years.

Let Congress pass such laws as the officers of the government in Utah have long been asking for; let President Taylor, Delegate Cannon, and a few of the other leaders of the Mormon church be sent to the penitentiary for a term of years, and it will have a salutary effect in inspiring respect for national authority.

Still the difficulty mentioned of a wrong public sentiment is not wholly removed. How shall this be remedied?—By the same means that are employed to correct wrong public sentiment on other moral questions.

This sentiment springs from ignorance or erroneous teaching, or both. Ignorance must be supplanted by knowledge, and erroneous instruction counteracted by that which is correct and wholesome.

There are three powerful engines for doing this work everywhere,—the school, the church, and the press. When these three work together, hand in hand, their success is certain.

Let us not despair, then. Legal suasion, backed by the strong arm of the nation in concert with moral suasion, which is sustained by the prayers, sympathies, and contributions of the Christians of every faith, will secure the right, and that must prevail.

In mentioning the three moral agencies, the school was purposely placed first; because from the peculiar exigencies of the case, this must be the pioneer.

To understand the reason for this, we must briefly consider the condition and teachings of the Mormon schools and churches.

It has been stated in the preceding pages, that the emigrants are generally from the ignorant and uneducated classes of Europe, and they have no opportunities for acquiring an education after they arrive, as many of the adult foreigners do who settle in other sections. Neither have they the same stimulus, even if they had the opportunity.

Then the schools are of the poorest kind. The teachers themselves are poorly prepared for their work. The highest Mormon school for training teachers and professional men is the Deseret University, located at Salt Lake, and it would compare unfavorably with the high schools of other sections. The school-houses are of the poorest kind, and are not furnished with the modern appliances for aiding the teacher in his work.

Everything about them is unattractive and repulsive. Moreover, none of these schools are free; but while a part of the support is raised by taxation, all the pupils are required to pay tuition. This, in a community where the people are so poor that the children never see a penny, but if they want a slate pencil, take an egg to the store to pay for it, helps to keep the children away.

John Taylor, the president of the Mormon church, is the superintendent of the schools in the Territory. Consequently, they are all managed in the interest of the church, and the children are all instructed in the dogmas of Mormonism.

The sermons in the churches are not such as to educate and awaken thought, but are largely denunciations of the national Government and of the Gentiles, arguments in favor of polygamy, and exhortations to obey the peculiar instructions of the priesthood. As shown by competent testimony, they are often low and obscene; and yet to this people, living in the very center of our own land, a part of our very nation, no effort was made to carry the gospel with its civilizing influences until the year 1865, and practically almost nothing was done until within the last decade!

CONGREGATIONAL CHURCH.

Rev. Norman McLeod, Chaplain of California Volunteers stationed at Camp Douglas, was the first to make an effort for the Christianization of this people. Jan. 22, 1865, he preached the first evangelical sermon in Salt Lake City, and soon after organized the Congregational Church and Society.

With the aid of the Young Men's Literary Association, funds were raised for the purchase of a lot, and the erection of a building, rightly named "Independence Hall," which served for church services, Sunday-school, lectures, etc. This Hall has served as the rallying place for the Gentiles from that time, and has been used as a starting point by several other denominations, as they have successively engaged in Christian work here. A full history of this Hall is in the Appendix.

Rev. Mr. McLeod organized a Sabbath-school of which Dr. J. K. Robinson was superintendent. He also delivered lectures upon polygamy which aroused a great deal of interest and controversy, and excited the anger of the Mormons.

In 1866 he went East to raise funds to build a church, and while there was called before a committee of Congress to testify in regard to the workings of polygamy. His testimony so increased the indignation of the Mormons that they threatened his life if he returned to the Territory. Meanwhile, Dr. Robinson, his Sunday-school superintendent, had been shot down in the street in cold blood, and Mr. McLeod's friends in the Territory advised him not to return, so the enterprise was abandoned for a time.

In 1872 he returned for a few months. In the fall of 1873 Rev. Walter M. Barrows was sent by the American Home Missionary Society to prosecute the enterprise anew. He remained until the summer of 1881, when he was called to New York to become the Assistant Secretary of the American Home Missionary Society. His church had then increased till its membership exceeded 150.

A Congregational church has also been organized at Park City, and a missionary stationed at Bountiful, and several others will soon be sent into the Territory.

SALT LAKE ACADEMY.

Mr. Barrows, noting the success of the few schools already established in the Territory under Christian auspices, and the similarity between the people here and in heathen lands, saw that the work must be carried on here in the same way as by foreign missionaries,—the church and the school must go together, hand in hand, and in many cases the school must be the forerunner and prepare the way for the church. The teacher must be a Christian missionary, and carry the Gospel.

To do this, he saw the need of Christian teachers trained on the ground, and directed his energies to the establishment of an unsectarian Christian school which should eventually grow into a college. As a result of his labors, Salt Lake Academy was incorporated in the summer of 1878, under the laws of Utah. Prof. Edward Benner, formerly connected with Drury College, Mo., was appointed principal. The Academy opened in September, 1878, with two teachers. It is now in its fourth year of successful work, and has two hundred and twenty pupils. The trustees are erecting a fine edifice to cost $30,000. It greatly needs endowment to enable it to carry on its work more successfully.

THE NEW WEST EDUCATION COMMISSION.

The necessity of establishing Christian schools in all parts of Mormondom was early seen and forcibly urged by Rev. Mr. Barrows in the *Home Missionary*, December, 1878. The writer of this chapter laid the subject before the assembled Congregational pastors of Chicago in April 1879, and delivered addresses in many of the larger cities of the interior. The Congregational Association of Illinois, June, 1879, appointed a committee to confer with the American Home Missionary Society, and urged immediate action. During the same season, President Tenney of Colorado College secured the appointment of a Christian Commission. But upon further consideration a new organization was found necessary, and the New West Education Commission was incorporated under the laws of Illinois, November 3, 1879, with headquarters in Chicago. Its purpose, as defined in its charter, is: "The promotion of Christian civilization in Utah and adjacent States and Territories, by the education of children and youth under Christian teachers, and also by the use of such kindred agencies as may at any time be deemed desirable." Rev. F. A. Noble, D. D., of Chicago, is the president, and Rev. Charles R. Bliss is the secretary and superintendent of its work.

This Commission has assumed the care of the academies at Salt Lake, Utah, and at Santa Fe and Albuquerque, New Mexico, which had already been established under the auspices of Colorado College. It has opened two others at Las Végas, New Mexico, and Trinidad, Colorado. The Commission has also opened flourishing primary schools at Salt Lake City, Farmington, Hooper, Stockton, Brigham, Lehi, Sandy, Bountiful, Coalville, and Weber; so that it now has under its care five academies with nearly six hundred pupils, and ten primary schools with about five hundred pupils, and this number is being increased as fast as the means are furnished. Their expenditures for the year ending September 1, 1882, are about $41,000.

The following statement in regard to one of these schools will illustrate their working and influence:—

In October, 1880, Miss Lydia M. Tichenor of Chicago, a graduate of the Cook County Normal School, who after several years of successful experience as a teacher in the public schools, had been laboring as church missionary of the Lincoln Park Congregational church, was sent by the Commission to open a school at Hooper, a Mormon town about thirteen miles southwest of Ogden.

She found here no Christian helper. Possessed in an eminent degree of tact and the power to influence others, and fired with the missionary spirit, she opened her school with seventeen pupils from six to eighteen years of age. None could write without a copy, or read writing. She had no chair, table, bell, clock, map, chart, text-books, chalk, or anything else for teacher's use, and scarcely an article of the kind needful for school purposes could be found in the place. Before the close of the year nearly eighty pupils were enrolled.

Soon after opening the day-school she organized a Sunday-school which she was obliged to teach entirely herself for a time. (This school was attended by nearly all her day scholars and by many others.) She skillfully employed some of the young men as clerk, etc., and soon a number of the Mormon young men began to come in. As their attendance was forbidden by the bishop, they obeyed him by stopping in the outer room where, however, they could hear all that was said.

At the request of the young people she began in the spring to hold religious service Sabbath evenings, at which she had very large and attentive congregations. Her work was conducted so wisely and well that even the Mormon bishop acknowledged in a conference of Mormon officials that the influence of her school was good.

Miss Tichenor has for some months been successfully employed by the Commission in addressing the Eastern churches and raising funds for their work. Meanwhile her school work goes forward.

The Commission is buying places for school purposes costing from $500 to $1500 each, which are also used by the home missionary who follows in the wake of the teacher. The secretary, Rev. Charles R. Bliss, writes: "It is an interesting fact that the New Academy building is on the site taken by the Mormon bishop Wooley. His residence was upon it, and in the very parlors he furnished and occupied we have a primary school, and I heard the little children singing Christian songs where he concocted plans for getting what he could out of Mormon dupes. There is poetic justice and a feeling of compensation in Divine Providence."

THE ROMAN CATHOLICS.

The second attempt to establish a mission in Utah was made by Rev. E. Kelly, a Roman Catholic priest, in the summer of 1866. Although he spent some time in Salt Lake, and raised money with which to purchase a lot, he did not succeed in founding a church.

In the spring of 1871, Rev. P. Walsh was appointed pastor of the Territory, and raised funds with which he erected a handsome church.

His successor, Rev. L. Scanlan, has erected churches in Ogden and Silver Reef, and opened schools at each of the three cities; also the Hospital of the Holy Cross at Salt Lake, and St. John's Hospital at Silver Reef.

At the Hospital of the Holy Cross, which was opened in 1876, three physicians are in charge; over

2000 patients are treated annually, and many surgical operations have been successfully performed.

THE PROTESTANT EPISCOPAL CHURCH.

The third missionary effort in the Territory was inaugurated by Right Rev. Daniel S. Tuttle, bishop of the Diocese in which Utah was included. He sent Rev. Geo. W. Foote and Rev. Thomas W. Haskins to Salt Lake City in May 1867. They found but two communicants of their own faith, and only twenty of all Christian denominations. They held their services in Independence Hall, and organized a Sunday-school which grew and flourished in spite of the Mormon priesthood.

St. Mark's Grammar School, the first Gentile school in Utah, was opened in July 1867, by Rev. Mr. Haskins, with only sixteen pupils; but in January, 1882, it had four hundred and eighty. A tuition fee was charged, but those unable to pay were admitted free. Schools have also been established under the auspices of the Episcopal church at Ogden, Logan, and Plain City.

In 1871 they erected a church edifice in Salt Lake City, at a cost of $45,000. A fine school edifice has also been erected, capable of accommodating nearly five hundred pupils. In 1881 Rowland Hall was started as a boarding school for girls.

Bishop Tuttle removed to Salt Lake City in July, 1867, and has resided there since. The statistics of the Episcopal church in Utah, as taken from his last annual report, August 1, 1881, are as follows:—

THE REDEEMING AGENCIES. 379

Clergymen in the Territory,	6
Churches in the Territory,	4
School-houses in the Territory,	4
Communicants,	359
Sunday-school Teachers,	48
Sunday-school Scholars,	710
Parish-school Teachers,	21
Parish-school Scholars,	711
Value of Church Property,	$161,400
Offerings for Church Purposes,	18,830

St. Mark's Hospital was started in 1872, and was the first ever opened in Utah. Rev. R. M. Kirby has been the superintendent of this from the first, with an ample corps of physicians; but has recently resigned. From three hundred to four hundred patients are treated in it yearly. All miners in the Territory can enjoy its benefits by paying into the hands of the Treasurer one dollar per month, which secures them board, medical attendance, and treatment when needed.

THE HEBREWS.

The Hebrew congregation numbers one hundred members. They have two benevolent societies which have disbursed over $2300 to the poor in a single year.

Utah is said to be the only place in the world where the Jew prides himself on being a Gentile. These Jewish citizens are liberal patrons of the Gentile schools, and have ever been firm supporters of the Government, and friends of every measure tending to the welfare and prosperity of the Territory.

METHODISM IN UTAH.

May 8, 1870, Rev. G. M. Peirce, the first Methodist preacher appointed to labor in Utah, arrived with his family at Salt Lake City and began the work of planting Methodism in Mormon soil. He

METHODIST EPISCOPAL CHURCH, SALT LAKE.

hired an unfinished hay-loft over a livery-stable and fitted it up for church services. October 16, 1871, ground was broken for the present church edifice which was erected at a cost of about $50,000, and includes auditorium and rooms for the Rocky Mountain Seminary. The church was dedicated the last of December, 1871, although only one story was finished, and was the first regular church dedicated in Utah.

The Methodists now have eight churches, with one hundred and eighty-nine members. They have seven church buildings and three parsonages, valued at about $63,000. They have eight Sunday-schools, with about seventy-two officers and teachers, and six hundred and thirty-five scholars. Their total contributions for benevolence, and incidental expenses, for the past year amounted to $3,433.89.

They established their first day-school September 20, 1870, at Salt Lake City, which has been carried on with varied success, but now seems to be well established under the care of Rev. T. B. Hilton, A. M. They have also opened schools at Ogden, Toelle, Provo, and Beaver. Rev. G. M. Peirce is Superintendent of Missions, and Rev. L. A. Rudisill Corresponding Secretary,—both located at Salt Lake City. There are now eleven clergymen and thirteen teachers employed by the Methodist Episcopal church in carrying on its mission work in Utah.

THE PRESBYTERIAN CHURCH.

The Presbyterians commenced their work in Utah in 1870, at Corinne, a Gentile town on the Central Pacific railroad.

Rev. J. Welch commenced work in Salt Lake City, in October, 1871, and organized a church of twelve members in November following.

In 1874 a church edifice was erected, the house and lot costing about $30,000. The church now has ninety-seven members, and Rev. Robert G. McNeice is the successful pastor.

In February, 1875, Rev. D. J. McMillan, a Presbyterian clergyman from Southern Illinois, who was spending the winter in Utah for his health, went into the Mormon town of Mt. Pleasant, where there was not a single Gentile family, and bought an unfinished building that had been erected for a dancehouse, and fitted it up for a school-room and a church. This was the first school opened by the Presbyterians in the Territory, and the first one in an exclusive Mormon community. Although at the peril of his life,* he remained at his post, and has pushed forward the work in Central and Southern Utah, until now the Presbyterians have more schools and churches than any other denomination in the Territory. He is now the General Superintendent of Missions.

April 12, 1875, Prof. J. M. Coyner of Indianapolis, Indiana, opened the Salt Lake Collegiate Institute in the basement of the newly erected Presbyterian church.

Opening with only thirty pupils, it has increased till at the present time it has two hundred enrolled.

It has a fine two-story building valued at $18,000, and capable of accommodating two hundred and twenty-five pupils, with a fully equipped boarding department which can accommodate forty pupils and teachers. Over six hundred pupils have been in attendance since its organization.

The Presbyterians have at the present time thirty-three schools, forty-six teachers, ten churches,

---

* See Appendix, page 414.

seventeen ministers, and thirty-one Sunday-schools, and have about two thousand children, chiefly of Mormon parentage, under their instruction. These schools and churches are scattered throughout the whole Territory.

THE BAPTISTS.

The Baptists organized their first church in Utah, May 20, 1881, with thirteen members, which membership has been nearly doubled. They are planning to erect a $5000 church during 1882. Rev. Richard Hartley is the pastor, and Rev. Dwight Spencer is also laboring in the Territory as a missionary. They hope to open a day-school during this year.

The Mormon leaders are of course very much opposed to these Christian schools, and forbid the people to patronize them, and often excommunicate them from the church if they persist in sending their children. But the more intelligent and liberal of the Mormons, as they come in contact with the Gentiles, see the need of having their children educated, and in many cases disregard the orders and anathemas of the church authorities.

Thus the schools serve as an entering wedge to help throw off the authority of the bishops and liberate the people from the slavery under which they have so long labored.

Many of the Mormons are ready to contribute to the support of the schools. When the school was opened in Park City, one Mormon contributed $50;

but as he had thirty-nine children it was said he could well afford to do so. A Mormon who has several wives recently offered two stone buildings to the New West Education Commission, rent free, and is willing to deed it to them outright for educational purposes.

Very few of the churches could have been established had not the school gone first and prepared the way. Moreover these schools are exerting a great influence upon the public schools sustained by the Mormons; as they see the necessity of improving them in order to keep their children from being drawn to the Christian schools.

There is now an open door all through Utah for the establishment of schools as fast as means can be obtained.

One of the most useful laws Congress could pass would be one which should authorize the President to appoint a Superintendent of schools, for the Territory, and invest him and the Governor and Secretary with absolute control over the schools, so that they should not be used to instruct children in the doctrines of the Mormon church. No measure could have a greater influence in civilizing this people and preparing them for Statehood. Indeed, this law should be made general, applying to all the Territories.

The Press also is exerting no small influence against this great evil, by showing up its iniquities and absurdities.

The *Salt Lake Tribune*, established in 1870, has done and is doing valuable service. It has a large circulation and deserves to be liberally sustained.

The *Rocky Mountain Christian Advocate*, established in 1876, and edited by Rev. G. M. Peirce and Rev. L. A. Rudisill, is the organ of the Methodist Episcopal church. It circulates in all parts of the country, and wherever it goes it utters no uncertain sound in regard to this crying sin.

The *Anti-Polygamy Standard*, started in 1881, is the organ of the Woman's National Anti-Polygamy Society. It has had great influence in swelling and directing the current of public opinion which is to result in the utter annihilation of this foul blot on our national history.

In addition to the influence of the local press, the leading journals of the country are taking up the question of polygamy in Utah, and discussing it as a living issue, which demands the attention of statesmen, and the thoughtful consideration of all who have at heart the welfare of our nation. This cannot fail to have a powerful influence in molding public opinion, and will prove a strong auxiliary in the crusade against the evil.

The mines, too, are attaining great importance, and by bringing a large number of Gentiles into the Territory are helping on all the other "redeeming agencies." Indeed, the financial aspect of the question seems destined to play an important part in the solution of the difficulty. The material resources of the Territory, aside from its mineral wealth, are attracting the attention of prospective settlers from various portions of Christendom. The effect of constant immigration will be the creation of a healthy public sentiment within the Territory itself, which, unless the remedy is sooner reached, will lead to an uprising, and the final overthrow of the iniquitous system.

Earnest Christians who are looking for a place where they can have good business prospects and where their influence is needed, should consider the claims of this Territory. As immigration societies were formed to help keep Kansas a free State, so the same plans might prove an efficient aid in the redemption of Utah.

INDEPENDENCE HALL,
SALT LAKE CITY, UTAH

Appendix.

Independence Hall. (By Hon. O. J. Hollister, Salt Lake City, Utah.)—The Pioneers in Providing for Social, Educational, and Religious Necessities of the Non-Mormons of Utah Territory. Decision of the Supreme Court.—Polygamy not Religion.—The Illustrations of this Work.—Judge McKean.—Perils of a Missionary.

THE homely adobe building on Third South, just west of Main street, belonging to the First Congregational church of this city, popularly known as Independence Hall, is one of the remarkable buildings of Utah. It was the first crystallization in bricks and mortar of Gentile tendencies in Salt Lake, social, religious, and political. It was the point, if not the seed, whence started the Christian churches and scores of connected schools now among the most powerful influences affecting the destiny of this Territory. The Sunday-school system of the Mormons, even now having an attendance of more than thirty thousand, had its direct and immediate incentive in the Sunday-school opened in Independence Hall by Charles H. Hempstead, Frank B. Gilbert, and William Sloan, in connection with the Rev. Norman McLeod's First Congregational church and society, and of which Dr. J. King Robinson was superintendent when he was assassinated. Sunday-schools had previously been attempted in one or two wards of the city, but they were dying or already dead when the thronging attendance of this school forced their revival, and the opening of the others followed until they became universal.

YOUNG MEN'S LITERARY ASSOCIATION.

One must recall the condition of Utah nearly twenty years ago to get at the origin of Independence Hall. The civil war was at its height, and the Mormons, in exclusive possession of Utah, were hoping for and expecting the fulfillment of Latter-day prophecy by the mutual destruction of North and South. General Connor arrived at Salt Lake in the second year of the war with the California Volunteers, and established Camp Douglas and a provost guard in the city. Gold was discovered in Idaho and Montana about this time, and the Volunteers scattered out and found mines in various parts of Utah. The commerce of the plains, carried on by huge wagon trains, was at its height, and Salt Lake City was an important point in its distribution. But at the beginning of 1864 it was still impossible to gather the Gentiles of the city and camp together in any capacity. There were no Christian churches, no mission schools, no Odd Fellows, no Masons, no clubs, no hotels, no society, politics, or religion; and from the fact that the First Presidency of the Mormon church has dared within the past year to curse, " in the name of Israel's God," the Saint who should sell a city lot to a Gentile, we may get some idea of the condition and outlook of Gentile interests in Utah seventeen years ago. Toward the end of 1864 (Nov. 17), a few bright and active spirits met for the second time in the Provost Marshal's office and organized the Young Men's Literary Association. One year later they celebrated their first anniversary by a dedicatory dance in the new Independence Hall, at which one hundred couple were present, and $292 cleared. There were few of the gentler sex among them. Their ball tickets were $2 for a gentleman with lady, but $5 for a gentleman alone. For its reunions, debates, readings, lectures, socials, and dances, the association rented at $100, then at $125, a month, the upper part of Daft's store,—the building now occupied by Day & Co. The active members were Frank B. Gilbert, D. D. Stover, R. A. Keyes, Wm. P. Appleby, Samuel Dean, Elias Ransohoff, Horace Wheat, Samuel Kahn, Charles H. Hempstead, William Sloan, John W. Kerr, J. Mechling, Howard Livingston, Samuel J. Lees, J King Robinson, Fred Auerbach, Nelse Boukofsky, John Cunnington, S. S. Walker, John Bowman, W H. Whitchill, and others, many of whom have gone to other parts or have finally laid down life's burden. All the Federal officers, most of the officers of the Volunteers at the camp, and all the distinguished gentlemen who visited the city in 1865, were members, either active or honorary.

FIRST CONGREGATIONAL CHURCH.

As near as can be learned at this moment, General Connor made the acquaintance of the Congregational minister, Rev. Norman McLeod, and through his influence the Y. M. L. A., before it was a month old, sent him an invitation to come to Salt Lake. He arrived January 19th, 1865, and on Sunday (the 22d) preached in the Association Hall, from the text, " Can any good come out of Nazareth? Come and see;" and this was the first Christian service ever held in Utah, so far as known to the writer. In the evening of the same day he preached at Camp Douglas, and thereafter for some time regularly in the city and at the camp. Within a month the First Congregational church and society were organized, and two Sunday-schools, one at the camp and one in the Association Hall, were established, the latter soon being cramped for room.

INDEPENDENCE HALL.

Naturally, the Church and Society and the Association began soon to look for permanent quarters. A lot was bargained for, and the Literary Committee of the Association, which, by the way, was its chief working organ, circulated a subscription paper on Main street—the first of such a series as never was presented to, and so generously patronized by, any equal number of men before. It soon footed up $4,000 (It is a pity the original, or a copy, has not been preserved), and toward the end of the season the house was quickly thrown together. The lot cost $2,500, the house probably about $5,000. Mr. McLeod went to California in October and raised $1,440 in gold, equivalent to perhaps $2,200 in currency; but there was left an indebtedness on the property of about $1,200, which it took just ten years to pay off, the rents barely meeting the interest and keeping it in repair. The deed runs from Samuel J. Lees to John Titus, P. Edward Connor, Wm. Sloan, Charles H. Hempstead, D. Fred Walker, John W. Kerr, Howard Livingston, Samuel Kahn, J. Mechling, Dr. Griswold, and George W. Carleton, Trustees of the First Church of Jesus Christ (Congregational) and of the First Christian Society connected with that church. The property is described as "the E. 6 rods, W. ½ of lot 6, block 51, containing 60 square rods, as platted in Great Salt Lake City survey." Early in 1866 Mr. McLeod went East, more as politician than pastor, the Y. M. L. A. voting him a send-off of $200. He visited Washington as a witness before a House Committee on Utah affairs, and in October following was returning to his post, when he was met at Leavenworth by letters announcing the assassination of Dr. J. K. Robinson, and directing him not to return just then, as it was believed to be unsafe for him to do so. He was instructed by the Trustees to resume his lecturing and soliciting for the common cause, which he did, raising $2,540 gross in five months. Expenses reduced this by about one-third, and the balance was afterward voted him as compensation in part for his services.

TURBULENT TIMES.

By this time the general situation had materially changed. The California Volunteers had been discharged, and Camp Douglas was garrisoned by "Galvanized rebels," Confederate prisoners who had enlisted in the Union service. Idaho and Montana had found sources of supply independent of Salt Lake, and business grew dull. The church reasserted itself, and inaugurated a small reign of terror by the assassination of Robinson and of Brassfield, and by other acts of violence. Gentiles left the Territory; their press, the "Vidette," lost its patronage, was obliged to reduce its size and force and all but surrender its principles, and some strong Gentile houses were bankrupted by church ostracism. The Federal officers appointed by President Johnson were indifferent Gentiles, if not Jack Mormons. The first attempts at mining had failed. All Gentile interests were in a bad way, and might have been crushed out had not the building of the overland railroad revived them. After the start, Mr. McLeod's work was more political than pastoral, and more abroad than in Utah. He entered into it with all his energies, and church work was neglected for eight years after 1865.

THE EPISCOPAL MISSION.

The Hall was still the center of religious and educational work. Reverends Thomas W. Haskins and George L. Foote came to Salt Lake in the spring

PUBLIC BUILDINGS IN SALT LAKE CITY.

of 1867 (Bishop Daniel S. Tuttle following in July,) to found an Episcopal mission. Sunday, May 3d, 1867, they held service in Independence Hall, and started a Sunday-school; and they continued both in the Hall, gradually gaining in strength, until they moved into the basement of their own church in June, 1871. They first used their present audience-room in September of that year.

ST. MARK'S SCHOOL.

They started St. Mark's Grammar School in what is now the Walker House cooking range, the old bowling-saloon of Dr. Robinson. They moved from that to Independence Hall, then to a house opposite the Walker House, then back to Independence Hall, which they occupied from September 1, 1868, to September 1, 1870, two years. When on November 1, 1872, they were ready to move into their new school-house, nearly opposite the City Hall, the Rev. Mr. Haskins wrote Major Hempstead a note, asking of him the favor of a short address, sketching the history of St. Mark's School, "which takes its root, you know," wrote Mr. Haskins, "from yourself and McLeod, as the day-school was a growth from the Sunday-school." From that day to this, every Christian mission in Utah has grown day-schools from its Sunday-schools in the same manner.

OTHER CHRISTIAN MISSIONS.

The Methodists now took the Hall for their day-school and used it nearly a year, and this was the starting point of the Rocky Mountain Seminary and all the Methodist schools in Utah. The Episcopalians still using the Hall on Sundays, the Methodists had their services over Faust's livery stable. During this year, 1871, the Trustees were disposed to sell the property for school purposes. They invited proposals from Mr. Haskins, and got them from the Presbyterians. Mr. McLeod consented, on condition that it brought its full value and the proceeds were not diverted from their original purpose. But no trade was made. The Presbyterians used the Liberal Institute, and finally built a church and a good school building of their own. They have since fairly taken the lead in educational work in Utah. The Hebrew Congregations have always used Independence Hall for their services. They have now become strong enough to contemplate putting up a building of their own, and also establishing a school in connection with it. The Josephite Mormons held their first meetings in Independence Hall, Brigham Young having refused them the use of any Mormon hall for that purpose. They have just completed a house of worship of their own. In 1867 the Hall was the scene of the first Gentile political meeting in Utah,—that which nominated Hugh McGroarty for Delegate to Congress. In 1872 a Gentile mass meeting was held on the grounds in front of the Hall, the city authorities declining to let it be held on the streets. The Woman's Anti-Polygamy Society was organized within its walls, and they have always been witnesses of its significant proceedings. The officers of Utah Lodge No. 1, I. O. O. F., were installed in Independence Hall, January 5, 1866, and this was the real beginning of Odd Fellowship in Utah, although a Lodge was organized with twenty-three members a year previous (Jan. 25, 1865). The Hall has often been the scene of festival and dance, of lectures, plays, concerts, shows, etc. In short, there was never a more useful building, homely as it is.

REORGANIZATION OF THE CHURCH.

About New Years, 1874, the Rev. Walter M. Barrows arrived to reoccupy the field for the Congregationalists under the auspices of the American Home Missionary Society. This had been attempted through Mr. McLeod in 1872, but the event proved that he was not the man for the work. Becoming aware of this himself, he resigned after a year's trial, leaving the enterprise itself under a cloud. Mr. Barrows had the furniture stored in the Hall (to such base uses had it come) removed as soon as possible, gathered a score of adherents, and toward the end of April announced a meeting for the purpose of reorganization. At this meeting were the ever-faithful Hempstead, Major I. O. Dewey, U. S. A., D. F. Walker, John T. Lynch, R. H. Robertson, O. J. Hollister, T. R. Jones, Henry C. Goodspeed, Frank Tilford, and Henry S. Greeley. Articles of incorporation were adopted, but they were superseded, July 2, by an incorporation under the laws of Utah, the gentlemen above-named being the incorporators.

The new Trustees assuming the indebtedness, which was finally paid off in January, 1876, the property was deeded to them. But Mr. Barrows, who left the church last June to become the Secretary of the Home Missionary Society, tells the story of the last few years in his pastoral letter of January 1, 1881, as follows:—

REV. WALTER M. BARROWS' WORK.

"Seven years ago last Christmas night I came to this city an entire stranger. After five months of preliminary work, our church was organized. We began a missionary church with twenty-six members. God has prospered us, and to-day we are a self-supporting church, with a membership of 118, and with a Sunday-school, the average attendance of which is now nearly 200. We have also had a hand in establishing the Salt Lake Academy, an institution of learning in which we already take great pride, and from which we expect greater things in the future. In connection with friends in the East, we have established in this city the first free school ever opened here, and in different parts of the Territory, five other schools. This progress has been made in the face of unusual difficulties and discouragements, but the outlook for the future is certainly hopeful. I believe we are in a position to-day where, with God's blessing, we can make greater progress in one year than we could in any three years that are past."

After this letter was penned, and before Mr. Barrows left, there was an accession, making the membership about 150. The society numbered 325, and not least missed to-day among the treasures the year has stolen from the church and society will be Mr. Barrows himself. Doubtless he was not faultless, but he had a breadth and manliness which peculiarly fitted him for this field. He had a faculty of ignoring trifles, and applying his strength only to essentials. He preached the necessity of a manly life rather than of nice professions. His scholarship, as well as general good judgment, made his treatment of any subject worthy of attention, and his semi-religious Sunday evening lectures were very popular, and justly so. He did not require notes, and his delivery was impressive. He kept well abreast of the progressive thought of the times, and took an active interest in whatever was of public concern. He never rested until he got the educational work of his church and society started. He is a man of taste and discretion, self-contained, with the masterful way that is inseparable from ability—a little cold in temperament, perhaps, and wanting in physical robustness, but withal a natural leader, who would be prominent and popular in any field of human effort. It is greatly to be regretted that he concluded to leave Salt Lake, and to the writer, doubtful if he has found or will find a field that more needs his services or in which he can be of greater usefulness. It is to be hoped that the church and society will soon fill his place, in every sense of the word. The Trustees at present are George A.

Lowe, Thomas R. Jones, J. R. Walker, Edward Benner, Frank Tilford, L. E. Holden, and H. C. Goodspeed; the officers, P. T. Van Zile, O. J. Hollister, and John T. Lynch. The ladies have a Ladies' Benevolent Society and a Woman's Home Missionary Society. The Rev. D. L. Leonard came out last summer from Minnesota to take charge of and extend the educational work of the church, backed by the Home Missionary Society and the New West Education Commission. Mr. Leonard has established six additional schools, making eleven in all.

THE EDUCATIONAL WORK.

This was begun in 1878 by raising $2,500 and building three school-rooms upon Independence Hall. The Salt Lake Academy was incorporated, and began its first year with an attendance averaging 100. It is now in its fourth year, with an average attendance of nearly 200. Since the first year it has used the audience-room as well as the new ones. Through the New West Education Commission the Academy has the past year obtained $13,000, and it has raised by subscription in Salt Lake $12,000, for the purpose of erecting an academy building. The foundation is completed, and the Academy expects to open its fifth year in a house of its own, ample for its uses, on a lot 16x20 rods in area, in a fine location, and then to go on as fast as possible to make of itself an institution equal in every respect to Eastern academies.

PAST, PRESENT, AND FUTURE.

The reader who has perused this narrative and read between the lines all it implies, will be forced to accredit the Gentiles of Salt Lake from the earliest times with extraordinary public spirit. Many of those mentioned above have gone elsewhere, some of them are dead, gentle Charley Hempstead for one, Frank Gilbert, Horace Wheat, Dr. Robinson, and R. H. Robertson; but their work lives and grows in almost geometrical progression. It required time and trouble and means to provide for the social, religious, educational, and political needs of the Gentiles of Utah. These men and their confreres still among us did not hesitate to make the requisite sacrifice, whatever it was. After this pioneer mission others followed, and they demanded labor and the sacrifice of time, trouble, and money; and these have been generously given. The calls for sixteen years have been weighty and incessant; subscription papers have been in almost constant circulation on Main street; the element that had to respond and that has responded was numerically weak and has labored under many and unusual disadvantages. But the missionary and educational work done and procured to be done by this element, ought to forever silence the charges of rapacity and self-seeking so flippantly made against it. It must have raised for churches and schools and hospitals altogether nearly half a million dollars. It must be now schooling more than three thousand children.

Ten years hence, with growth in proportion, it will have 200 schools and an attendance of 10,000 pupils. The indirect influence of this work is simply incalculable. With railroads, mining, and a free press, it has made a new country of Utah. It is the continuation and extension of this work that is to ultimately drive barbarism from the Territory, and make it a flourishing American State. Laws cannot do it, force cannot; but darkness vanisheth quickly when light shineth. "The people that walked in darkness have seen a great light: upon them hath the light shined." Had the pioneers neglected this work, we should still have had it to do, and against tenfold obstacles. Let every one feel, then, that he owes something to the community, and let the splendid example set by those who blazed the way, and the magnificent results apparent, encourage him to discharge the debt to the best of his capacity and opportunity. As he grows older, his work in this line will be that which he will regard with the most satisfaction. And it is a good investment from a purely business stand-point. Does any one suppose, for example, that the Walker Brothers would to-day be building a magnificent opera house in Salt Lake had not they and others invested money in the Independence Hall mission sixteen years ago? An educated, reading, free-thinking progressive community is the best, even if money-making is one's sole object.

SIDNEY R. RIGDON, THE FIRST MORMON PREACHER.

DECISION OF THE SUPREME COURT OF THE UNITED STATES IN THE CASE OF GEORGE REYNOLDS, OF UTAH, CONVICTED OF BIGAMY.

There are those who cannot see how the Government can interfere with polygamy, since it is claimed by the Mormons to be a part of their religion. For the benefit of such persons, we give below the decision of the Supreme Court, as delivered by Chief Justice Waite in this case, so far as it pertains to this point:—

V. *As to the defense of religious belief or duty.*

On the trial, the plaintiff in error, the accused, proved that at the time of his alleged second marriage he was, and for many years before had been, a member of the Church of Jesus Christ of Latter-day Saints, commonly called the Mormon church, and a believer in its doctrines; that it was an accepted doctrine of that church "that it was the duty of male members of said church, circumstances permitting, to practice polygamy; * * * that this duty was enjoined by different books which the members of said church believed to be of divine origin, and among others the Holy Bible, and also that the members of the church believed that the practice of polygamy was directly enjoined upon the male members thereof by the Almighty God, in a revelation to Joseph Smith, the founder and prophet of said church; that the failing or refusing to practice polygamy by such male members of said church, when circumstances would admit, would be punished, and that the penalty for such failure and refusal would be damnation in the life to come." He also proved "that he had received permission from the recognized authorities in said church to enter into polygamous marriage; * * * that Daniel H. Wells, one having authority in said church to perform the marriage ceremony, married the said defendant on or about the time the crime is alleged to have been committed, to some woman by the name of Schofield, and that such marriage ceremony was performed under, and pursuant to, the doctrines of said church."

Upon this proof he asked the court to instruct the jury that if they found from the evidence that he "was married as charged—if he was married—in pursuance of, and in conformity with, what he believed at the time to be a religious duty, that the verdict must be, 'not guilty.'" This request was refused, and the court did charge "that there must have been a criminal intent, but that if the defendant, under the influence of a religious belief that it was right,—under an inspiration (if you please) that it was right,—deliberately married a second time, having a first wife living, the want of consciousness of evil intent, the want of understanding on his part that he was committing a crime, did not excuse him; but the law in such case inexorably implies the criminal intent."

Upon this charge and refusal to charge, the question is raised whether religious belief can be accepted as a justification of an overt act made criminal by the law of the land. The inquiry is not as to the power of Congress to prescribe criminal laws for the Territories, but as to the guilt of one who knowingly violates a law, which has been properly enacted, if he entertains a religious belief that the law is wrong.

Congress cannot pass a law for the government of the Territories which shall prohibit the free exercise of religion. The first amendment to the constitution expressly forbids such legislation. Religious freedom is guaranteed everywhere throughout the United States, so far as Congressional interference is concerned. The question to be determined is whether the law now under consideration comes within this prohibition.

The word "religion" is not defined in the Constitution. We must go elsewhere, therefore, to ascertain its meaning, and nowhere more appropriately, we think, than to the history of the times in the midst of which the provision was adopted. The precise point of the inquiry is, What is the religious freedom which has been guaranteed?

Before the adoption of the Constitution, attempts were made in some of the colonies and States to legislate not only in respect to its doctrines but to its precepts, as well. The people were taxed against their will for the support of religion, and sometimes for the support of particular sects to whose tenets they could not and did not subscribe. Punishments were prescribed for a failure to attend upon public worship, and sometimes for entertaining heretical opinions. The controversy upon this general subject was animated in many of the States, but seemed at last to culminate in Virginia. In 1784 the House of Delegates of that State, having under consideration "a bill establishing provision for teachers of the Christian religion," postponed it until the next session, and directed that the bill be published and distributed, and that the people be requested "to signify their opinion respecting the adoption of such a bill at the next session of assembly."

This brought out a determined opposition. Among others, Mr. Madison prepared a "Memorial and Remonstrance," which was widely circulated and signed, and in which he demonstrated "that religion, or the duty we owe the Creator," was not within the cognizance of civil government. (Semple's Virginia Baptists, Appendix.) At the next session the proposed bill was not only defeated, but another "for establishing religious freedom," drafted by Mr Jefferson (1 Jeff. Works, 45; 2 Howison's Hist. of Va., 298.), was passed. In the preamble of this act (12 Hening's Stat., 84), religious freedom is defined, and after a recital "that to suffer the civil magistrate to intrude his powers into the field of opinion, and to restrain the profession or propagation of principles on supposition of their ill tendency, is a dangerous fallacy which at once destroys all religious liberty," it is declared "that it is time enough for the rightful purposes of civil government for its officers to interfere when principles break out into overt acts against peace and good order." In these two sentences is found the true distinction between what properly belongs to the Church and what to the State.

In a little more than a year after the passage of this statute the convention met which prepared the Constitution of the United States. Of this convention Mr. Jefferson was not a member, he being then absent as Minister to France. As soon as he saw the draft of the Constitution proposed for adoption, he, in a letter to a friend, expressed his disappointment at the absence of an expressed declaration insuring the freedom of religion (2 Jeff. Works, 355.), but was willing to accept it as it was, trusting that the good sense and honest intentions of the people would bring about the necessary alterations. (1 Jeff. Works, 79.) Five of the States, while adopting the Constitution, proposed amendments. Three, New Hampshire, New York, and Virginia, included in one form or another a declaration of religious freedom in the changes they desired to have made, as did also North Carolina, where the convention at first declined to ratify the Constitution until the proposed amendments were acted upon. Accordingly, at the first session of the first Congress the amendment now under consideration was proposed with others by Mr. Madison. It met the views of the advocates of religious freedom and was adopted. Mr. Jefferson afterward, in reply to an address to him by a committee of the Danbury Baptist Association (8 Jeff. Works, 113.), took occasion to say: "Believing with you that religion is a matter which lies solely between man and his God, that he owes account to none other for his faith or his worship, that the legislative powers of the Government reach actions only, and not opinions, I contemplate with solemn reverence that act of the whole American people which declared that their Legislature should 'make no law respecting an establishment of religion or prohibiting the free exercise thereof, thus building a wall of separation between Church and State. Adhering to this expression of the supreme will of the nation in behalf of the rights of conscience, I shall see with sincere satisfaction the progress of those sentiments which tend to restore man to all his natural rights, convinced he has no natural right in opposition to his social duties.' Coming as this does from an acknowledged leader of the advocates of the measure, it may be accepted almost as an authoritative declaration of the scope and effect of the amendment thus secured. Congress was deprived of all legislative power over mere opinion, but was left free to reach actions which were in violation of social duties or subversive of good order."

Polygamy has always been odious among the northern and western nations of Europe, and until the establishment of the Mormon church, almost exclusively a feature of the life of Asiatic and African people. At common law the second marriage was always void (2 Kent's Com., 79.), and from the earliest history of England, polygamy has been treated as an offense against society. After the establishment of the ecclesiastical courts, and until the time of James I., it was punished through the instrumentality of those tribunals, not merely because ecclesiastical rights had been violated, but because upon the separation of the ecclesiastical courts from the civil, the ecclesiastical were supposed to be the most appropriate for the trial of matrimonial causes and offenses against the rights of marriage, just as they were for testamentary causes and the settlement of the estates of deceased persons.

By the statute 1, James I., chap. 11, the offense, if committed in England or Wales, was made punishable in the civil courts, and the penalty was death. As this statute was limited in its operation to England and Wales, it was at a very early period re-enacted, generally with some modifications, in all the colonies. In connection with the case we are now considering, it is a significant fact that on the 8th of December, 1788, after the passage of the act establishing religious freedom, and after the convention of Virginia had recommended as an amendment to the Constitution of the United States the declaration in a bill of rights that "all men have an equal natural and unalienable right to the free exercise of religion, according to the dictates of conscience," the Legislature of that State substantially enacted the statute of James I., death penalty included, because as recited in the preamble, "it hath been doubted whether bigamy or polygamy be punishable by the laws of this commonwealth." (12 Hening's Stat. 691.) From that day to this we think it may safely be said there never has been a time in any State of the union when polygamy has not been an offense against society, cognizable by the civil courts and punishable with more or less severity. In the face of all this evidence it is impossible to believe that the constitutional guaranty of religious freedom was intended to prohibit legislation in respect to this most important feature of social life. Marriage, while from its very nature a sacred obligation, is nevertheless in most civilized nations a civil contract and usually regulated by law. Upon it society may be said to be built, and out of its fruits spring social relations and social obligations and duties, with which government is necessarily required to deal. In fact, according as monogamous or polygamous marriages are allowed, do we find the principles on which the government of the people rests, to a greater or less extent. Professor Lieber says, Polygamy leads to patriarchal principle, and which, when applied to large communities, fetters the people in stationary despotism, while that principle cannot long exist in connection with monogamy. Chancellor Kent observes that this remark is equally striking and profound. (2 Kent's Com., 81, note. e.) An exceptional colony of polygamists under an exceptional leadership may sometimes exist for a time without appearing to disturb the social condition of the people who surround it, but there cannot be a doubt that, unless restricted by some form of constitution, it is within the scope of the power of every civil government to determine whether polygamy or monogamy shall be the law of social life under its dominion.

In our opinion the statute immediately under consideration is within the legislative power of Congress. It is constitutional and valid as prescribing a rule of action for all those residing in the Territories and in places over which the United States have exclusive control. This being so, the only question which remains is, whether those who make polygamy a part of their religion are excepted from the operation of the statute. If they are, then those who do not make polygamy a part of their religious belief may be found guilty and punished, while those who do must be acquitted and go free. This would be introducing a new element into criminal law. Laws are made for the government of actions, and while they cannot interfere with mere religious belief and opinions, they may with practices. Suppose one believed that human sacrifices were a necessary part of religious worship, would it be seriously contended that the civil government under which he lived could not interfere to prevent a sacrifice? Or if a wife religiously believed it was her duty to burn herself upon the funeral pile of her dead husband, would it be beyond the power of the civil government to prevent her carrying her belief into practice?

So here, as a law of the organization of society under the exclusive dominion of the United States, it is provided that plural marriages shall not be allowed. Can a man excuse his practices to the contrary because of his religious belief? To permit this would be to make the professed doctrines of religious belief superior to the law of the land, and in effect to permit every citizen to become a law unto himself. Government could exist only in name under such circumstances.

A criminal intent is generally an element of crime, but every man is presumed to intend the necessary and legitimate consequences of what he knowingly does. Here the accused knew he had been once married, and that his first wife was living. He also knew that his second marriage was forbidden by law. When, therefore, he married the second time, he is presumed to have intended to break the law. And the breaking of the law is the crime. Every act necessary to constitute the crime was knowingly done, and the crime was, therefore, knowingly committed. Ignorance of a fact may sometimes be taken as evidence of a want of criminal intent, but not ignorance of the law. The only defense of the accused in this case is his belief that the law ought not to have been enacted. It matters not that his belief was a part of his professed religion, it was still belief, and belief only.

In Regina vs. Wagstaff (10 Cox. Crim. Cases, 531.), the parents of a sick child who omitted to call in medical attendance because of their religious belief that what they did for its cure would be effective, were held not to be guilty of manslaughter, while it was said the contrary would have been the result if the child had actually been starved to death by the parents, under the notion that it was their religious duty to abstain from giving it food. But when the offense consists of a positive act which is knowingly done, it would be dangerous to hold that the offender might escape punishment because he religiously believed the law which he had broken ought never to have been made. No case, we believe, can be found that has gone so far.

[Reynold's counsel also claimed that the decision should be set aside because the judge in his charge to the jury improperly directed their attention to the consequences of polygamy. The following is the part of the decision pertaining to that point]:—

VI. *As to that part of the charge which directed the attention of the jury to the consequences of polygamy.*

The passage complained of is as follows: "I think it not improper, in the discharge of your duties in this case, that you should consider what are to be the consequences to the innocent victims of this delusion. As this contest goes on, they multiply, and there are pure-minded women, and there are innocent children—innocent in a sense even beyond the degree of the innocence of childhood itself,—these are to be the sufferers; and as jurors fail to do their duty as these cases come up in the Territory of Utah, just so do these victims multiply and spread themselves over the land."

While every appeal by the court to the passions or the prejudices of the jury should be promptly rebuked, and while it is the imperative duty of a reviewing court to take care that wrong is not done in this way, we see no just cause for complaint in this case. Congress in 1862 (12 Stat., 501.), saw fit to make bigamy a crime in the Territories. This was done because of the evil consequences that were supposed to flow from plural marriages. All the court did was to call the attention of the jury to the peculiar character of the crime for which the accused was on trial, and to remind them of the duty they had to perform. There was no appeal to the passions, no instigation of prejudice. Upon the showing made by the accused himself, he was guilty of a violation of the law under which he had been indicted; and the effort of the court seems to have been, not to withdraw the minds of the jury from the issue to be tried, but to bring them to it: not to make them partial, but to keep them impartial.

Upon a careful consideration of the whole case we are satisfied that no error was committed by the court below, and the judgment is consequently affirmed.

ILLUSTRATIONS.

Most of the illustrations are sufficiently referred to in the body of the work, but one or two need a word of reference.

Mrs. A. G. Paddock is a noted writer on Mormonism, and in addition to numerous articles in the papers, has written "In the Toils," and "The Fate of Madam La Tour," two stories, vividly portraying the evils of Polygamy.

Hon. James B. McKean is known in Utah as the Martyred Judge. His ancestors on his father's side were of Scotch descent, and on his mother's were connected with the Huguenots of France. He was born in Hoosic, N. Y., 1821. He was a lawyer by profession, and served four years as county judge.

In 1858 the Republicans of the fifteenth district elected him Representative to Congress and re-elected him in 1860. He took an active part in the great civil war. During President Johnson's administration he was tendered the appointment of Consul to San Domingo, which, however, he declined.

In 1870 President Grant appointed him Chief Justice of the Supreme Court of Utah,—a position for which he was not an applicant, but which he was induced to accept, and held for five years.

Judges Strickland and Walker ordered the United States Marshal to summon the jurors in the trials of Mormon offenders, and only Gentiles or apostate Mormons were placed on the juries. Thus it was possible to indict and convict many of the leading Mormons. Their counsel had objected to this as contrary to the laws of the Territory. Judge McKean gave an able opinion sustaining the action of his associates. On appeal to the Supreme Court of the United States, however, this decision was reversed, and those who had been convicted, were released. The Mormons were triumphant, and the Gentiles despondent.

Judge McKean was the first man to lay hands on the Lord's Prophet. Brigham Young was arrested, by his order, for contempt of the authority of the Court, and imprisoned for twenty-four hours.

The Mormons were astonished, and the Gentiles elated. It seemed as though the day of better things had come, but for some unknown reason President Grant, to the great joy of the Mormons, removed the brave and upright judge, and the cause of justice and righteousness received a blow from which it has never recovered.

Some account of Rev. D. J. McMillan's work is given in chapter twenty-four, but the following extract from a paper will show the perils of Missionary work among the Saints even as late as 1875. Mr. McMillan vouches for the truth of the extract:—

"In support of a charge made in *Harper's Magazine* that Brigham Young, before a full congregation, in July, 1875, ordered his hearers to kill the Rev. Mr. McMillan, a Presbyterian minister in Utah, the *Salt Lake Tribune* tells at length the story of the meeting in question. It was a meeting called in the San Pete valley to receive President Young, seven or eight of the apostles, and some lesser lights. George Q. Cannon, Brigham Young, Jr., Daniel H. Wells, Lorenzo Snow, Erastus Snow, Orson Hyde, and A. M. Musser were in the party. After several other matters had been treated by Young, he took up the McMillan matter, and said:—

"'There is a mischievous stranger, a Presbyterian minister, in this valley. He has no business here. The Lord has given to me these valleys, and to those whom I choose to have occupy them; this Presbyterian minister has no business here. The Saints do not know how vile a character this man has. In the best society in the United States, not one child in ten can identify his father. Mistresses are luxuries which are conceded to all orthodox ministers. One prominent clergyman keeps twenty-eight mistresses, and though I don't know this minister who has come here, he is one of the same stripe. I am informed that Saints have gone to hear this man preach, and have sent their daughters to his school. The next thing you will know he will send sorrow and distress to the hearts of the mothers of these girls.' (Then followed something too obscene for publication.) 'You must not be deceived by the fact that this man seems a gentleman and a moral man; there is just where the danger lies. He is a wolf in sheep's clothing. What would you do were a wolf to enter the field where your sheep are? Why, you would shoot him down. Kill him on the spot. Inasmuch as souls are more precious than sheep, it becomes you to be correspondingly more diligent in ridding yourselves of this intruder. I need not tell the Saints how this is to be done. They know well enough.' Then with uplifted hands, he said: 'You must obey me the same as though Jehovah had spoken; for my voice is the voice of Jehovah.' Those were the words delivered to quite 2,000 people,—a primitive people,—taught from youth up to believe the speaker was the vicegerent on earth of the Infinite God.

"George Q. Cannon followed, indorsing everything that Young had said; and, referring to the law of 1862 against polygamy, said it was a dead letter and always would be. He referred to the fact that Congress had never unseated him, as a proof that his people are shielded by the Almighty, and that the law would never be enforced. A meeting of the mothers in the valley was called for that evening, and at the meeting, Cannon, Snow, and others spoke, the burden of the speeches being to devise means through which the people might get rid of Mr. McMillan.

"The next night a mob gathered around Mr. McMillan's house and stoned it, and the next night a murderer, who was seeking an entrance into the house was driven away with a pistol. Later, an ambuscade was laid for the minister, which he escaped by taking another road. Many of the apostate Mormons in the valley advised Mr. McMillan to leave, and some friendly Mormons told him to always go armed and never expose himself. The most of the pupils were taken from the school, and it was months before the full number was restored. The foregoing is a simple statement of facts, gathered from the note-book of the man who was assailed, who sat by and heard Young's denunciation, and George Q. Cannon's indorsement of all that his chief said."

www.ingramcontent.com/pod-product-compliance
Lightning Source LLC
Chambersburg PA
CBHW022115300426
44117CB00007B/727